THE ONGOING BURDEN *of* SOUTHERN HISTORY

MAKING THE MODERN SOUTH

David Goldfield, *Series Editor*

THE ONGOING BURDEN *of* SOUTHERN HISTORY

Politics and Identity in the Twenty-First-Century South

Edited by

ANGIE MAXWELL, TODD SHIELDS,

and JEANNIE WHAYNE

LOUISIANA STATE UNIVERSITY PRESS
BATON ROUGE

Published by Louisiana State University Press

Manufactured in the United States of America
FIRST PRINTING

DESIGNER: Barbara Neely Bourgoyne
TYPEFACE: Adobe Garamond Pro
PRINTER: McNaughton & Gunn, Inc.
BINDER: Acme Bookbinding, Inc.

Library of Congress Cataloging-in-Publication Data
The ongoing burden of southern history : politics and identity in the twenty-first-century South / edited by Angie Maxwell, Todd Shields, [and] Jeannie Whayne.
p. cm. — (Making the modern South)
Includes index.
ISBN 978-0-8071-4756-6 (cloth : alk. paper) — ISBN 978-0-8071-4757-3 (pdf) — ISBN 978-0-8071-4758-0 (epub) — ISBN 978-0-8071-4759-7 (mobi) 1. Southern States—Politics and government—21st century. 2. Southern States—Social conditions—21st century. 3. Southern States—Civilization—21st century. 4. Woodward, C. Vann (Comer Vann), 1908–1999. Burden of southern history. I. Maxwell, Angie, 1978– II. Shields, Todd, 1968– III. Whayne, Jeannie M.
F216.2.O54 2012
975'.044—dc23

2012007907

The paper in this book meets the guidelines for permanence and durability of the Committee on Production Guidelines for Book Longevity of the Council on Library Resources. ♾

CONTENTS

PREFACE: Why Woodward Still Matters vii
Angie Maxwell, Todd Shields, and Jeannie Whayne

ACKNOWLEDGMENTS xv

1 Therapist of the Public Mind: Woodward and the Most Burdensome Burden 1
James C. Cobb

2 Woodward's Southerner: History, Literature, and the Question of Identity 31
Leigh Anne Duck

3 A Lighter Burden? Southern Political Identity in the Shrinking South 62
Wayne Parent

4 The History of the Present 80
Robert C. McMath

5 Woodward's Losers: Disappearing Democrats in Southern Political History 116
Patrick G. Williams

6 The End of Woodward's Second Reconstruction? African American Political Participation in the South 131
Charles S. Bullock III

7 Woodward's New Intellectual Stream:
The Enfranchisement of the Freed Slave Population 153
Hanes Walton Jr., Josephine A. V. Allen, Sherman C. Puckett, and Donald R. Deskins Jr.

CONTRIBUTORS 189

INDEX 195

PREFACE
Why Woodward Still Matters

> The time is coming, if indeed it has not already arrived, when the Southerner will begin to ask himself whether there is really any longer very much point in calling himself a Southerner.
>
> —C. Vann Woodward, *The Burden of Southern History* (1968)

In the half century since the publication of Arkansas native C. Vann Woodward's landmark collection *The Burden of Southern History* (1960), academic debates regarding the existence, breadth, and impact of southern distinctiveness have remained constant and vigorous. In that single volume, Woodward defines white southern identity during a tumultuous period of regional history, tackling questions of equality, the legacy of Reconstruction, the heritage of Populism, and the place of the South within the nation. In an effort to assess the influence of Woodward's classic collection, an interdisciplinary group of noted southern studies scholars gathered at the University of Arkansas in April 2010 for the third installment of the Blair Legacy Conference series, cosponsored by the Diane D. Blair Center of Southern Politics and Society and the Winthrop Rockefeller Institute. This installment was titled "C. Vann Woodward: Politics and Identity in the 21st-Century South." The series has previously considered the impact and legacy of Arkansas native President William Jefferson Clinton (*The Clinton Riddle*) and preeminent political scientist V. O. Key Jr. (*Unlocking V. O. Key, Jr.: Southern Politics in the Twenty-First Century*). Both of those volumes were published by the University of Arkansas Press.

At the most recent gathering, each contributor reconsidered the bold ideas put forth by Woodward fifty years earlier, highlighting both Woodward's limitations and his relevance in the modern South. Though cited and quoted extensively, Woodward's work is rarely deconstructed directly, particularly by those outside of his chosen field of history. Specifically, these chapters apply Woodward's ideas to southern politics, where identity and behavior remain clearly distinct and increasingly "red." For it is here, in the political arena, where old habits seem to die hard in the South and where southern identity in the twenty-first century may still be operating at full steam. Chapter 1, by keynote scholar James C. Cobb, and the chapters put forth by Leigh Anne Duck, Wayne Parent, Robert C. McMath, Patrick G. Williams, Charles S. Bullock III, and Hanes Walton Jr. and coauthors demonstrate the ongoing complexity of Woodward's original *Burden.* In short, Woodward still matters. And this collection demonstrates why.

In November 1908, Comer Vann Woodward was born in the eastern Arkansas town of Vanndale, which was named for his mother's family. He attended high school in Morrilton, Arkansas, less than twenty miles from Petit Jean Mountain, where Winthrop Rockefeller later established his remarkable farm and institute. Woodward completed his college degree in philosophy at Emory University in Atlanta, Georgia, where his uncle and namesake was both a sociology professor and the dean of students. After graduation, he accepted a job teaching English at the nearby Georgia Institute of Technology. In Atlanta, his association with Will Alexander, head of the Congress of Interracial Cooperation, further developed his sense of social justice, which eventually led him to aid in the defense of Communist Angelo Herndon, who had been arrested for protesting the conviction of the Scottsboro nine.

After losing his teaching position, Woodward worked for President Franklin Delano Roosevelt's Works Progress Administration, and during this period his passion was sparked for the interplay between race, class, and demagoguery in the South. Specifically, Woodward began writing a biography of Tom Watson, a Georgia Populist and white supremacist who became a U.S. senator and a vice-presidential candidate. With a research grant and access to Watson family archives, Woodward pursued a Ph.D. in history at the University of North Carolina, Chapel Hill. The dissertation manuscript became Woodward's first book, *Tom Watson, Agrarian Rebel,* published by Macmillan in 1938.

Woodward's first job out of graduate school was at the University of Florida, where he began work on the book *Origins of the New South, 1877–1913,* part of the History of the South series published by Louisiana State University Press. His writing was delayed by his service in the Office of Naval Intelligence during World War II, after which he resumed his academic career at Johns Hopkins University. His reputation as an expert in southern studies made him a popular voice in the civil rights movement, from its early years onward. For example, he served as a consultant for Thurgood Marshall during the *Brown v. Board of Education* trial. *Origins* was followed by Woodward's groundbreaking treatment of segregation, *The Strange Career of Jim Crow* (1955). The revisionist framework of Reconstruction presented in *Origins,* coupled with the long evolution of segregation detailed in *Strange Career,* created a new vision of the southern past on which Woodward elaborated and which he further defined in the essays that made up *The Burden of Southern History.*

The final phase of Woodward's career was spent at Yale University, during which he received the 1982 Pulitzer Prize for editing *Mary Chesnut's Civil War.* During his tenure there, he also served as president of both leading professional organizations for historians—the Organization of American Historians and the American Historical Association—as well as the Southern Historical Association. At the time of his death in December 1999, he was still considered one of the leading scholars of the field; his ideas were still driving the ongoing debates at the center of southern history, politics, and literature.

Chosen as the keynote speaker of the April 2010 conference, James C. Cobb, the B. Phinizy Spalding Distinguished Professor of History at the University of Georgia, provides the opening chapter to this collection. In "Therapist of the Public Mind: Woodward and the Most Burdensome Burden," Cobb argues that to understand Woodward's intent in *Burden,* readers must first examine his method in *The Strange Career of Jim Crow.* As he clarifies Woodward's intent, Cobb exposes a somewhat timeless thesis of *Burden.* He contends that Woodward wanted to expand the definition of southern distinctiveness—to give southern whites an identity not solely based on white supremacy—and that he saw southern identity as having a public, political, and progressive purpose. Moreover, Cobb asserts that Woodward's subsequent versions of *Burden,* as well as his own commentary about his choices, reveals that this kind of "therapy" became a burden to him. He feared his optimistic views had maintained denial. Cobb ultimately concludes that scholars must return to Woodward's essays in *Burden* and reconsider their meaning for the twenty-first century.

Leigh Anne Duck, associate professor of English at the University of Mississippi, turns to Woodward's literary essays and revised editions of *Burden* in an effort to reconstruct his original conception of southern identity. In "Woodward's Southerner: History, Literature, and the Question of Identity," she challenges misinterpretations of Woodward's intent and argues for a pragmatic Woodward concerned with promoting a usable past for white southerners. However, Duck does not shy away from exposing Woodward's deficiencies—specifically, his overly generalized portrait of southerners. But she finds in Woodward's revisions an effort to track the impact that his conception of the South had had on the political reality experienced by African American and white southerners alike. In a similar vein, though with a different method, Wayne T. Parent, Russell B. Long Professor of Political Science at Louisiana State University, attempts to locate the remaining elements of Woodward's southern identity as presented in *Burden* fifty years ago. Challenging recent scholarship in his chapter, "A Lighter Burden? Political Identity in the Shrinking South," Parent points to the demise of southern distinctiveness, and in an effort to understand the political realignment of the South with the Republican Party, Parent uses the 2008 presidential election, and specifically the candidacy of the first African American nominee, to test the ongoing presence of a southern "burden."

Focusing more specifically on political identity, Robert C. McMath, dean of the Honors College and professor of history at the University of Arkansas, employs two of Woodward's essays—"The Irony of Southern History" and "The Populist Heritage and the Intellectual"—to explicate the collapse of New Deal liberalism and the consequential rise of the "new American right." Moreover, in his chapter, "The History of the Present," McMath skillfully delineates differences between the contemporary Tea Party movement and the nineteenth-century Populists championed and defended by Woodward. McMath's colleague Patrick G. Williams, associate professor of history at the University of Arkansas, also reflects backward, although he offers a more nuanced picture of southern Democrats. In "Woodward's Losers: Disappearing Democrats in Southern Political History," Williams contends that Woodward's insistence on a usable southern past—most notably, his inclination toward progressive southern rebels—contributed to a lack of scholarly treatment of the Redeemer Democrats who recaptured control of the Reconstructed South. Also significant to Williams's argument is his attention to the economic appeal of the low-tax, small-government moniker of these post–Civil War southern Democrats. His effort to trace the roots of contemporary conservative policies in the region's past exposes yet another dimension of the southern "burden," shaped, indirectly, by Woodward's choices.

Shifting focus, Charles S. Bullock III of the University of Georgia, who is holder of the Richard B. Russell Chair in Political Science and is Josiah Meigs Distinguished Teaching Professor, revisits one of the central concerns that arise in the late-1960s revised editions of Woodward's *The Burden of Southern History*—the end of the civil rights movement. In his chapter, "The End of Woodward's Second Reconstruction? African American Political Participation in the South," Bullock traces the rise in African American voter registration and turnout, made possible by the 1965 Voting Rights Act, to counter Woodward's pessimistic view of the movement's accomplishments. Specifically, Woodward drew a parallel between the waning interest in the South that followed Reconstruction and the diminishing interest in civil rights initiatives following the major legislative victories of 1964 and 1965. Bullock, moreover, reevaluates Woodward's notion of success and highlights the long-term progress that Woodward could not foresee. Offering a counterinterpretation of Woodward's vision, Hanes Walton Jr. and his coauthors, Josephine A. V. Allen, Sherman C. Puckett, and Donald R. Deskins Jr., test Woodward's predictions regarding the consequences that large influxes of African American voters would have on the American democratic system. In this final chapter, "Woodward's New Intellectual Stream: The Enfranchisement of the Freed Slave Population," Walton and his colleagues contend that Woodward was optimistic about the ability of the party system to absorb these new voters. Analyzing three historical moments, including the 2008 election, when such influxes were prominent, Walton and coauthors ultimately concur with Woodward's prospective assessment that despite the burden of southern history, American democracy would prevail.

This collection as a whole situates Woodward within the modern political landscape of the South, while investigating his personal motives, reconsidering his definition of southern distinctiveness, and interrogating his omissions. The product of this interrogation is a more nuanced understanding of Woodward himself, of the ideas made famous in *The Burden of Southern History,* and of the legacy of those ideas for candidates, political parties, and voters. W. E. B. Du Bois once warned, "As the South goes, so goes the nation." Du Bois feared that the permitted oppression of labor, particularly African American labor, would infect the country as whole. But the phrase has been co-opted by many political scientists who study the South when they point to the impact that the southern voting bloc has in national elections. Despite the ongoing contestation of southern distinctiveness so popular at this time, scholars of political behavior and identity still see the distinct voting trends in the South as indicative of an underlying regional culture that reflects a unique history. For decades, this distinctiveness was attributed primarily to the one-party politics that dominated the South for much of the twentieth century. And although Woodward's essays in *The Burden of Southern History* do not rely on the measurements that consume social scientists, his effort is to expose the cultural forces operating behind and maintaining the Solid South.

Republican inroads brought two-party competition to the region within a few years after *Burden*'s publication. But the competition was short-lived, and white southern voters have helped usher in another era of one-party domination at the national level and increasingly at the state and local levels. The reemergence of a second Solid South requires that scholars revisit classic works like *Burden* in an effort to understand the way in which identity, conservatism, and race have shaped political values in the region. As Leigh Anne Duck contends in her chapter, Woodward was guilty—specifically in the original edition of *Burden*—of promoting a collective and generalized southern identity devoid of diversity. It was only in the revised editions that he directly commented on issues of social justice and acknowledged the distinct experiences of African American southerners. Woodward, because his focus was on white southerners, often failed to acknowledge the multifaceted nature of African American political participation in the South. Moreover, McMath, in his careful reading of Woodward's revision of *Burden,* reveals that Woodward's effort to establish a usable past for southerners—a southern identity that could prove instructive to the rest of the country—haunted him. Woodward feared that his initial optimism and the promotional nature of his commentary on southern identity was being misused to maintain a status quo in the region that disenfranchised African American southerners. His growing pessimism, as Charles Bullock argues, did not allow him to foresee the progress the African American candidates could and did make in the years following the 1965 Voting Rights Act. And although this progress is often threatened, it speaks, as Hanes Walton notes, to the very nature of democracy—which Woodward did acknowledge and which, perhaps, gave him solace.

The democratic spirit, particularly at the grassroots level, is what drew Woodward emotionally and intellectually to the Populists. He saw the rebellious nature of their politics as a vision of southern potential. And Woodward's commitment to defining the Populist impulse resulted in a lack of attention paid by him to the appeal of the Redeemer Democrats, who reestablished southern Democratic dominance after the Civil War. Patrick Williams fills in this gap, demonstrating why the economic conditions and class ideology that often fueled populist fervor were, ironically, part of the Redeemer heritage as well. Moreover, Bob McMath sees Woodward's treatment of the Populists as instructive beyond its specific interpretation of this one movement. McMath finds in Woodward's essays a useful framework for understanding the rise and fall of social movements in the South and in the country, even the contemporary Tea Party movement; they are distinct from the Populists yet clarified when placed under Woodward's lens.

Woodward still matters because his ideas are still useful. Wayne Parent even finds a way to measure and to locate Woodward's southerner, in what he calls a "shrinking South." Smaller, perhaps, but still relevant, particularly in the public arena of politics, which, in fact, consumed much of Woodward's attention and concern. He was, as Jim Cobb claims, "a therapist of the public mind." Such a role inevitably became a burden to him, but the ideas that resulted from his struggle continue to influence southern political culture in the twenty-first century.

ANGIE MAXWELL
TODD SHIELDS
JEANNIE WHAYNE

ACKNOWLEDGMENTS

The Ongoing Burden of Southern History: Politics and Identity in the Twenty-First-Century South is dedicated to the organizations that made its publication possible. Without the support of the Diane D. Blair Center of Southern Politics and Society at the University of Arkansas—specifically, Jim Blair—and the Winthrop Rockefeller Institute, we would remain academics with good ideas and few resources. Their financial and moral support allows us to reach beyond disciplinary boundaries and ask questions about the legacy of the leaders who shaped our past and continue to affect our present.

The Diane D. Blair Center of Southern Politics and Society was established by an act of the U.S. Congress in the fall of 2001; only a few research centers in the country have been so established. It was named in honor of Diane Divers Blair, who taught in the Political Science Department at the University of Arkansas for thirty years. Diane, a daughter of William Keeveny Divers and Minna Rosenbaum Divers, was born October 25, 1938, and raised in Washington, D.C. She graduated cum laude from Cornell University in 1959 and was a member of Phi Beta Kappa. She worked in Washington, D.C., in the early sixties as a contract analyst for the President's Committee on Government Contracts, as a research assistant for a Senate Special Committee on Unemployment, and as legislative secretary and speechwriter for Senator Stuart Symington of Missouri. Relocating to Arkansas in 1963, Diane immersed herself in numerous civic and political organizations, as well as the modern literature club, and she received her master's degree in political science from the University of Arkansas in 1967. She is listed in "America's Who's Who in Government and Politics" and in the "World's Who's Who of Women." She debated Phyllis Schlafly before the Arkansas Legislature on Valentine's Day 1975 on behalf of the Equal Rights Amendment, and in 1992 Diane was selected to cast one of Arkansas's ballots in the Electoral College.

Diane established a record of accomplishment simply unparalleled in its combination of serious scholarship and practical involvement in both local and national politics. In May 2000, Diane was awarded an honorary Doctor of Laws by the University of Arkansas; she was twice nominated to the board of the U.S. Corporation for Public Broadcasting by President William Jefferson Clinton and twice confirmed to that position by the U.S. Senate. She served two terms as chair of the Corporation for Public Broadcasting, and the corporation has now named its governing board after her. She was appointed by Governor Dale Bumpers in 1971 to serve as chair of the Governor's Commission on the Status of Women; by Governor David Pryor in 1976 to chair a Commission on Public Employee Rights; and by Governor Bill Clinton in 1980 to serve as a member of the Arkansas Educational Television Network commission, which she served until 1993—and chaired from 1986 to 1987. In 1992 she took leave from the University of Arkansas to serve as senior researcher for the Clinton presidential campaign and again took leave in 1996, when she served as senior adviser to the Clinton-Gore reelection campaign.

In addition to establishing a breakneck record of service to her state and nation, Diane was an accomplished scholar, teacher, and mentor. She published two books, the first an analysis of Senator Hattie Caraway, the first woman elected to the U.S. Senate, entitled *Silent Hattie Speaks: The Personal Journal of Senator Hattie Caraway.* Her second book, *Arkansas Politics and Government: Do the People Rule?* continues to be a primary text used in Arkansas high schools, colleges, and universities. In addition, she authored fourteen chapters in edited volumes and authored or coauthored more than ninety articles in various publications. Her research interests focused primarily on women and politics, state and local government, and the politics of Arkansas and the South. In 1993 she served as a guest scholar at the Brookings Institution in Washington, D.C. Diane was three times named the "Outstanding Faculty Member" by University of Arkansas students, and in 1982 she was one of the first recipients of the Fulbright College Master Teacher Award. In 1995 she was honored by the Midwest Political Science Association for the body of her work in political science. The Southern Political Science Association now has a competitive annual award called the Diane D. Blair award, which is given to a scholar, chosen by committee, who successfully combines rigorous analyses of contemporary politics with a commitment to political activism. Diane D. Blair was a champion of interdisciplinary research and critical thinking, and she reached across the academic aisles often and with ease. The Blair Center reflects her academic model and strives to approach the study of the American South from a variety of angles and to reveal the undercurrents of politics, history, and culture that have shaped the region over time.

The newly forged partnership between the Rockefeller Institute and the Blair Center promises to increase the number and quality of future symposia and considerably increase the scholarly attention given to the contemporary South across multiple disciplines. Like Diane Blair, Winthrop Rockefeller had eclectic interests. He was committed to improving the South and convening scholars and activists in order to better understand the political and social troubles that held the South during the 1950s. It was 1953 when Rockefeller chose to make Arkansas his home. Through his leadership and philanthropy, he positively transformed the state's politics, economy, culture, and education.

As the nonconformist fourth son of one of the most powerful families in America, Winthrop Rockefeller spent his first forty-one years searching and living beyond family expectations. After withdrawing from Yale, he went to work as a roughneck in the Texas oil fields. Rockefeller then enlisted in the army and served in World War II, where he received the Bronze Star with Oak Leaf Cluster and the Purple Heart. After returning from the war, Rockefeller married Barbara "Bobo" Sears, and they had a son—his only child—Winthrop Paul. During his time in the military, he befriended an Arkansan named Frank Newell. In the summer of 1953, Frank invited Winthrop to Arkansas for a reprieve from the hustle and bustle of New York City. Following the trip to Arkansas, Rockefeller was never the same.

He moved to Arkansas and built a new life for himself atop his beloved Petit Jean Mountain. Demonstrating remarkable purpose and vision, he developed a premier working cattle farm called Winrock Farms. Rockefeller hosted thousands of visitors from across the nation to his innovative farm, a site that served as a model for progress and an inspiration for change in the state of Arkansas. Rockefeller was also an Arkansas pioneer of philanthropy: his Rockwin Fund supported worthy causes across the state. In a letter to his son, he wrote of his family: "While we lived comfortably with that which we inherited and earned, we had the responsibility to see that these resources were also used wisely in the service to our fellow man." Rockefeller's philanthropy focused on strengthening America's place in the world and building Arkansas.

Rockefeller was not politically ambitious, but he was determined to do anything he could to enact positive change in Arkansas. As chairman of the Arkansas Industrial Development Commission, he helped create ninety thousand new jobs. Rockefeller ultimately realized that his efforts would have to include political and election reform to facilitate the change he envisioned. His election in 1966 made him the thirty-seventh governor of Arkansas and the first Republican governor since Reconstruction. He was reelected to a second term in 1968. With a lifelong commitment to civil rights, Governor Rockefeller appointed the first African American state government department head, and he was the only southern governor known to hold a public memorial service after the assassination of Martin Luther King Jr.

Rockefeller filed for a third term in 1970 but was defeated by Dale Bumpers. Upon leaving office, Governor Rockefeller said he wanted historians to think of him as more than a political phenomenon. He wanted to be remembered as "a catalyst who hopefully served to excite in the hearts and minds" of the people "a desire to shape [their] own destiny." The legacy of Governor Rockefeller continues today through the work at Winthrop Rockefeller Institute, which was established in 2005 by the University of Arkansas System with a grant from the Winthrop Rockefeller Charitable Trust. By integrating the resources and expertise of a statewide university system with the legacy and ideas of Governor Winthrop Rockefeller, this educational institute and conference center creates an atmosphere where collaboration and change can thrive.

The Institute's 188-acre campus located on Petit Jean Mountain was once part of the home and cattle farm of Governor Rockefeller, giving it a remarkably distinguished heritage on which to build. In the twenty years he lived on Petit Jean, Rockefeller hosted more than two hundred conferences and meetings. These conclaves addressed an astonishing range of concerns—from educational needs and rural economic development to how to clean up Arkansas's political system and harmonize the races. Today, the Institute continues to build upon the legacy of its namesake by providing an environment conducive to open discussion, stimulating new perspectives, and developing future-oriented results.

We would also like to acknowledge our departments, the Department of History and the Department of Political Science, in the J. William Fulbright College of Arts and Sciences at the University of Arkansas, for their unwavering support of our endeavors. No successful gathering of notable scholars happens without the graciousness of one's colleagues. We are grateful for your attendance, feedback, and open doors.

THE ONGOING BURDEN *of* SOUTHERN HISTORY

I

Therapist of the Public Mind

Woodward and the Most Burdensome Burden

JAMES C. COBB

> Since the last World War old racial attitudes that appeared more venerable and immovable than any other have exhibited a flexibility that no one would have predicted. One by one, and in astonishingly rapid succession, many landmarks of racial discrimination and segregation have disappeared, and old barriers have been breached.
>
> —C. Vann Woodward, *The Burden of Southern History* (1993)

Drawing on Woodward's books, articles, and correspondence, James Cobb traces the evolution of his role as a "therapist" of the southern mind. Cobb focuses most of his attention on two of Woodward's works, making the connection between The Strange Career of Jim Crow, *where race was central, to two specific essays in* The Burden of Southern History, *where Woodward argued that by focusing on the broader historical—as opposed to the narrower racial—dimension of their regional identity, white southerners could teach the rest of the nation about restraint and humility, a lesson badly needed amid the saber rattling and megalomania of the McCarthy era. Woodward's storied rise to prominence in the profession did nothing to undermine his dedication to shaping public opinion, both within the South and without. In fact, Cobb argues, Woodward's desire to influence his readers' thinking often outdistanced the evidence he could marshal in support of his arguments. In* The Strange Career of Jim Crow, *Woodward famously contended that segregation had developed relatively recently in the South and that it was a "stateway" instigated by law rather than a "folkway" derived from cultural experience, his implication being that once relieved from the onerous segregation statutes, southerners would throw off the Jim Crow system. Meanwhile, in both "The Search for Southern Identity" and "The Irony of Southern History," Woodward urged southerners to embrace their experience with defeat and humiliation in the Civil War in order to offer guidance to the rest of the nation, caught up in the dangerous and deadly cold war. Over the course of time, as evidenced in two subsequent editions of* The Burden of Southern History, *Woodward's optimism steadily dimmed. The civil rights movement turned violent and moved north, Martin Luther King Jr. was assassinated, and many black activists rejected integration in favor of separatism. At the same time, few white southerners appeared to have learned the lessons that Woodward believed their history could teach them. From Cobb's point of view, Woodward continued throughout his life to urge Americans "to reflect soberly on their past before reacting rashly to their present."*

After reading the galleys for *The Burden of Southern History* in 1960, Henry Nash Smith came away thoroughly convinced that C. Vann Woodward "possesses southern history so completely that in his writing it ceases to be mere learning and becomes the form and content of thought at its most sophisticated level." This was high praise indeed for a collection of previously published essays that might well have struck some at the time as simply an attempt to piggyback on the success of Woodward's *The Strange Career of Jim Crow*, which had appeared five years earlier and, after multiple printings, was already out in the first of three revised editions.[1]

At first glance, the two books appeared to have relatively little in common. *Strange Career* owed its enormous appeal—and eventual sales in excess of a million copies—to its relevance to the nation's ongoing struggle with the problem of race. Race seemed decidedly less integral to *Burden*, where Woodward tried to persuade white southerners that their real claim to regional distinctiveness lay not in their traditional dominion over black southerners but rather in a larger, defeat- and poverty-ridden historical experience that actually left them peculiarly equipped to offer their fellow Americans some valuable lessons in humility and restraint. Yet Woodward's concerted efforts in *Burden* to get southern whites to stop defining themselves through their allegiance to the Jim Crow system are very much of a piece with his emphasis in *Strange Career* on that system's relatively recent origins. Considered in the context of Woodward's own somewhat "strange" career, the connections between these books also reflect his extraordinary transition from a traditional scholar writing primarily for his peers to what he called "a therapist of the public mind," who broke free of academic constraints to reach out to a broader general audience with a new vision of the past and its potential to suggest more constructive responses to the present.

The Burden of Southern History won both prizes and critical acclaim and went on to rack up impressive sales figures of its own, but its appearance was not the only propitious career development for C. Vann Woodward in 1960. When George W. Pierson took over as head of Yale's History Department in 1956, he knew that his alma mater's reputation in history had fallen well behind Harvard's. Pierson had earned his Ph.D. from Yale in 1933 and taught there ever since, and he committed himself to injecting some new bloodlines into what he realized was a thoroughly inbred bunch. He managed to build on the recent appointment of Harvard-trained colonialist Edmund Morgan by hiring another Harvard Ph.D., political historian John Morton Blum, away from M.I.T. in 1957. When Pierson's fellow Yale alumnus southern historian David Potter decided to leave Yale for Stanford in 1960, Blum and Morgan immediately descended on Pierson, insisting that "there was only one way to replace David." That was by bringing in C. Vann Woodward, then at Johns Hopkins and, in Blum's view, "already the premier historian of the American South." Although Woodward had earned his Ph.D. in the relative backwaters of Chapel Hill, by Blum's account the acutely pedigree-conscious Pierson took only "a minute" to concur, and he proceeded on the spot, without further consultation with anyone, to call Woodward and offer him a Sterling professorship, "the most prestigious and remunerative chair available at Yale."[2]

The dispatch with which the offer to Woodward was handled was entirely in keeping with what seems to have been a truly charmed career up to that point. This outcome was all the more remarkable given that, at the outset, Woodward's career had given promise of needing all the charm it could get, for he had surely embarked on it with as little enthusiasm for the undertaking as could be imagined. From his undergraduate days at Emory through his indifferent pursuit of an M.A. in "public law" at Columbia thereafter, Woodward had consistently made little effort to conceal his disdain for the traditional constraints and expectations of the academy.[3]

He had entered graduate school in history at the University of North Carolina in 1934 simply because he saw influential sociologist Howard Odum's promise of a Rockefeller Foundation Fellowship as the best means of supporting himself while he finished his book on Georgia Populist Tom

Watson, whose papers, it so happened, had recently been deposited in the newly opened Southern Historical Collection in Chapel Hill. Although it later became his dissertation, Woodward had begun his work on Watson with "no academic purpose in mind" and only "the faintest formal preparation in American history," acquired in an exceedingly dull course at Emory that had "been more than enough to discourage further curiosity." For him, history was not so much a chosen field as one dictated by his choice of a biographical subject, which, in turn, eventually forced him to accept the fact that, as he put it, "a Southern historian I must be—or somehow become."[4]

Much to his dismay, Woodward found little additional inspiration for this task when he arrived in Chapel Hill to discover the masters of the southern historical establishment merely parroting the "received wisdom" that had long sustained the "New South" sociopolitical and economic system "founded on the ruins of Reconstruction" and still securely in place in the 1930s. While studying at North Carolina, he mercilessly bombarded his old Emory undergraduate chum Glenn Rainey with complaints about having to read "prose so pedestrian, pages so dull, chapters so void of ideas," not to mention the useless "rigamarole" of classes that did nothing more than interfere with his writing. After a year in Chapel Hill, he declared that he had not "gleaned a single scholarly idea from any professor here." Blending disgust with sarcasm, he wrote Rainey, "History, I find, is a collection of facts. Should have looked into that before going so far. Nothing but contempt for the facts! Opinion all that matters. Proper attitude." The very next day after his mediocre performance on his oral exams, an unrepentant Woodward declared that he was purging himself of unwanted information by "indulging in extravagant forgetting. No niggardly date here and a dictator there, but whole dynasties at a time—Poof! There go the Hapsburgs. Poof! The Hohenzollerns. (I made the mistake of forgetting Hanoverians before the orals.)"[5]

His contemporaries recalled that not much in graduate school had "really influenced" Woodward, who had arrived "with a definite point of view" and little interest in anything other than his Watson biography. He had crammed for exams with borrowed notes, showed interest only in information pertaining to the "post–Civil War South," and disappointed faculty because "he simply did not know many facts of history." Be that as it may, owing in part to the work he had done on Watson before he arrived, in early May 1937, less than three years after he began his formal Ph.D. studies at the University of North Carolina, C. Vann Woodward had defended his dissertation, "The Political and Literary Career of Thomas E. Watson." A right sizable contribution to scholarship, the two-volume work topped out at a hefty 556 pages, and its author was advised by both University of North Carolina Press director William T. Couch and his sociologist mentors Howard Odum and Rupert Vance that at least 150–200 of those pages would have to go before he could even hope to see it in print. Both Odum and Vance had nonetheless encouraged him to go ahead and send the full manuscript to a publisher in order to get a read on what cuts and revisions might be necessary. Thus, in July, roughly two months after it was approved by his doctoral committee, he shipped his unrevised dissertation to Macmillan, where editors had agreed to review it at Odum's request. Convinced that such a high-profile press would never really consider publishing it without big cuts and perhaps a heavy subsidy as well, Woodward expected no more than some helpful suggestions out of Macmillan.[6]

Within the space of another two months, however, in early September, just as he was settling rather uncomfortably into his teaching position at the University of Florida, he received a letter from Macmillan, not only offering to publish his manuscript, but telling him, "we like the book about as it stands, and we hope you do not change it too much." Having gotten what amounted to an author's dream letter, Woodward proceeded then to push his luck by cramming an additional fifteen pages into his text, and less than a year after his dissertation was deemed adequate to secure his Ph.D., the young author was reading a glowing review of *Tom Watson, Agrarian Rebel* by influential historian Allan Nevins in the *New York Times.* Numerous such public commendations were no doubt gratifying, but surely no more so than a brief note from his primary academic inspiration Charles A. Beard, lauding Woodward as "a flash of light in a fog of academic mediocrity."[7]

Still intent on making his name as a biographer rather than a traditional academic historian, Woodward spent the next year mostly casting about for a new subject. After months of flirting with the likes of John C. Calhoun and John Randolph of Roanoke, he had just about settled on socialist leader Eugene V. Debs when he received a rather surprising invitation to replace the original author of the post-Reconstruction "New South" volume in the new History of the South series, a joint venture of the University of Texas and Louisiana State University Press. All of the authors chosen for the other volumes were much older and better established than the thirty-one-year-old Woodward, who by this time had reconciled himself, albeit grudgingly, to the fact that even as a successful biographer, he would still have to make his primary living as a university professor. Accordingly, he realized that the chance to "have my say on the period" and "lay down the main lines of interpretation" was "more important professionally than anything I could write just now."[8]

He was surely correct, although it would be twelve years before the book appeared. Woodward's research and writing were interrupted by three years of wartime service in the Office of Naval Intelligence, during which time he did the work that culminated in his second book, *The Battle for Leyte Gulf,* which was published in 1947. Upon his release from military service, with a Guggenheim Fellowship guaranteeing that his first year would be free for research, Woodward accepted an associate professorship at Johns Hopkins in 1946 and rose to full professor the following year. He continued to work on what eventually became two books; one of them, *Origins of the New South,* covered the period 1877–1913, and the other, *Reunion and Reaction,* explored the causes and context of the Compromise of 1877, which brought Reconstruction to its ostensible end. After publishing both of these important books in 1951, Woodward was invited to deliver the prestigious Walter Lynwood Fleming Lectures in Southern History at Louisiana State University. The next year brought both the Bancroft Prize for *Origins of the New South* and the presidency of the Southern Historical Association.[9]

Woodward's rising international profile resulted in opportunities to teach at the University of Tokyo in 1953 and to serve first as Commonwealth Lecturer at the University of London in 1954 and then as Harmsworth Professor of American History at Oxford for the 1954–55 academic year. The single most momentous career opportunity to come Woodward's way, of course, was the invitation to deliver the James W. Richards Lectures at the University of Virginia in the fall of 1954. With the aftershocks of that May's historic Supreme Court school integration decree far from dissipated and its implications by no means fully understood, large and receptive audiences turned out to hear Woodward's take on the origins of segregation. Sensing the timeliness of the topic and the dearth of any such historically informed commentary on a matter of urgent contemporary concern, Oxford University Press pounced on Woodward's lectures, and roughly six months after he gave them, they were in print as *The Strange Career of Jim Crow.*[10]

Reviewers were overwhelmingly positive, many of them seemingly swept along by Woodward's suggestion that Jim Crow's roots were neither historically deep nor as culturally affirmed as many had presumed. If, instead of rising more naturally out of experience, racial segregation had simply been implanted by law, then surely it might well be uprooted in the same fashion. Initial sales were solid but unspectacular, but as the civil rights movement began to gain momentum, Oxford had difficulty keeping the book in stock.[11]

Woodward had become a major force within his profession by the end of the 1950s, and his word on whom to hire and what to publish was already being widely sought. Roger Shugg informed him in 1959 that his "good opinion" of Stanley Elkins's controversial dissertation on slavery had completely "cancelled out the highly critical opinion" of another historian who had read the manuscript for the University of Chicago Press. Woodward had already signed a contract with Little, Brown, and Company for a book on Reconstruction, but he asked to be released from his contract in 1958 because W. W. Norton had offered him a considerably larger advance to do the same book; Little, Brown eventually tripled its initial figure. At the same time, when word got out that he was thinking of putting together the volume of his previously published essays that became *The Burden of Southern History*, he was besieged by inquiries from a host of commercial publishers, including Little, Brown and Knopf, even though he had already signed a contract with Louisiana State University Press.[12]

Woodward had already turned down offers from Berkeley, Wisconsin, Columbia, Chicago, and Princeton, to name but a few, by the time that Yale came calling in 1960, and it was only after an intense courtship of both Woodward and his wife, Glenn, that he finally decided to leave Baltimore for New Haven. He did not actually step into the classroom at Yale until 1962, having negotiated an initial year free from teaching responsibilities. However belated, his arrival would, as Michael O'Brien put it, quickly establish Yale as "the headquarters of Southern history."[13]

Not only had he reached what the thoroughly unreconstructed University of Georgia historian E. Merton Coulter snarkily described as "the pinnacle in Yankeeland," but fifty-two-year-old Comer Vann Woodward from Vanndale, Arkansas, had also reached the pinnacle in his chosen field, and from that point on, practically until the end of his life, hardly any front-rank institution made a senior appointment in southern history without consulting him. At times it seemed that Woodward was nothing less than the "go-to guy" for aspiring authors hoping to see their books touted in the *New York Times Book Review* and the *New York Review of Books*. In these publications and elsewhere, he regularly reviewed his own students' work and that of his close friends with little apparent regard for any questions of propriety that such a practice might raise. The same attitude prevailed as he wrote tenure and promotion evaluations for his students and other protégés.[14]

In a career where irony and references thereto were not exactly scarce, it was nonetheless striking that by the time he arrived at Yale to begin his long reign as the patriarch of southern history, Woodward's days of writing traditional scholarly monographs had actually been over for roughly a decade. He went on over the better part of the next four decades to pen literally hundreds of essays and essay reviews, some of them in academic journals, but the overwhelming majority in influential popular publications, ranging from the *New York Times* to *Harpers* to the *Saturday Review.* Meanwhile, save for several spurts of research in the early 1960s on his never-to-be-completed book on Reconstruction and the flurry of work on coediting the previously unpublished Mary Chesnut diaries in 1984, after 1951 Woodward's time in the archives was scant indeed and little in evidence in his writings. Roughly four and a half of the ninety-six boxes that constitute the C. Vann Woodward papers at Yale contain research notes of any sort, and the overwhelming bulk of those involving primary sources relate to work completed by 1951 or earlier. None of his eight additional books, composed largely of previously published and typically footnote-free essays, give evidence of archival work that was likely done after the publication of *Origins of the New South,* and the same is true of all except one of his eleven articles in traditional historical or social science journals published over the next forty-odd years.

There are several considerations that might help us understand this apparent shift in Woodward's focus as the 1950s unfolded, or perhaps to determine whether it was, in fact, all that significant or pronounced. On an elemental, personal level, archive avoidance hardly seems out of character for someone who, as we have already seen, was not at heart a terribly avid hunter and gatherer of historical information. Given the choice, Woodward clearly preferred massaging ideas to digging for evidence. One of the greatest of his multitudes of complaints about graduate school, after all, had centered on both books and professors equally "void of ideas." Several years after graduate school, while teaching at the University of Virginia, he commiserated with a young Englishman who had studied at Virginia and who discovered, to his dismay, that "in America as in England . . . ideas" were "about the last thing professors of history care[d] for." Woodward heartily agreed, condemning "the research for research's sake school" and observing, "Some of the young American scholars are going to have to stage a deliberate revolt from this academic Philistinism or our scholarship will lapse into an untimely dotage."[15]

To a certain extent, Woodward was surely objecting here simply to the penchant of an older generation of historians for gathering information, as Barbara Fields might put it, simply "for the pure antiquarian hell of it" rather than for the meaning it might actually convey. Moreover, as he offered this criticism, Woodward himself was engaged in the massive multi-archival effort that eventually produced both *Origins of the New South* and *Reunion and Reaction.* In this case, however, he had been urged by History of the South Series editors, especially E. Merton Coulter, to shun primary research in favor of simply summarizing the accumulated wisdom of those senior scholars whose writings consistently reaffirmed the New South's historiographical order and, by implication, the region's racial and political status quo. Thus, if, as he put it, he hoped to turn "the orthodox credo . . . upside down," Woodward realized he had little choice in the matter—it was to the archives he must go.[16]

It was clear early on as well that Woodward would never be content with simply tilting with the academic establishment. He frequently forsook the relative security of the ivory tower to push forcefully and directly for social justice, particularly racial justice, in the public arena. He was a lifelong admirer of W. E. B. Du Bois, and at age twenty-four he had been involved in rallying support for black communist organizer Angelo Herndon, who was convicted of attempting to incite insurrection in Atlanta in 1932. In April 1940, just thirty-one years old and not quite three years out of graduate school, Woodward had testified before the House of Representatives Committee on the Judiciary in support of abolishing the poll tax, speaking in behalf of "the agrarian masses who have not a sufficient voice in their own state governments, much less in their representatives in Congress."[17]

Having just arrived on campus in 1947, Woodward quickly lodged a protest against segregation at the Johns Hopkins Faculty Club. As chairman of the Southern Historical Association's Program Committee in 1949, he also saw to it that John Hope Franklin became the first black scholar to read a paper before that group. Three years later, as the sitting president of the SHA, Woodward managed, with strategic support from local friends and influential members, to move the presidential address and banquet to a nearby country inn when the host hotel in Knoxville refused to serve dinner to an integrated audience. He was soon working with the NAACP's Legal Defense Fund to prepare the historical briefs that became part of the plaintiff's case in *Brown v. Board of Education*. In 1965 he joined the last leg of the fabled Selma to Montgomery march, and in 1981 he returned to Congress to testify in behalf of renewing the Voting Rights Act.[18]

Given his zeal for social activism, it was not terribly surprising that, in addition to attempting "revisionary subversion" of the reigning orthodoxy in southern historiography, even when he was operating largely as a traditional scholar, Woodward had also tried to use his writings to reach beyond the academy and directly influence contemporary public opinion and policy. His efforts to make the past tell a broader popular audience what he thought it needed to hear in the present profoundly influenced the scholarly response to these writings over time.

Surely the least intentionally didactic of his books on southern history—either in the academic realm or the broader public context—was the first. A half century after his Watson biography appeared, Woodward characterized it as his fledgling attempt to launch an "oblique" assault on "the ramparts of the establishment in Southern historiography" by "looking into all the dark, neglected, and forbidden corners of Southern life shunned by the New South school." He had also expected, so he claimed, that readers would pick up on the obvious comparisons between the plights of "the rednecks, lintheads, and Samboes" of the 1890s and the "Okies and Arkies" of the 1930s. In reality, of course, he had chosen the topic and written most of the manuscript with no such purpose or expectation in mind. Even as the book went to press, Woodward remained primarily enthralled with Watson's personal "story," and he fairly bragged about yielding "only when I had to" when his adviser, Howard Beale, urged him to provide more of the "transitions, summaries, etc." that would assist scholarly readers in grasping the larger historical and historiographical implications of his work.[19]

Although most reviewers saw Watson's story simply as a personal tragedy symbolic of a regional one, Woodward's study did make an implicit case that southern Populists should be taken seriously as legitimate actors in a dramatic Beardian contest between the shrewd and powerful business/industrial "haves" and the game but outmanned agrarian "have-nots." He also made the demise of southern Populists, and of Watson in particular, seem a classic example of the devastating impact of racism on political and personal behavior in the South. To many critics, however, Woodward ultimately pushed his argument a counterfactual too far by suggesting that Watson's early overtures to black voters were significant enough to justify seeing the Populists as a "forgotten alternative"—a potential colorblind coalition of "those who have less," such as that later envisioned by political scientist V. O. Key—that had been cruelly smothered in its cradle by the agents of the emerging Redeemer–New South elites.[20]

These infanticidal Populist-slaying Redeemer–New South leaders became the villains of *Origins of the New South.* Woodward began by disputing the traditional wisdom that the Redeemers, with whom latter-day southern politicians were quick to claim spiritual kinship, were descendants of the old aristocratic antebellum planter regime that was still venerated by many southern whites in the 1950s. On the contrary, he argued, those who seized the levers of political and economic power in the wake of Reconstruction were merely the self-serving representatives of an ascendant and grasping new middle class. While the broader implications of *Tom Watson, Agrarian Rebel,* were not so universally clear, *Origins* all but defied careful readers to miss the connection between the contemporary South's multitude of problems and deficiencies and the transgressions of the Redeemers. They, after all, had deliberately divided the region's black and white masses, condemning them to generations of unrelenting racial and class repression and thoroughly callous economic exploitation as the colonial subjects of northeastern capital. In similar fashion, of course, their self-styled political heirs were still using race to thwart class consciousness and maintain their restrictive grip on the South's material and human development as the second half of the twentieth century began. Reiterating his message a decade after *Origins* appeared, Woodward insisted that "the Modern South" was still "continuous in its economic, political and racial institutions with the order established in 1877." *Origins of the New South,* Avery O. Craven observed, was a book that "wrecks most of the old notions that have grown up about Southern life after the Civil War."[21]

Purposeful notion-wrecking can be a risky business, for it tempts historians into the kind of excesses that send salivating revisionists into feeding frenzies. By insisting so adamantly that there was "little but a nominal connection" between the greedy, scheming Redeemers and the still-hallowed old planter group, Woodward had hoped by implication to undermine the ancestral legitimacy of the neo-Redeemers who continued to run the South in the 1950s. In doing so, however, he also sparked more than a generation's worth of historiographical jousting on the mere matter of Redeemer genealogy, ultimately at the expense of potentially more fruitful exploration of their actual aims, motives, and interests, irrespective of their pedigrees. Moreover, by assigning so much responsibility to the Redeemers for the sorry way things turned out for the twentieth-century South, Woodward had ignored or slighted factors over which they had little or no influence, such as the abysmal scarcity of capital in the postbellum South, the declining growth rate of world cotton demand, or the more dynamic northern economy's greater competitive attraction for large-scale investors. Conceding that he might have gone a little over the top in his campaign against the standard New South historiographical dogma, Woodward admitted many years later, "The familiar line of southern historiography was the one I was trying to overthrow, so I had to speak out rather forcibly to be heard. In such circumstances it's perhaps natural to overemphasize some points, and I think I did that." While *Origins of the New South* has shown remarkable staying power, its presence on today's graduate and undergraduate reading lists may say more about its readable, informative narrative than its abiding interpretive power.[22]

This was clearly not the case in the 1950s, however. The NAACP lawyers in the *Brown* case drew heavily on the interpretations offered in both *Origins* and *Reunion and Reaction* as they contended that after Reconstruction, "the Negro" had been "effectively restored to an inferior position through laws and practices, now dignified as 'custom and tradition.'" In *Origins,* Woodward had suggested that "coercion of sovereign white opinion" had actually been a "more pervasive" influence on the rise of segregation than had "state and local law." Yet three years later in *The Strange Career of Jim Crow,* he took great pains to present racial separation as largely a product not of long-standing custom and social pressure, but of relatively recent legislation, suggesting that its status was less venerable, and therefore perhaps more tenuous, than many believed.[23]

In October 1954, as he reflected on the recently delivered lectures that would soon become *The Strange Career of Jim Crow,* Woodward confided to Howard Beale that he had "sensed a powerful concern over the subject, a genuine eagerness of troubled people to know what to think and feel and say about a deeply disturbing problem. In this situation I felt the historian would play a legitimate role as therapist of the public mind, could probe the public memory and bring to light the repressed if unpleasant truth." Oxford University Press's request to publish the lectures as quickly as possible seemed to reaffirm Woodward's perception that such therapy was urgently needed, but his revelation was not simply his acknowledgment of a rare, fleeting opportunity for an academic to teach the general public a timely historical lesson. Rather, in retrospect it seems more like a relatively forthright indication of his ambition to escape the traditional scholarly tedium of footnotes, bibliographies, and archival burrowing and draw instead on his prodigious facility with words and ideas in order to make the past more relevant and usable for Americans outside the academy as they confronted the challenges and anxieties of a turbulent present.[24]

Woodward's desire to serve as public therapist ultimately led him well beyond the realm of southern history to take on a variety of concerns, national and global, foreign and domestic, political and social. Yet as *The Strange Career of Jim Crow* and many of his subsequent writings in both *The Burden of Southern History* and elsewhere made so abundantly clear, nothing would ever engage him nearly so deeply and passionately as the struggle to destroy segregation and racial discrimination and create an effectively colorblind America. *Strange Career* became, without doubt, his most influential book, but here, as with *Origins,* the implications of Woodward's approach also suggested that historians who seek to use the past to shape contemporary public opinion should always remember that in doing so, they are likely to be engaging and affecting scholarly opinion as well.

In this case, Woodward's desire to sway popular thinking on a matter of monumental contemporary social import, and of great personal urgency to him as well, was clear at the outset when he announced in the preface to *Strange Career* that he was looking to offer a much-needed "corrective" to "the national discussion over the questions of how deeply rooted, how ineradicable, and how amenable to change the segregation practices really are." He proceeded then to assail the prevailing public perception that, as an ancient "folkway" rooted deeply and inextricably in tradition and historical experience, segregation was, in fact, simply impervious to efforts to destroy it with "stateways," which in this case meant the official actions of the courts or Congress. This *folkways uber alles* doctrine held such broad popular sway at that point that its adherents included both 1956 Democratic presidential nominee Adlai Stevenson, who warned against "upsetting habits or traditions that are older than the Republic," and his incumbent opponent, Dwight D. Eisenhower, who simply announced, "You cannot change people's hearts merely by law."[25]

Woodward had clearly identified a significant obstacle to winning broader public support for the civil rights cause. Clearly, historians should not be held solely responsible for a lack of initiative or imagination among their peers or successors. Still, by setting up his historical analysis with a view to weighing in on an important but rather simplistic and superficial popular debate over whether state-ways could influence folkways, Woodward exaggerated the actual importance of any difference between the two. In addition, because legitimate scholarly examinations of the topic were so scarce at that point, by addressing a question that he had raised simply to engage a broad public audience, he also set a full generation's worth of professional historians largely to exploring the when and how of segregation rather than the why.

Beyond that, in *The Strange Career of Jim Crow,* what his old friend David Potter called Woodward's powerful "urge to find constructive meanings in the past for the affairs of the present" and his faith in the power of ideas had simply gotten the better of his "historical realism," leading him to advance an argument that he simply lacked sufficient evidence to sustain. *Strange Career* came into the world unblushingly naked of footnotes and remained so, but this may have been a rare case of a work's academic credibility actually being enhanced by its lack of formal documentation, given that the sparsity of supporting evidence would have been more immediately apparent with notes than without them.[26]

Forrest McDonald's description of *Strange Career* as "an example of a historian's letting what his heart told him influence what his research showed him" was certainly insightful, although McDonald appeared to presume that Woodward had actually done enough research on this topic to show him much of anything. Indeed, although he had committed to the lectures more than a year earlier, scarcely three months before they were to be delivered, he had done no preparation whatsoever but was planning to talk about the relatively recent racial, political, and economic changes that had marked "the end of an era of Southern history that began with the end of Reconstruction." In reality, what became the most broadly influential historical treatment of American race relations since the Civil War would not have passed muster as a research paper in one of Woodward's own graduate seminars at either Johns Hopkins or Yale. Among Woodward's contemporaries, only David Potter either noticed or chose to point out that his friend's argument for greater fluidity in racial interaction prior to the Jim Crow legislation of the 1890s rested on a grand total of seven sources (all of which had already appeared either in *Origins* or in contemporary works by Vernon Wharton and George Tindall), including, to wit, the accounts of two northern travelers and one from Great Britain, plus those of two southerners, one white and one black, and, finally, two southern newspaper editorials.[27]

By the most charitable appraisal, this was an exceedingly frail body of evidence for so muscular an argument. Moreover, Woodward had brazenly cherry-picked the words within these sources, excising his quoted material with such surgical precision that within the space of sometimes no more than a single sentence in the original document, even the casual reader could have found other observations and sentiments that, if not flatly contradictory, clearly weakened Woodward's case.[28]

For the most part, general readers paid little attention to the way Woodward used his sources or to the relative paucity thereof, but many of them who had picked up on the book's relatively encouraging implications and tone were sorely dismayed as the ugly reality of massive resistance set in. With her husband actively involved in defending participants in the Montgomery Bus Boycott in December 1955, Woodward's friend Virginia Durr warned him that his "'Jim Crow' book" seemed "a little optimistic from the point of view of Montgomery, Alabama," leading the author to gently concede that after witnessing more than a year's worth of public reaction to the initial *Brown* ruling, he "would not be as hopeful as I was then." Woodward's concession did nothing to silence the pit-bullish Durr, however, who reminded him again in early 1963 to "be humble, you did prophesy wrong in the Jim Crow book and all hell has broken loose since then."[29]

Although Woodward had expressed great enthusiasm in the immediate aftermath of his lectures for serving as "a therapist for the public mind," he complained on more than one later occasion that his book had been read so widely by "the truly uninformed who needed all the help they could get," and thus "what had originated as a modest communication to a Southern academic audience had swelled into a mass paperback publication for a national and quite mixed audience of vast numbers." "Searching for the cheering and hopeful message," he observed with no hint of irony, "truly naïve" popular readers had simply "sought quotable passages to confirm views, advance an argument, make a point. In *The Strange Career of Jim Crow,* they often discovered what they sought and used it as they wished."[30]

Woodward's complaints about nonacademic readers who found too much cause for optimism in his text might have carried more weight had he not repeatedly taken his argument into the popular reading arena shortly after *The Strange Career of Jim Crow* first appeared. By 1956 he was pointing out to readers of the *Nation* that "many of those who are presently defending the Jim Crow laws as ancient and immemorial folkways are older than the laws they are defending." Over the latter half of the 1950s, he penned several more articles that generally accentuated the positive over the negative even in the face of swelling white opposition and the ugliness in Little Rock. Strident calls for last-ditch resistance notwithstanding, in language that seemed to have been lifted directly from the text of *Strange Career,* Woodward insisted there actually was "no uniformity of opinions" among contemporary white southerners but rather "a considerable degree of diversity as well as some fluidity."[31]

Finally, Woodward's claim that it was primarily the large popular audience attracted by *The Strange Career of Jim Crow* that had come away irrationally exuberant over the prospect of segregation's speedy demise hardly squares with the reading it got from a good many of his fellow academics, even African American scholars like Rayford W. Logan, who thought the new cracks discovered in Jim Crow's armor might be chalked up to "the relative recency of many of the segregation laws." Meanwhile, black sociologist E. Franklin Frazier lauded Woodward's demonstration that "the race problem was *made* and men can *unmake* it as they are attempting it today."[32]

Both academic and general readers found further cause to believe that Jim Crow's demise, if not yet a fait accompli, was nonetheless imminent in "The Search for Southern Identity" (originally published in 1958), the lead essay in *The Burden of Southern History,* where Woodward noted that "one by one, in astonishingly rapid succession, many landmarks of racial discrimination and segregation have disappeared, and old barriers have been breached." If, as he had maintained in *Strange Career,* racial subordination and separation were not as firmly fixed in southern tradition as many believed, it followed then that whites who abandoned their defense of Jim Crow were not also abandoning their regional heritage in the process. Here Woodward was urging white southerners to reject U. B. Phillips's contention, advanced thirty years earlier, that the "central theme of southern history" and "the cardinal test" of southern identity was "a common resolve, indomitably maintained," that the South "shall be and remain a white man's country." Doubtless responding to contemporary charges that the intensifying push for racial integration was a direct assault on "the Southern way of life," Woodward likened the situation in the late 1950s to that of the late 1850s when another embattled South had another "morally discredited Peculiar Institution in its hands." Reminding white southerners of what had happened when loyalty to slavery became synonymous with loyalty to the South, he foresaw similarly disastrous consequences if southern leaders succeeded a century later in doing the same with segregation. As in 1860, the South's racial institutions were once again "under condemnation from the rest of the country and the rest of the world," and Woodward warned, "If Southernism is allowed to become identified with a last ditch defense of segregation, it will increasingly lose its appeal among the younger generation."[33]

Woodward was acutely aware that, for all the exceptions he might point out, most white southerners shared a common impulse to resist practically any significant threat to the status quo, racial or otherwise. Hoping to harness this ingrained defensiveness to a more positive purpose, he suggested that while the region's leaders had contrived to make saving segregation seem tantamount to saving southern identity, the real threat to southern distinctiveness lay in "The Bulldozer Revolution," which, fueled by rapid industrial and metropolitan growth, was steadily "plow[ing] under cherished old values of individualism, localism, family, class, and rural folk culture." He urged his fellow southerners to counter these powerful homogenizing forces by dropping their futile defense of segregation as the touchstone of southern identity and embracing something that gave their regional heritage real affirmative meaning and value. Woodward had already offered a hint as to just what that might be in "The Irony of Southern History," his 1952 presidential address to the Southern Historical Association, which had appeared the following year in the *Journal of Southern History* and now served as the concluding essay in *The Burden of Southern History*. In "Irony," Woodward cleverly inverted the prevailing paradigm in debates about southern distinctiveness, arguing that in a broader global context, it was not the South but the rest of the nation's experience that was actually peculiar because not only did southerners have no place in the great "American legend of success and victory," but it was "not shared by any other people of the civilized world." On the other hand, while the South's experience with military defeat, occupation, and reconstruction set it apart from the rest of America, it also established common ground "with nearly all the peoples of Europe and Asia."[34]

Although he had effectively established the basis for a new southern identity grounded in fundamental historical differences, in "Irony" Woodward simply used his premise to argue that in light of the South's repression of criticism and dissent from the proslavery line in the 1850s, historians of the region should be particularly well positioned to provide a dispassionate but informed critique of the McCarthyite witch-hunting of the 1950s. They might also draw on the thwarted idealism of the Reconstruction era to make cold war strategists more aware of the pitfalls that might await them as they sought to overthrow undemocratic regimes and to indoctrinate "liberated peoples."[35]

In "The Search for Southern Identity," Woodward took this argument a step further, urging all southerners to see their "un-American past" with its legacies of failure, defeat, and guilt as both the basis of a new regional self-awareness and a powerful antidote to cold war assumptions of American innocence, virtue, and invincibility. It soon became apparent, of course, that Woodward had failed to persuade very many southerners to acknowledge the lessons of their own past, much less to impart them to other Americans. It should not escape notice, however, that in the most widely read essay in *The Burden of Southern History*, he had also sought to push white southerners' historic commitment to maintaining their racial system out of the spotlight and uncouple it from efforts to preserve their distinctive regional identity.[36]

In one way or another, the remaining essays in the collection also managed to move southern racial practices toward the periphery, emphasizing the limited egalitarianism of northern abolitionists or Radical Republicans; suggesting that for all their superficial Yankee-baiting and rhetorical excess, white southerners also had some valid, substantive criticisms of northern values and practices; and lauding southern writers for their profound respect for the power of the past. In sum, nothing in the first edition of

The Burden of Southern History undermined in the least Woodward's earlier suggestions that the prospects for effecting Jim Crow's demise might be brighter than many believed. Indeed, "The Search for Southern Identity" presented that demise as practically a done deal and urged southern whites to squander no further energy in trying to rationalize or defend the indefensible.[37]

Woodward's purpose in challenging U. B. Phillips in this essay, as he later explained, was much the same as his purpose in the lectures that became *Strange Career.* That was not to deny, on one hand, the enduring reality of racism, or racial subordination, which he deemed a "'given' in the southern condition," requiring "no proof or demonstration." On the other hand, "What *did* need proof and demonstration at the time was that there were ever any exceptions, any evidence against the once prevalent (and now reviving?) assumption 'that things have always been the same,'" or as Phillips put it, "'that it shall be and remain' the same." After all, Woodward reasoned, "if there had been no exceptions, no breaks, and things had always been the same, there was little hope of change."[38]

In response to Woodward's rationale for this highly selective and unapologetically presentist treatment of the past, David Potter simply asked, "What has the historian to do with hope?" For Potter, the problem with such an approach in this case was that it "implied that the degree of the historian's emphasis upon the identification of the South with slavery and later with segregation should be determined not by the actual extent of the South's [historical] commitment to these practices, but by the effect [of] such an identification" on the racial attitudes and behavior of contemporary southerners. To be sure, if Woodward might be accused of using history as propaganda, then he must at least be credited with propagandizing for a manifestly good cause. Hence, the repeated allusions by historians to Rev. Martin Luther King Jr. reportedly praising *The Strange Career of Jim Crow* as the "historical Bible of the Civil Rights movement" in his moving speech upon the completion of the historic Selma-to-Montgomery march in 1965. Contrary to numerous secondary accounts, if transcripts of his remarks are accurate, King apparently did not actually invoke the biblical metaphor on this occasion. However, with Woodward and many other prominent historians in the crowd, he did praise *Strange Career* for exposing segregation as nothing more than "a political stratagem employed by the emerging Bourbon interests in the South to keep the southern masses divided and southern labor the cheapest in the land." For all the emotional satisfaction this must have given him, Woodward must surely have winced just a bit at hearing his thesis so egregiously oversimplified and also in knowing that, whatever his intent, the hope he had given his readers had even at that point already soured into discouragement and discontent for many of them.[39]

Sensing that he may have gone a bit overboard in accentuating the positive, by the time the second edition of *Burden* appeared in 1968, Woodward was less upbeat in his assessment of what the Second Reconstruction had actually managed to achieve and notably less sanguine about what might lie ahead. The southerners to whom he referred in *Burden* were always white, since, in his view, blacks had yet to "achieve articulate expression of their uniquely un-American experience" as southerners. This assertion would doubtless have surprised Zora Neale Hurston, Jean Toomer, and Langston Hughes, not to mention Woodward's friend Ralph Ellison and even Richard Wright, to name but a few influential black writers. To his credit, though, Woodward was certainly prescient in suggesting that "the Negro" would one day acknowledge "that he is also a southerner as well as an American."[40]

In the first edition of *The Burden of Southern History* and the early editions of *Strange Career,* Woodward had seemed to take it for granted that when whites either chose or were forced to pull down their discriminatory barriers, grateful, longsuffering blacks would simply embrace the opportunity for full interaction with whites on equal terms. This, after all, was what the ultimate goals of the *Brown* decision and the civil rights movement, as it stood at the end of the 1950s at least, seemed to be. It is important to remember, however, that at that point the Montgomery Bus Boycott was the only major instance of organized civil rights protest Woodward had witnessed. There was certainly little basis for anticipating the bitter, broadly distributed confrontations and violence sparked by the sit-ins, the Freedom Rides, the Birmingham protests, the organizing activities of Freedom Summer, and the bloodshed in Selma. Nor could one have anticipated at that point the sometimes bitter divisions in black opinion on the most effective and appropriate strategy and terms for securing racial equality. Moreover, with such overwhelming attention focused on the struggle in Jim Crow's backyard, not much attention was given to the prospect that pent-up anger and frustrated expectations would set northern cities aflame in the mid-1960s.

Woodward had only begun to process all these unforeseeable or unexpected outcomes when he penned an essay in November 1966, asking "What Happened to the Civil Rights Movement?" Beset by negative white reaction across the nation and undercut by the excesses of a few black leaders and the violence in the streets of America's major cities, after the passage of the Voting Rights Act of 1965 the Second Reconstruction had quickly ground to a halt in what he judged to be a "triumph of tokenism." Despite his disappointment, Woodward still managed to find reason to hope that the energy and drive of the younger activists of the Second Reconstruction might eventually spark a Third. However, the assassination of Rev. Martin Luther King Jr. forced him to append a hasty postscript to the essay as it appeared in the second edition of *The Burden of Southern History* in 1968, conceding that the "loss" of King "necessarily modifies even the cautious words of optimism with which the above essay was concluded in 1966." Acknowledging that at his death King was still more readily associated with the Second Reconstruction than with the Third, "which was [still] struggling to be born," Woodward noted that during the final year of King's life, the martyred black leader had been "striving heroically to redirect his leadership from a Southern to a Northern or national orientation." In doing so, King was moving past the issue of legal rights to focus on "economic objectives" and to "embody the new aspirations and needs in his own rhetoric of nonviolence and hope and to resist their embodiment in the idiom of the ghetto, in the rhetoric of despair, alienation, racism and violence." Hardly sounding confident, Woodward conceded, "Whether [King] would have succeeded in his strivings we will never know."[41]

Woodward also ventured "A Second Look at the Theme of Irony" in the 1968 edition, finding irony aplenty in the fact that self-righteous northern crusaders intent on righting the South's racial wrongs had suddenly glanced over their shoulders to see "their own cities on fire" because "the very people whose liberation they were about to achieve and whose eternal gratitude they assumed they had won in the South were now in open rebellion against them in the North." In a tone more bitingly sarcastic than ironic, Woodward noted that as the "seething black ghettoes continued to erupt," eclipsing anything seen in the South to that point, a growing number of northern "Moderates or Liberals" had begun to redefine their objectives, explaining that "while racial integration may be desirable in the South, conditions in the metropolitan North made it impractical in the foreseeable future." Until such time as integration seemed feasible, they would accommodate themselves in the North to the racial separation they had vowed to eradicate in the South, evoking, Woodward observed wryly, "the old separate-but-equal dialectic of Southern segregationists, so recently discredited and abandoned."[42]

A year after the second edition of *Burden* appeared, Woodward's presidential address to the Organization of American Historians was a truly remarkable example of the kind of unflinching, go-against-the-grain candor all too rarely witnessed in the academy. Making a thorough and persuasive case that the traditional "whites-only" or "whites-mostly" approach to their history had done a great disservice to all Americans regardless of race, he called for "an infusion of 'soul'" as "an essential corrective in line with the tradition of countervailing forces in American historiography."[43]

That said, however, Woodward made no secret of his concerns about separate Afro-American studies programs featuring courses emphasizing the agency of even the most downtrodden blacks and taught solely by black instructors, who alone were said to be capable of supplying the "black perspective." In 1967 Woodward had declared his friend William Styron's *The Confessions of Nat Turner* "the most profound fictional treatment of slavery in our literature" and had praised Styron's "native instinct for the subtleties and ambivalences of race in the South." He had grown steadily more outraged as, on one hand, black academics assailed Styron for presuming, as a white man, to write a novel about the leader of America's best-known slave revolt. Accordingly, on the notion of "exclusive preemption of a subject by reason of racial qualification," Woodward was both forceful and blunt. Not only was "Negro history . . . too important to be left entirely to Negro historians," but "to disqualify historians from writing Negro history on the grounds of race is to subscribe to an extreme brand of racism," precisely the kind of racial discrimination, one might add, that Woodward had labored so mightily to discredit.[44]

Turning to guilt-ridden white historians dedicated to seeing "full justice done at long last to Negro achievements and contributions," Woodward warned, "It is a misguided form of white philanthropy and paternalism that would attempt to compensate by exaggerating or by celebrating ever more obscure and deservedly neglected figures of the past." Reacting to the growing presence and respectability of Afrocentrism in American academe, Woodward also cautioned against "impulses of guilt and self-flagellation that encourage the depreciation of all things European or white in our own civilization and turn its history into a chorus of *mea culpas.* The demagoguery, the cant and the charlatanry of historians in service of a fashionable cause can at times rival that of politicians." Woodward's concerns on this score only intensified as he heard from black graduate students teaching at other institutions about the alarming "incidence of fraud, farce, and frustration" that seemed to accompany the explosive growth of black studies programs and curricula.[45]

One need not presume to play therapist to Woodward's mind to observe that nothing is so striking about his writings on race after the 1960s and throughout the rest of his life as his repeated, almost pyrophobic allusions to flames and fire as he lamented the violence that left so many cities in the mid and late 1960s "literally aflame." Although on rare occasions he seemed almost to take satisfaction in observing what he called the resultant "withering of self-righteousness along the Massachusetts-Michigan axis," he knew full well that what he saw going up in smoke when northern cities were "set aflame by looting and embattled mobs" was his own dream of a racially integrated, colorblind society.[46]

Here again, he need not look to the streets to see his dream reduced to ashes. In his mind he could see it perishing right before his eyes on university campuses where "black intellectuals were loudly demanding black withdrawal, separation, nationalism, exclusion of all whites, and pre-emption of all teaching and monopoly of all writing of black history by blacks." Such an outcome was clearly a bitter disappointment for someone whose principal goal, as his former student J. Mills Thornton observed, had always been "a society in which race was recognized as an identity imposed by others, rather than something innate."[47]

In the third and final edition of *The Burden of Southern History,* Woodward offered a second retrospective on "The Irony of Southern History" forty years after its initial appearance in the *Journal of Southern History.* One thoroughly inescapable irony that clearly brought him a little satisfaction was the relative "peacefulness" and alacrity with which racial integration and reconciliation had proceeded in the South as compared to the rest of the country after 1965. "Perhaps," Woodward observed, "alterations of this degree and depth have occurred elsewhere in history in the relations between people of such widely disparate origins and status over so brief a period, but they do not readily come to mind." Sweet as this ironic outcome might have been in some respects, however, there was always for Woodward the bitter offsetting reality of "the national resort to violence by the black people who in 150 major riots looted and put to the torch the slums of cities from one coast to the other for four summers." Thus was "the triumph of the non-violent strategy" followed by "militant threats to 'burn down America'" and the "about-face ordered by black-power leaders of the militant persuasion who renounced King's aim of racial integration and proclaimed an aggressive racial separatism and nationalism."[48]

Woodward's anger and frustration with the proponents of black separatism or Afrocentrism would not cool, and he continued to decry all such attempts to promote black unity at the expense of further integration with whites. This was abundantly clear in his remarks titled "Recent Paradoxes of American Race" at a conference on race and ethnicity at the German Historical Institute in September 1994. Here once again he deplored "the rise of movements for black power and racial separation" and quoted the incendiary rhetoric of black intellectuals like James Baldwin, who asked in *The Fire Next Time,* "Do I really want to be integrated into a *burning* house?" Impressed by Woodward's candid assessment of race relations and the state of black leadership at that point, W. W. Norton president Donald Lamm asked him at the end of 1994 to take a year to explore the prospect of a short book highlighting these paradoxes and the concerns they raised. As an enticement, Lamm promised a fifty-thousand-dollar advance, the first ten thousand of which Woodward could keep even if the project should "lose its appeal" to him.[49]

In response, Woodward began gathering some relevant notes from contemporary sources. Before the allotted year had expired, however, he wrote Lamm in October 1995, noting that the [O. J.] Simpson and Rev. [Louis] Farrakhan "TV melodramas" had helped him focus even greater attention on the project. He even listed some additional "paradoxes" that had occurred to him, such as efforts to achieve "black unity by embracing slaveholders 'one-drop' [of black blood] definition of black" and using "Africa, the most disunited of continents as [a] model for black unity in [the] U.S." Yet, just when Woodward appeared to have made the case for writing the proposed book, he pointed out that presenting any of the paradoxes he raised would inevitably entail "some degree of criticism or reproach for blacks," none of which, of course, would be "welcome," especially if it came with a candid discussion of the sensitive matter of the Simpson trial with its "use of money and race to subvert justice and [to] disgrace trial by jury" or "plain speaking about Farrakhan . . . and his blatant racism." The response from blacks, so he imagined, would be a pained: "This from Woodward . . . one white southerner we have been taught to regard as a friend. But look at what he is saying now!" Woodward insisted that up to this point he had "never let hostility to my views stop me from putting them into print." Still in raising these controversial issues he would also be matching wits with "pundits" and other experienced contemporary analysts while writing not as "a historian with command of the evidence" but rather more as a "journalist" or "sociologist," and just a few weeks shy of his eighty-seventh birthday, he concluded, "to come forth in either or both roles in such times as this would be a poor way to end a long career as a historian."[50]

Yet, at the very end of that career, at the tender age of eighty-nine, Woodward was doing exactly what he told Lamm that he wanted to avoid, as he gave vent once more to his bitter disappointment with America's racial present and his grave concerns about its racial future. As it happened, I was on hand to hear these remarks, delivered, strangely enough, on the tiny island of Ærø, off the coast of Denmark. The occasion was the 1997 meeting of the European Southern Studies Forum, an organization consisting primarily of European scholars whose deep interest in the American South simply affirmed Woodward's prescient observations in "The Irony of Southern History" about the global relevance of the southern experience. In his remarks comparing the post-Reconstruction periods of the 1890s and 1990s, Woodward noted that while "optimism [had] briefly soared" in the wake of the landmark civil rights legislation of the 1960s, it had quickly become clear that these hopeful expectations rested on "false assumptions." One of these fallacies, he conceded, perhaps with oblique reference to *The Strange Career of Jim Crow,* was "that the legal end of an institution meant the end of the abuses outlawed."[51]

From this self-referential admission, he launched into his now-familiar narrative of black disappointment and division, including the requisite reference to "flaming cities" and a condemnation of the white backlash reflected in the Republican-stacked Supreme Court's efforts to undermine school integration. Actually cheered on by a black justice, the Court had recently rendered school desegregation a "lost cause," Woodward reported, but Clarence Thomas was far from "alone among the black people" who favored "resegregation." Distressed that "ethnic nationalism" had soundly trumped "*e pluribus unum*" in a nation supposedly dedicated to "assimilation for all," the old ironist could not resist pointing to the contrast between the racially diverse group assembled at the Lincoln Memorial in 1963 to listen to Reverend King's message of integration and healing and the crowd, twice as large and all black, which gathered at the same spot in 1995, "facing the opposite way—in more than the literal sense," to hear Reverend Farrakhan "spread his gospel of nationalism, separatism, racism and hatred."[52]

These observations, which appeared in print shortly before Woodward's death in 1999, were quite likely his last published words on this or perhaps any other subject. Standing on the cusp of a new century he did not live to see, the old warrior who had put his scholarly reputation on the line for the cause of racial integration and cooperation by straining so earnestly to find reason for hope in the supposedly forfeited opportunities of the distant past could find little in the recent past or present to justify such feelings. As he ultimately conceded, by using his writings to influence public opinion outside the academy, Woodward had clearly given those within it "the impression of neglecting the rule for the exceptions" and thereby placed himself squarely in the critical crosshairs of his trigger-happy professional peers. Woodward's well-known advocacy of clear, constructive criticism as vital to the scholarly process was both a virtue and a necessity, given the strong challenges his work encountered during the last half of his career. By 1982 John Cell was not the least bit hesitant in declaring that Woodward's argument for notably more fluid racial interaction in the South prior to the Jim Crow legislation of the 1890s "contradicts most, though certainly not all, of the available evidence about the lives of most southerners in the generation after the Civil War." Woodward's thesis was nowhere in evidence in Stephen Hahn's 2003 study of black political struggle and did not make it out of the footnotes in Michael J. Klarman's *From Jim Crow to Civil Rights* in 2004.[53]

If it is fair to say that Woodward's efforts to rewrite the South's past have been subjected to sharp and frequently telling revisionist attacks, it is surely necessary nonetheless to add that both the number and the general quality of these challenges to his work are themselves something of a tribute to his scholarly accomplishments. As Richard H. King put it, "Woodward's achievement was to seize the historical moment in the early 1950s and to redirect southern historiography from the pietistic, monumentalist mainstream . . . into more liberal-critical channels." In doing so, he made revisionism not only respectable but a vital part of the process for southern historians. Beyond this, the soaring prose of dozens upon dozens of his essays does indeed show a committed and accomplished public therapist patiently probing, prodding, and sometimes gently rebuking his readers for their recalcitrance or self-righteousness, always urging Americans, regardless of region or race, to reflect soberly on their past before reacting rashly to their present. For this, he surely deserves our lasting thanks and praise as one of the most profoundly and constructively influential American intellectuals of the twentieth century.[54]

It is all the sadder, then, to think that as the curtains fell on that century and, almost simultaneously, on his remarkable life, he seemed to take what he called the "failures" and "cruelly shattered" dreams of "the Second Reconstruction" so personally. In May 1960 as he reviewed the original jacket copy for *The Burden of Southern History,* Woodward objected to a reference to the book's "ironic perspective" because, on occasion, "irony is wrongly confused with mockery or sarcasm." Yet not only was one of the two pivotal essays in the volume centered on the theme of irony, but consciously or not, he had also chosen a strikingly ironic title (actually suggested by fellow historian Daniel Boorstin) for a book in which he had endeavored to show that instead of a crippling encumbrance, the South's past was actually replete with vitally important lessons for all Americans. Even at the end of his days, however, perhaps the most critical of the unlearned lessons of that past, the tragic consequences of an obsession with racial identity, continued to torment and frustrate the mind and heart of one who had truly made what he always contended was not simply his region's but his nation's most burdensome historical burden his own.[55]

NOTES

1. C. Vann Woodward, *The Burden of Southern History,* 3rd ed. (orig. published 1968; Baton Rouge: Louisiana State University Press, 1998), back cover.

2. John Morton Blum, *A Life with History* (Lawrence: University of Kansas Press, 2004), 157; William Palmer, *From Gentleman's Club to Professional Body: The Evolution of the History Department in the United States, 1940–1980* (Lexington: University Press of Kentucky, 2009), 55–56.

3. For an overview of Woodward's early career, see James C. Cobb, "'On the Pinnacle' in Yankeeland: C. Vann as a (Southern) Renaissance Man," *Journal of Southern History* 67 (November 2001): 715–40.

4. C. Vann Woodward, *Thinking Back: The Perils of Writing History* (Baton Rouge: Louisiana State University Press, 1986), 20, 21, 22.

5. Ibid., 23, 22; C. Vann Woodward to Glenn W. Rainey, October 27, 1934; April 29, 1935; May 17, 1936, box 22, folder 1, Glenn W. Rainey Papers, Special Collections Department, Robert W. Woodruff Library, Emory University.

6. J. Carlyle Sitterson, transcript of interview by John Herbert Roper, November 10, 1979, folder 7; Bennett H. Wall, transcript of interview by John Herbert Roper, April 11, 1979, folder 9, John Herbert Roper Papers, Southern Historical Collection, University of North Carolina Library; C. Vann Woodward to "Jack," July 15, 1937, folder 4; Woodward to Rainey, September 11, 1937, folder 1, box 22, Rainey Papers.

7. Woodward to Rainey, September 11, 1937, box 22, folder 1, Rainey Papers; Allen Nevins, "Tom Watson and the New South: Crucial Economic, Social, and Political History as Reflected in His Career," *New York Times Book Review,* April 3, 1938, 1, 26; Charles A. Beard to C. Vann Woodward, September 20, 1938, box 7, folder 70, C. Vann Woodward Papers, Archives and Manuscripts, Sterling Library, Yale University.

8. Woodward to Rainey, March 26, 1939, box 22, folder 1, Rainey Papers.

9. Julia Ann Oxner Hall, "C. Vann Woodward: American Educator" (Ph.D. diss., University of Mississippi, 1977), 44–48; C. Vann Woodward, *The Battle for Leyte Gulf* (New York: Macmillan, 1947); *Reunion and Reaction* (New York: Little, Brown, 1951).

10. Hall, "American Educator," 51–52; C. Vann Woodward to Howard K. Beale, October 22, 1954, box 28, folder 6, Howard K. Beale Papers, Wisconsin State Historical Society, Madison, WI.

11. Sheldon Meyer to C. Vann Woodward, February 26, 1960, box 71, folder 113, Woodward Papers.

12. Roger W. Shugg to C. Vann Woodward, February 20, 1959, box 50, folder 589, Woodward Papers; Arthur Thornhill Jr. to C. Vann Woodward, April 15, 1959, box 71, folder 11, Woodward Papers.

13. Michael O'Brien, "Making the South New: Sympathy and Scholarship in C. Vann Woodward," *Times Literary Supplement,* April 14, 2000, 18.

14. E. Merton Coulter to J. Fred Rippy, October 25, 1961, box 48, folder 5, Special Collections Division, E. Merton Coulter Papers, University of Georgia Library. On Woodward's influence, see, for example, Woodward to Raymond Walters Jr., December 22, 1966, box 38, folder 416; Woodward to R. B. Silvers, February 22, 1964; April 14, 1969, box 71, folders 117–18; Woodward to David M. Kennedy, February 3, 1984, box 62, folder 758, all in Woodward Papers.

15. Woodward, *Thinking Back,* 21; Woodward to Rainey, May 17, 1936, box 22, folder 1, Rainey Papers; Esmond Wright to C. Vann Woodward, October 15, 1940; Woodward to Wright, December 1, 1940, box 60, folder 736, Woodward Papers.

16. Woodward, *Thinking Back,* 63.

17. C. Vann Woodward, "Statement in Favor of Abolishing Poll Taxes," *Congressional Digest,* 20 (1941): 309–10 .

18. Cobb, "'On the Pinnacle,'" 732–33; Ferdinand Hamburger Jr. to C. Vann Woodward, January 15, 1948, box 228, folder 327, Woodward papers; "Voting Rights Act" [Woodward's House subcommittee testimony], 1981, box 79, folder 57, Woodward Papers.

19. Woodward, *Thinking Back,* 42; Woodward to Rainey, May 7, 1937; January 10, 1937(8) [This letter is incorrectly dated, probably because it was written so early in the new year.]; December 4, 1942, box 22, folder 1, Rainey Papers.

20. Woodward, *Strange Career of Jim Crow,* 2nd ed. (New York: Oxford University Press, 1966), 60–65; V. O. Key, *Southern Politics in State and Nation* (New York: Alfred A. Knopf, 1949), 307.

21. C. Vann Woodward, "New South Fraud Is Papered by Old South Myth," *Washington (DC) Post,* July 9, 1961, E3; Avery O. Craven, "The South in Critical Days after the Civil War—Debunking Some Legends," *Chicago Tribune,* January 20, 1952, pt. 4, p. 5.

22. C. Vann Woodward, *Origins of the New South, 1877–1913* (Baton Rouge: Louisiana State University Press, 1951), 20; Jan De Blieu, "A Past Apart," *Emory Magazine,* October 1984, 10.

23. Richard Kluger, *Simple Justice: The History of Brown v. Board of Education and Black America's Struggle for Equality* (New York: Alfred A. Knopf, 1975); Woodward, *Origins,* 212.

24. Woodward to Beale, October 22, 1954, box 26, folder 8, Beale Papers.

25. Woodward, *Strange Career,* ix, 134, 163.

26. David M. Potter, "C. Vann Woodward and the Uses of History," in *History and American Society: Essays of David M. Potter,* ed. Don E. Fehrenbacher (New York: Oxford University Press, 1973), 166.

27. Forrest McDonald, *Recovering the Past: A Historian's Memoir* (Lawrence: University Press of Kansas, 2004), 105; C. Vann Woodward to Rupert B. Vance, June 21, 1954, box 57, folder 684, Woodward Papers; Potter, "C. Vann Woodward," 163.

28. George B. Tindall to C. Vann Woodward, March 20, 1965, box 63, folder 652, Woodward Papers. For Woodward's selective use of evidence, compare Woodward, *Strange Career,* 18, with A South Carolinian [pseud.], "South Carolina Society," *Atlantic Monthly* 391 (June 1877): 676; and Woodward, *Strange Career,* 24, with Charles Dudley Warner, "Impressions of the South," *Harper's New Monthly Magazine* 71 (September 1885): 550.

29. Virginia Durr to C. Vann Woodward, December 5, 1955; Woodward to Durr, December 9, 1955; Durr to Woodward, February 25, 1963, box 16, folder 183, Woodward Papers.

30. Woodward, *Thinking Back,* 93.

31. C. Vann Woodward, "Young Jim Crow," *Nation,* July 7, 1956, 10; C. Vann Woodward, "The Disturbed Southerners," *Current History* 32 (1957): 279; see also C. Vann Woodward, "The New Reconstruction in the South," *Commentary* 21 (1956): 501–8; and C. Vann Woodward, "The South and the Law of the Land," *Commentary* 26 (1958): 369–74.

32. Rayford W. Logan, review of *The Strange Career of Jim Crow,* by Woodward, *American Historical Review* 61 (1955): 212; E. Franklin Frazier, review of *The Strange Career of Jim Crow,* by Woodward, *Saturday Review* 38 (June 11, 1955): 13.

33. Woodward, *Burden of Southern History,* 10–12.

34. Ibid., 10, 209, 188, 190.

35. Ibid., 209.

36. Ibid., 21.

37. See "The Historical Dimension," 27–39; "Equality: The Deferred Commitment," 69–88; "The Political Legacy of the First Reconstruction," 89–107; "A Southern Critique for the Gilded Age," in Woodward, *Burden of Southern History.*

38. Woodward to Roper, September 6, 1977, folder 30, Roper Papers.

39. Ibid.; Potter, "C. Vann Woodward," 159–60; Woodward, *Thinking Back,* 92; Rev. Martin Luther King Jr., "Our God Is Marching On!" (speech, Montgomery, AL, March 25, 1965), www.mlkonline.net/ourgod.html (accessed August 29, 2011).

40. Woodward, *Burden of Southern History,* 22.

41. Ibid., 172, 186.

42. Ibid., 225–28.

43. C. Vann, Woodward, "Clio with Soul," *Journal of American History* 56 (June 1969): 16.

44. Ibid., 16–18; Woodward is quoted in John White, "The Novelist as Historian: William Styron and American Negro Slavery," *American Studies* 4 (1971): 233.

45. Woodward, "Clio with Soul," 18; Woodward to Robert Engs, September 8, 1970, box 86, folder 18, Woodward Papers.

46. Woodward, *Burden of Southern History,* 225 (first quotation), 237; C. Vann Woodward, "The South Tomorrow," *Time,* September 6, 1977, 99 (second quotation); Woodward, *Thinking Back,* 92 (third quotation).

47. J. Mills Thornton III, "C. Vann Woodward: November 13, 1908–December 17, 1999," *Civil War History* 46 (2000): 337–40.

48. Woodward, *Burden of Southern History,* 246, 237–38.

49. Woodward, "Recent Paradoxes of American Race" (unpublished manuscript), box 70, folder 105, Woodward Papers; Donald S. Lamm to C. Vann Woodward, January 27, 1995, box 70, folder 104, Woodward Papers.

50. Woodward to Lamm, October 21, 1995, box 70, folder 104, Woodward Papers.

51. C. Vann Woodward, "Post-Reconstruction Periods Compared: 1890s and 1990s," in *The Southern State of Mind,* ed. Jan Nordby Gretlund (Columbia: University of South Carolina Press, 1999), 220.

52. Ibid., 220–21.

53. Woodward to Roper, September 6, 1977, folder 7, Roper Papers; John W. Cell, *The Highest Stage of White Supremacy: The Origins of Segregation in South Africa and the American South* (Cambridge: Cambridge University Press, 1982), 92; Michael J. Klarman, *From Jim Crow to Civil Rights: The Supreme Court and the Struggle for Civil Rights* (New York: Oxford University Press, 2004), 18, 51; Steven Hahn, *A Nation under Our Feet: Black Political Struggles in the Rural South from Slavery to the Great Migration* (Cambridge, MA: Harvard University Press, 2003).

54. Richard H. King, "The Last Southern Historian: C. Vann Woodward," *Intellectual History Newsletter* 22 (2000): 83.

55. C. Vann Woodward to Donald R. Ellegood, May 17, 1960, box 68, folder 81, Woodward Papers.

2

Woodward's Southerner

History, Literature, and the Question of Identity

LEIGH ANNE DUCK

> Historians are more skeptical of the alleged "lessons of history" than the laity, and they should know better than anyone else that when there is a choice between the "right" lesson and the "wrong," mankind has a strong predilection for the latter.
>
> —C. Vann Woodward, *The Burden of Southern History* (1993)

In "Woodward's Southerner: History, Literature, and the Question of Identity," Leigh Anne Duck deconstructs Woodward's vision of southern identity presented in The Burden of Southern History. *She begins with the misperceptions that remain rampant regarding Woodward's take on the southern heritage. She delineates Woodward from his literary colleagues, the Fugitive-poets-turned-Agrarian-intellectuals at Vanderbilt (Robert Penn Warren and Allen Tate, for example), who championed a whitewashed, innocent southern past. And she also contends that Woodward was not an advocate of abandoning one's southern identity in favor of a national allegiance, a position still attributed to him at times. Rather, Duck paints a more complicated and nuanced picture of Woodward's southerner, exposing the historian's inner desire to see white southerners find an authentic but usable past—one that "might be put to intellectually, politically, and ethically generative use." Despite her effort to balance Woodward's intent with his reception, Duck turns a critical eye toward Woodward's omissions. Noting that Woodward honed his vision of southern identity in his essays on southern literature—a field consumed with defining southern identity at that time—Duck also points out Woodward's lack of discussion of African American literature, specifically. She sees this omission as a casualty of his efforts to define a shared culture: "Woodward's inattention to African American writing parallels his treatment of regional identity more broadly; in seeking a politically productive account of southern commonality, he neglects meaningful differences." But these differences were not lost on Woodward, Duck concludes. His evolving perspective, argues Duck, is revealed in his revised editions of* The Burden of Southern History, *where he not only calls for a Second and a Third Reconstruction that would move the South beyond Jim Crow, but he also highlights the ongoing injustices facing African Americans in the South in the post-civil-rights era. After her thorough evaluation of Woodward's vision of southern identity and its political function, Duck concludes that "had Woodward imagined that, 150 years after the Confederacy lost the Civil War, the nation would still be debating that entity's merits, he might not have suggested that a specifically 'southern' identity might constitute the best hope for promoting the values of modesty, caution, and justice in national politics."*

In March 2010, as the book review and opinion editor for the *New York Times* was seeking to contextualize debates over the new social studies curriculum in Texas, he was moved to cite the late C. Vann Woodward concerning the relationships among history, politics, and collective identity. The Texas State Board of Education (SBOE) had garnered national attention not only because textbook producers are purported to cater to Texas's demands in constructing volumes for multiple states,[1] but also because SBOE members so unabashedly sought to shape historical knowledge in support of contemporary political agendas. (During one meeting, argument became so heated that a Republican accused more conservative members of "re-writing history"; in an interview, the leader of the conservative faction proclaimed education "too important not to politicize.") Sam Tanenhaus, writing for the *Times,* situated this controversy in a long series of conflicting efforts to articulate and institutionalize an American identity, but he feared this particular incident might indicate that "after so many years of increasingly bitter polarization, Americans stand on the brink of a collective identity crisis and no longer share a set of common ideas about the true character of the country and the true meaning of democracy."[2] It is this concern that Tanenhaus sought to address via Woodward's famous essay "The Search for Southern Identity" (1958), written amid regional turmoil over racial desegregation. Considering the midcentury South a "parallel phenomenon" to the contemporary nation, Tanenhaus recommends Woodward's solution: "What Southerners should do, Mr. Woodward urged, is subordinate their regional attachment to the country's 'national myths,' for instance the American 'success story' that had inspired so many others."

But Tanenhaus could not have been more wrong about Woodward's recommendations, which, as the historian later explained, were prompted less by his concerns about southern culture than by his "fear of and revulsion at the mood into which the country at large had fallen."[3] Thus, although Woodward notes the "powerful urge among [U.S.] minority groups to abandon or disguise their distinguishing cultural traits and conform as quickly as possible to some national norm," he does so with considerable alarm; rather than promoting regional adherence to "the national legends of opulence and success and innocence," Woodward seeks chiefly to challenge that understanding of national identity.[4] He observes that such beliefs are, to a great extent, facilitated by presenting the South as an aberration: if the United States has experienced conspicuous "economic abundance," for example, the South is equally distinctive for its "generations of scarcity and want," and while the United States may celebrate its victory over such "Old World ills" as "tyranny, monarchism, aristocracy, and privilege," the South cannot deny having "lived intimately with a great social evil" (16–20).[5] Woodward paints here with a surprisingly broad brush, as he was surely aware that neither poverty nor injustice (including slavery) had been restricted to the South; writing shortly after the notorious acquittal of Emmett Till's murderers, he also overlooks that regional understandings of "evil" appeared far more diverse than he suggests. But in *The Strange Career of Jim Crow* (1955), Woodward had already intimated his desire to call a more liberal South into being by inscribing a more liberal history, and he later admitted that in "The Search for Southern Identity," he chose to dwell in "the hypothetical" as a way to address national politics.[6] Accordingly, although he begins the essay by questioning whether "Southern heritage" remains meaningful to the region's residents, he concludes, "To deny a Southern identity . . . would also be to deny to America participation in a heritage and a dimension of historical experience that America very much needs, a heritage that is far more closely in line with the common lot of mankind than the national legends"; as he later explained, he hoped such a regional identity might be able to resist "engulfing nationalism."[7]

One can only guess at the cause of Tanenhaus's flagrantly inaccurate paraphrase, but he may have been engaging in the practice he attributes to the broader public, concerning whom he argues: "As Americans struggle to see where they are going, they continue to gaze fondly at the past—and to see in it what they like." Nonetheless, in suggesting the salience of Woodward's thought to "America's seemingly endless culture wars," Tanenhaus usefully highlights Woodward's series of meditations on the relationship between history and collective identity. Observing Woodward's influence on scholarship in southern and U.S. history, Matthew D. Lassiter and Joseph Crespino have recently and persuasively argued that his insistence on southern distinctiveness has proved deleterious: overstating differences and neglecting similarities between region and nation, such descriptions have been used to bolster precisely the narratives of national innocence and benevolence that Woodward sought to disrupt.[8] But Woodward also claims, at a more general level, that a certain relationship to the history of a region could produce a beneficial form of identity that would be imbued—less by learning than simply by "heritage"—with insight into the dangers of hubris and the importance of justice in political life. This position also merits questioning, and indeed, as the following section of this essay demonstrates, such assumptions were often challenged by Woodward himself. Although *The Burden of Southern History* (wherein "The Search for Southern Identity" serves as an opening gambit) often presents history as a basis of identity, many of his writings depict it more tepidly as a potential source for perspective or, as evidenced by my epigraph, as a set of narratives that must always be viewed critically or even skeptically.

This ambiguity in Woodward's thought has been noted,[9] but his model of a regional identity emerging from historical experience remains influential, in part because much contemporary thought—scholarly and otherwise—has since embraced ideas of "collective memory."[10] Such approaches to the past—in which history is not so much investigated as absorbed through interpersonal or perhaps institutional interaction—were also at stake in the Texas SBOE debates.[11] One may question whether a middle-school history class could be a "critical site for the generation and inflection of affective bonds," as Kerwin Klein describes the implications of "memory," but that was the hope of some SBOE members. Thus, when many conservative revisions passed, one supporter proclaimed, "American exceptionalism is back!"—suggesting that students not only would learn a specific version of the nation's history, but they would also become intimately invested in an idealistic narrative concerning what the nation has been and is now. Woodward, in contrast, sought to understand how the South's "unmastered past"—defined by Gavriel Rosenfeld as "a historical legacy that has acquired an exceptional, abnormal, or otherwise unsettled status in the collective memory of a given society"—might be put to intellectually, politically, and ethically generative use. But through these speculations, he, too, expressed his desire that a certain relationship to the past would yield a reliable approach to contemporary politics.[12]

Thus, to consider *The Burden of Southern History* today is in part to contemplate the role of humanistic knowledge in politics and education, concerning which Woodward is ambivalent. Indeed, his account of southerners' attachment to their past may reflect less his historical scholarship—which is often quite skeptical of such attachments—than his literary leanings; he took his model of southern identity, after all, not from empirical observation, nor from historical research, but from some of the region's recent literature. In suggesting that to "accept the past and its burden," one must do so as a resident of the region with personal connections that are deeply implicated in its history, Woodward was influenced by his friend Robert Penn Warren: that line comes from the conclusion of Warren's *All the King's Men,* in which the narrator forgives his mother for her adultery and deception, his biological father for his confusion and corruption, and the father who raised him for his unhelpful idealism.[13] But this kind of emotional and symbolic relationship to the past is of questionable use to the historian, as the narrator of that novel (a former doctoral student) quite literally demonstrates; Warren's own career, which includes both determined efforts at racial liberalism and, at different moments, unabashed segregationist and Confederate nostalgia, further demonstrates how an imaginative and emotional relationship to the past may yield wildly divergent political attitudes. And if Woodward erred in suggesting that Warren's oeuvre might provide a viable and coherent model of identity for actual southerners, as opposed to just fictional characters, he erred even more substantially in failing to recognize the work of black writers. The section of this essay titled "Literary Diversity and the Limits of Woodward's Vision" observes that even as Woodward wrote, authors such as Richard Wright and Ralph Ellison were famously and vigorously asking similar questions—with very different answers—concerning regional identity and national politics.

The purpose of this essay is not to criticize Woodward's skills as a reader; on the one hand, related errors are abundantly apparent in the annals of literary criticism, and on the other, he was perhaps more cautious of disciplinary difference than seems necessary. (In a review of Joel Williamson's *William Faulkner and Southern History* [1993], he suggests, rather mildly, that "historians are capable of adding insights to literary criticism" [269].) But history—regional, political, and literary—has not treated Woodward's hypothesis concerning southern identity gently, and in order to consider the relevance of his work to the twenty-first century, one must also recognize the omissions and even sheer willfulness inherent in his initial model. As my concluding section suggests, Woodward may have been prescient in his belief that central issues in national politics could be framed through reference to a specifically regional past; now, as then, however, appeals to "memory" and "heritage" often subtend political positions antithetical to those espoused by Woodward. The fate of Woodward's theory in recent years supports, ironically, what Woodward often argued even alongside his account of southern identity: although forms of knowledge associated with the humanities, such as history and literature, can provide important perspectives on political questions, they cannot be uncritically mobilized as political guides without distorting their content, which is necessarily complex and often ambiguous. And yet, since the significance of purportedly "southern" history for national politics remains acute, the *new* burden of southern history (or southern studies more broadly) may be to hew more closely to the methods of this skeptical Woodward—the one who often looks askance at his writings on identity.

DESIRE AND ANXIETY IN WOODWARD'S QUEST FOR A REGIONAL IDENTITY

Even in the text of "The Search for Southern Identity," Woodward argues the need for caution in "spawning new myths in place of the old"; his later writings render this early enterprise all the more surprising (16). In 1958, he suggests that southerners' "unique historic experience as Americans" should provide "the basis for continuity of their heritage" as well as "contributions" to a nation that elsewhere manifests dangerous "habits of mind" (16, 19). In his presidential address to the American Historical Association of 1969, however, he inveighed against such quests for a "usable past," arguing that efforts to emphasize a sense of "continuity" over "disjuncture" constituted a "fatal betrayal of the craft." Woodward was wary of narratives about history that convey a sense not only of what happened in the collective under question, but also what kind of entity it has become; he often referred to such accounts of the past as "myths," which are, as he explained in 1961, "charged with values, aspirations, ideals, and meanings." In that essay, he concedes that because myth helps a collective to grapple with the political questions of its identity and purpose, such historical narrative can be "a precious thing," but he insists nonetheless that "serious history is the critique of myths." In still later writings, he describes myth-based ideas of U.S. identity as perpetually exaggerated, misleading, resistant to meaningful analysis, and even treacherous. On the one hand, he argued that "Americans evidently have some special problems of a self-destructive nature in dealing with national guilt," and on the other, he attributed the nation's "aggressive foreign policy" to its cycles of "fatuous complacency and self-righteousness."[14]

This longer history of Woodward's thought compels us to attend (as he later complained few critics had) to the "subjunctive mood" in "The Search for Southern Identity": in his intellectual autobiography, he explained that he could attribute insight to regional identity only hypothetically because he could find little evidence that it had any influence. The essay's initial readers could certainly be forgiven for overlooking his verb constructions because Woodward published this work at a moment when the region's segregationists were vigorously asserting that southern traditions and autonomy should not be opposed; in that context, readers might have been more struck by the essay's opening queries as to whether "the Southern heritage [has] become an old hunting jacket that one slips on comfortably while at home but discards when he ventures abroad" (3). But Woodward's affable, speculative tone belies a determined stance concerning what southern identity should *not* be: he had already, in 1955, challenged the idea that racial segregation constituted a "deeply rooted" aspect of regional heritage, arguing instead that Jim Crow's duration coincided with the life spans of older (but not elderly) southerners, and he later lamented that as "The Search for Southern Identity" was going to press, "All over the South the lights of reason and tolerance and moderation began to go out under the resistance demand for conformity."[15] In other words, the organic and beneficial regional identity that Woodward hypothesized in "The Search for Southern Identity" was almost immediately challenged—to the extent that it might even exist—by a hegemonic and reactionary performance of embattled southern whiteness.

Even more than *The Strange Career of Jim Crow,* which has since been criticized for its unduly optimistic account of the region's racial history,[16] "The Search for Southern Identity" seems surprisingly sanguine. Woodward expresses confidence that the region's myths—by which he means those of white southerners—have been debunked, such that none could boast of the beauty and benevolence of antebellum slavery or bemoan the evils of Reconstruction; he further suggests that the region's shame since attendant upon slavery should effectively prevent "Southernism" from becoming "identified with a last ditch defense of segregation" (12–13). Undoubtedly accurate for some white southerners of the era (true, after all, for Woodward himself), his premise that "Lost Cause" mythology had lost its sway remains untrue for others to this day. Echoing Woodward fifty years later, literary critic Scott Romine concludes, "What comfort, indeed, from memories of slavery, Reconstruction, racial violence, Jim Crow, rickets, and widespread poverty? And yet nostalgia continues unabated as everyday practice and as industry."[17] But Woodward's optimism regarding the decline of neo-Confederate romanticism is crucial to his argument: it is only by assuming a chastened version of regional identity that he imagines "regional heritage" to "prove of enduring worth" (25). If white southerners did not, as he would have them, accept their history as proof of their fallibility, then their myths would be at least as destructive as those of the nation—as, he noted, they had proved to be in the past (21).

"The Search for Southern Identity" is, then, so hedged round with contingencies that it would be no surprise if it had suffered the fate Woodward feared; in his preface to the first edition of *The Burden of Southern History* (1960), he acknowledges that "few . . . efforts" to proclaim the "distinctiveness" of "the heritage, or the collective character, or the general outlook of a particular geographical grouping of people . . . have stood up very well under the test of time" (xxiii). Nor did his project of national critique require him to fabricate a regional identity, for an earlier essay in the same collection offers a version of his thesis that relies less heavily on "heritage" and focuses more on the role of the historian. In "The Irony of Southern History" (1953), Woodward complains—as scholars still do—that "the regional historian is likely to be oppressed by a sense of his unimportance. . . . As a standpoint from which to write American history [the South] is regarded as eccentric and . . . something of a handicap to be overcome" (187). But whereas contemporary southern historians, such as Laura F. Edwards, challenge this situation by insisting that "the dynamics of southern history are inseparable from central themes in U.S. history,"[18] Woodward sought to take advantage of "eccentricity" (187). "The Irony of Southern History" effectively conveys that southern history's trove of object lessons in strategic, political, and moral "blind[ness]" might constitute correctives to contemporary national fallacy (195). Still, Woodward is not content with comparison, expressing instead his continuing desire for a subject position that would manifest resistance to the "national legend of success and victory" (209).

Why, given his insistent skepticism, does Woodward repeatedly turn to the concept of identity? Must one feel ancestrally tied to a place—the successor to its "heritage," a term with which Woodward begins—in order to learn from its history? Woodward never even gestures toward such an argument without noting its empirical implausibility: the most amusing irony in "Irony of Southern History" is that, although Woodward would like to claim that southern history provides distinctly useful insight, he readily admits that southerners are not "any wiser than their countrymen" (195). (Surveying the attitudes Woodward cites at this moment—particularly reflexive optimism and support for military intervention—Bruce Collins argues that the South has still not become any wiser in subsequent decades.)[19] It could be, of course, that Woodward is simply attracted to the idea of a collective identity: in "The Search for Southern Identity," he makes clear that he would consider its loss—amid "social change and cultural erosion"—unfortunate (4). And yet it is not entirely clear what he means, as he mixes terms that suggest cohesion ("identity," "heritage") with those that seem to allow for more diversity and change, such as "cultural landscape" (5). Michael O'Brien points out that, on the whole, Woodward insisted on the importance of dissent and discontinuity in history, which may explain why this essay on heritage and identity—so similar, in many ways, to more recent work in collective memory—maintains consistent differences. Like the later French historian Pierre Nora, for example, Woodward finds collective memory—or, in his terminology, "myth"—to be a source of comfort and a promise of continuity and guidance, but Nora, who believes collective memory to be effectively lost, expresses less concern about its "dictatorial" behavior than mourning for its ability to bind social groups and provide meaning to experience.[20] Woodward, describing a region in which uncritical dedication to the Lost Cause was, by his own account, responsible for "jeopardiz[ing] and discredit[ing]" regional identification altogether, is more circumspect regarding the merits of group cohesion and commitment. In "The Search for Southern Identity," his penchant for irony appears in his claim that "regional identification" depended chiefly on "faults" (12, 5).

But although he complains that southern society does not yet bear out his argument that the region's history provides special insight concerning ethical political behavior, he finds evidence to support his claim of "the South's distinctive heritage" through its "magnificent body of literature": literary southerners—whether writers or characters—demonstrate precisely the characteristics he hopes someday to observe in actual southerners more generally (24). In "A Southern Critique for the Gilded Age," he notes three northern writers (Herman Melville, Henry Adams, and Henry James) who invent southern characters to serve as "a useful foil" for "the mediocrity, the crassness, and the venality" they believed to have "overtaken their own society since the Civil War" (137). More to the point, in "The Historical Dimension" (1956), he describes "an almost obsessive concern of [contemporary white] Southern writers with the past in the present," which leads them not to "defend the values or the prejudices or the errors" of the past but rather to "penetrate the romantic haze of an older generation as well as the cynical stereotypes of our own" (36, 38–39). This attribute of southern writing had inspired him early in his career: for a "Southerner who was graduated about 1930," he explains, "the most brilliant manifestation" of the region's "intellectual awakening . . . was in the field of letters and literary criticism" (28). And as he wrote the essays for *The Burden of Southern History,* that literature had "placed its writers in the vanguard of national letters" (24): Faulkner's work, for example, had once been derided as a representation of regional pathology, but it was embraced at midcentury as a model for how a future-oriented national culture might benefit from contemplating its past.[21]

But in using southern literature as a model for regional identity, Woodward introduces new problems in his argument—though none, incidentally, that are unique to his disciplinary background (16). As Michael Kreyling demonstrates in *Inventing Southern Literature,* decades' worth of work in southern literary criticism was devoted to elaborating and institutionalizing "the orthodox narrative of [southern] identity"; this narrative varied some across time, but the literature consulted was produced chiefly by white men, and where such writers were openly critical of the region—or even overtly anticonformist—their work tended to be ignored or domesticated. Kreyling locates the origins of this project in the work of the Nashville Agrarians, whom Woodward cites prominently also, a problematic source for a writer who seeks a specifically liberal version of southern identity; in their manifesto, *I'll Take My Stand* (1930), the Agrarians argued explicitly that the region should "defend the traditional Southern life."[22] To be clear, Woodward is writing in the 1950s, after the group had divided and many of its members had ceased political commentary; further, one prominent member of the group had by this time changed his position regarding the particularly pertinent issue of racial segregation. In *I'll Take My Stand,* where one writer complained about black sharecroppers, several distorted the history of slavery, and others ignored black southerners altogether, only Robert Penn Warren defended Jim Crow explicitly, but in *Segregation: The Inner Conflict in the South* (1956), he describes the end of segregation as a difficult but necessary societal change. Woodward dedicated *The Burden of Southern History* to Warren, and the version of southern identity that he embraces is nothing like the defensive model once promulgated by the Agrarians: instead, he imagines that southerners must necessarily accept "the somber realities of hardship and defeat and evil," an awareness "closely in line with the common lot of mankind" (24–25). Even so, Woodward's effort to assign a single identity-formation to a diverse region fulfills the "possibilities for embarrassment" of which his preface warned (xxvi).

LITERARY DIVERSITY AND THE LIMITS OF WOODWARD'S VISION

Although *The Burden of Southern History* predates by decades what is now described as the "memory boom" or "memory industry" in several fields of the humanities and social sciences, Woodward was intimately familiar with one of its central precepts: his approach to southern history exemplified his conviction that to study history, as Edward Said later wrote of collective memory, was to enter "a field of activity in which past events are selected, reconstructed, maintained, modified, and endowed with political meaning." Woodward came of age, after all, at a time when accounts of the post–Civil War South were dominated, in the words of W. E. B. Du Bois, by a narrative that served "to paint the South as a martyr to inescapable fate, to make the North the magnanimous emancipator, and to ridicule the Negro as the impossible joke in the whole development."[23] Woodward's work helped to challenge that view, as he hints in "The Search for Southern Identity"; it is in his own *The Origins of the New South* (1951) and *The Strange Career of Jim Crow* (1955) where "rude hands [are] laid upon the hallowed memory of the Redeemers who did in the Carpetbaggers, and doubt [is] cast upon the antiquity of segregation folkways" (13). Ironically (and thus in keeping with Woodward's preferred intellectual approach), it may be in part because of Woodward and his contemporary John Hope Franklin that historians of the region were less swayed by a narrow definition of southern identity than their colleagues in literature departments were.[24] Although Woodward's interest in the region's distinctiveness was certainly influential, his insistence on challenging destructive hegemonies was also.

In a less palatable irony, however, Woodward overlooked the extent to which the literary avatars of his preferred identity formation had supported a nostalgic view. His main critical source for the view that southern writers are attuned to "the past in the present" was the conservative Agrarian Allen Tate, who, in *I'll Take My Stand,* admired the South's "feudal" tradition but lamented that the broader society was not still infused with it; he advocated a "violent and revolutionary" movement to restore what he very vaguely dubbed "a private, self-contained, and essentially spiritual life." Here, the only thing Tate seems to have learned from the past is that he wishes to restore it; its actual characteristics remain unclear. To be clear, Woodward relies on a later essay of Tate's, but, as Susan Donaldson argues, "The Profession of Letters in the South" (1935) ignores the historical impact of writing by southern white women and black southerners; it also pauses to "remark" that the only factor rendering southern "chattel slavery" worse than European peasantry was its greater "barrier between the ruling class and the soil."[25] Failing to recognize just how "peculiar" Tate's "historical consciousness" was (24), Woodward further neglected the fate of this identity formation in Faulkner's fiction. Initially interested in the power of commemoration to maintain the presence of the dead in a society, Faulkner's novels become increasingly skeptical of this practice as his career develops: for the characters in his most celebrated novels, "historical consciousness" is typically painful and often pathological.[26]

Ironically, then, the historical awareness that Woodward hoped might prove instructive was associated—in the very works he found so inspiring—with, on the one hand, the kind of defensive and mystifying exclusivity that he spent much of his career combating and, on the other, with a most painful kind of working-through, the success of which is usually dubious. Even more ironically, Faulkner's work has gone on to provide what seems to be an almost reflexive catchphrase for residents of the United States (and even beyond) who wish to acknowledge the continuing significance of the past: since its publication in *Requiem for a Nun* (1951), writers and speakers from Woodward to Barack Obama have quoted Faulkner's famous phrase "The past is never dead. It isn't even past."[27] In the novel, however, that line is attributed to a white lawyer who seems needlessly to demand that a white female relative, Temple Drake Stevens, recount a painful personal history to the governor; he has told her this narration might save a black woman, but she later discovers her errand was always doomed to fail. Thus, the context for that statement is, at best, a justification for a patriarchal power-play; Noel Polk reads this backward-looking authority figure as "sadistic." The point of the novel is not necessarily that the past is dead: Temple's early efforts to "fumigate an American past" are not successful either.[28] But the common implication that awareness of the past gives one any power to ameliorate or even understand its effects is probably more glib than could be supported by any of Faulkner's novels; a source of aesthetic inspiration for the novelist, history is rarely, in his work, a source of insight or even succor for characters.

Inattentive to the more negative aspects of "historical consciousness" as manifest in white southern writing, Woodward is oblivious to that found in the work of black southerners. As has been noted, "The Search for Southern Identity" often uses the word "Southerners" in ways that seem surely intended as reference to white southerners: Woodward could not have believed, for example, that black southerners had ever "cherished . . . the Plantation Legend of antebellum grace and elegance" (13). He makes clear, however, that the "Bulldozer Revolution," which "demolishes the old to make way for the new," affects everyone in the region, perhaps especially "rural Negroes, the most mobile of all Southerners" (6–7). This largely silent movement between inclusion and exclusion in his use of the term renders many instances ambiguous: certainly, black southerners had shared the region's experience of "poverty" and had observed reasons for "pessimism," but they might well be pleased about the South's "overwhelming military defeat" and, given the history of slavery and segregation, their feelings about "rural folk culture" might, in many cases, vary also (16, 21, 19, 10). In other words, Woodward writes in a way that allows for—and could be argued to assert—cross-racial commonality while also signaling, intentionally or not, his general focus on white southerners. This general ambiguity renders his one announcement of racial difference all the more stark: "There *are* Americans, after all, who were not 'born free.' They are also Southerners. They have yet to achieve articulate expression of their uniquely un-American experience. This is not surprising, since white Southerners have only recently found expression of the tragic potentials of their past in literature. The Negro has yet to do that. His first step will be an acknowledgment that he is also a Southerner as well as an American" (22).

Ironies abound here, not least that, although Woodward quietly jettisons many of the aristocratic biases he might have imported from Tate, he prominently succumbs to his source's habit of neglecting narratives of slavery, many of which are famous for their eloquence in describing the experience of oppression in America. Of course, that omission occurs in part because Woodward accepts Tate's assessment that southern literature only begins to achieve its potential in a later period; from there, Woodward errs by generalizing concerning a field of which he knows too little. But while one can accept that a busy historian with a penchant for white southern writing might not bring to mind such writers as Zora Neale Hurston or George Wylie Henderson, whose publishing careers declined in the 1940s, it is hard to understand how he could overlook Richard Wright, whose 1945 autobiography, a Book of the Month club selection, dealt exclusively with his experiences in Mississippi and Tennessee, including much consideration of whether Wright could identify with locales he found oppressive. Woodward's disregard for Ralph Ellison's *Invisible Man* (1952) is even more perplexing because that novel won the National Book Award just five years before Woodward published this essay; further, although Ellison's identification with the South was ambivalent, his protagonist does indeed, after first attempting to "slough off [his] southern ways of speech" and culinary preferences, finally—albeit anxiously—take the step Woodward advocates, reconciling himself to the pleasures of the hot buttered yam.[29] But the "invisible man's" experiences in the South—like those in the North—are brutal and alienating; he finally admits to appreciating black southern culture, but that affection symbolically leaves a bitter aftertaste, as he throws his second yam into the street.

Woodward's inattention to African American writing parallels his treatment of regional identity more broadly; in seeking a politically productive account of southern commonality, he neglects meaningful differences. (Michael Kreyling points to a similar problem in literary critics' early efforts to incorporate African American writers into a southern canon.)[30] Studying what he describes as struggles over "collective memory" between black and white southerners, W. Fitzhugh Brundage argues, "By insinuating their memory into public space, groups exert the cultural authority, express the collective solidarity, and achieve a measure of the permanence that they often crave." Unquestionably, the display of memorials and the organization of commemorative events testify to priorities in historical narrative and interpretation; they stake claims as to what persons and events matter in history. Woodward implicitly acknowledges the importance of such material and spatial practices by using the metaphor of "monuments" to describe "regional distinctiveness" (5), and such spatial metaphors are apt in a region whose "civic spaces" had, as Brundage demonstrates, long been "fill[ed] . . . with monuments glorifying the Confederacy and other episodes of white heroism." Woodward challenges that glorification, using the term "monuments" to describe, inter alia, white supremacist practices—"the poll tax, the white primary, the Jim Crow car, the lynching bee"—which "the Southerner," white or black, may find "deplor[able]" (5). But he fails to note that these practices, though potentially abhorrent to all, threaten and disenfranchise a specific group of the region's residents; similarly, albeit symbolically, monuments to the Confederacy produce a version of southern memory and identity that is explicitly hostile to African Americans. (However unpleasant antebellum life may have been for a wide array of southerners, no one fought to preserve the enslavement of white people.) Woodward's neglect of the differences between historic sites valued by black and white southerners, as well as their differing interpretations of various sites, is even more vexing in light of the fact that Confederate monuments were spared amid the "Bulldozer Revolution" that, in his view, threatened the continuity of southern identity. Many black neighborhoods, however, were razed, along with—as Brundage argues—"landmarks of black history."[31]

In more recent decades, efforts to interpret the region's history have broadened, allowing for vigorous contention and dialogue between, among others, black and white southerners. Literature has played an important role in this process, but in this case—perhaps more than ever—it demonstrates the tenuousness and incompleteness of any single narrative concerning the past. Ironically (again), given the gender Woodward invokes to describe his generic black southern writer, many of the African American writers who first identified their work closely with the South—even if they resided elsewhere—were women, including Toni Morrison, Alice Walker, and Gloria Naylor. As Madhu Dubey argues, many of their works describe pastoral settings infused with fulfilling "cultural traditions"; in that way, they "share much with the broader trend toward southern regionalism."[32] But this is not simply to say that Woodward's goal has been fulfilled. As Dubey further explains, the formal strategies of these works emphasize their fictive nature, such that the black southern experience they depict appears hypothetical, inaccessible, or simply otherworldly.[33] If, as Arlene Keizer argues, many contemporary works of African American (and Afro-Caribbean) literature seem to ground something like a black identity "in the past" of plantation slavery—"something like" because these works probe, in many ways, the question of how coherent a group can be—they also tend to do so in overtly experimental ways; as A. Timothy Spaulding argues, such "narratives simultaneously politicize the non-mimetic devices and genres they use in their texts and aestheticize the act of writing history."[34] Rather than, in Woodward's terms, acknowledging the Negro as southerner, they produce new literary forms through which to speculate about racial and regional experiences.

By foregrounding their innovation and idiosyncrasy in representing history, these authors are not submerging the actual past in a sea of relativism but rather addressing the potential political consequences of their projects. The rigorously historicist time-travel of Octavia Butler's *Kindred* (1979), the wrenchingly lyrical recitations of Gayl Jones's *Corregidora* (1975), the sardonic and whimsical parody of Alice Randall's *The Wind Done Gone* (2001), and the revisionist magic realism of Zakes Mda's *Cion* (2007)—to name only a tiny number of the novels in this enterprise—explore not only the difficulties of understanding a painful and poorly documented past, but also, and perhaps more centrally, the ways in which representations of that past can be used and abused. Arguments concerning black southerners' experience during slavery and segregation often proceed, after all, to assess contemporary African Americans as either "damaged" or heroically resistant (a claim that serves not only as praise but also as directive, since this quality is generally said to emerge from specific cultural or communal practices).[35] To propose an authoritative "identity" or "heritage," then, would be to align oneself with restrictive and sometimes racist political or cultural platforms, encountering problems that Woodward doesn't consider. Ironically, however, rather similar concerns had appeared in the work of Faulkner and some other white southerners, who aptly—and experimentally—explored whether and how an individual could value southern heritage and tradition without embracing the region's history of oppression. Woodward, entranced with the intellectual and aesthetic value of the questioning, neglected to consider whether such persistent and chastened backward gazes might be viable in the realm of politics or even, simply, life.

THE STRANGE CAREER OF WOODWARD'S SOUTHERNER

Later—and thus in essays appended to subsequent editions of *The Burden of Southern History*—Woodward became less sanguine concerning the potential for southern identity to yield insight into national politics. The multiple causes for this shift involved ironic outcomes in regional and national history: in "Look Away, Look Away" (1993), for example, he notes that just at the long-deferred moment when rural black southerners were gaining political rights, their districts had been so transformed by agribusiness that residents were left in abject poverty, turning to the construction of prisons and the disposal of other states' toxic wastes in order to rebuild their economies (253–55). Other ironies included the "backlash against black rights" in the "Northern and Western states," the poor living conditions confronting black migrants to the North,[36] the desire among some black southerners to resuscitate segregated schools over which they could exercise greater control, and the increase in white southern Republicanism, which he obliquely aligns with that party's retreat from racial justice (251, 248, 253, 256). Woodward appeared to feel gratified by the ways in which Lyndon Johnson—"as Southern in origins, accent, personality, and political style as a politician with aspirations for national leadership could have been at mid-twentieth century"—"implement[ed] the Second Reconstruction," facilitating the passage of multiple civil rights acts as well as legislation for the War on Poverty (238–39). But in a previous essay—"A Second Look at the Theme of Irony" (1968)—he expressed equal despair over Johnson's "pursuit of the national myths of invincibility and innocence" in his prosecution of the war in Vietnam (230).

By the close of the revised volume, then, Woodward has less to say about southern identity, but his essays from the 1960s, wry as they are, do convey some sense of mission for the historian. In "What Happened to the Civil Rights Movement" (1967), Woodward flirts with cynicism as he describes the "reaction" against the progress made toward racial justice, but although he mockingly boasts of the "armchair consolations" that prepare irony-clad historians for cycles in societal change, he ultimately refuses "glib[ness]" and assesses possibilities for a "Third Reconstruction," which would address the nation's economic inequality (172–73, 177). (In a moving postscript, he notes that the assassination of Martin Luther King Jr. "necessarily modifies even the[se] cautious words of optimism," since King had been "striving heroically" toward this economically oriented movement "which was struggling to be born" [186].) In "A Second Look at the Theme of Irony," he returns to his hopes for a Third Reconstruction, suggesting that "the un-American and ironic experience of the South with history" might provide crucial lessons for the "revolution in attitudes" and "wholesale abandonment of myths" that would necessarily accompany such social change (233). He still suggests that persons wishing to understand the challenges posed by the nation's present and future could find great insight by studying the region's past, and he even finds hope in the fact that, after the civil rights movement, the (white) "South has had to learn anew the bitter lesson history tried with only limited success to teach a century earlier—how to accommodate itself to conditions that it had repeatedly sworn it would never accept" (229).

This position merits reconsideration at a time when numerous scholars question whether the "southernness" of southern history (or studies), as has been practiced, might be a problem. On the one hand, Charles Joyner—speaking, as Woodward did in his time, rather hypothetically—argued in 2003 that for U.S. southerners, "confronting the tragic past has the potential to impart a deeper and more compassionate understanding of the modern world and of the universal human condition." On the other, in 2005, James C. Cobb suggested that "continuing to focus on why the South is not like the rest of America may actually prevent southern historians from fully understanding why the South is like it is (or was like it was)." Reaching the same conclusion from a perspective oriented toward scholarship on the United States, Lassiter and Crespino argue that a focus on southern distinctiveness "obscures much more than it reveals about fundamental questions of modern American history." Such concerns appear as well in other fields, and meanwhile, across an array of disciplines, scholars seek to better understand connections between the U.S. South and other parts of the world: "Like others building critically on Woodward's foundations," write literary critics Jon Smith and Deborah Cohn, they take seriously his claim that the southern experience shares much with the history of other locales.[37] This approach might initially seem to conflict with Woodward's avowed goal to provide insight for the nation, but given his rather unabashed penchant for seeking historical topics relevant to contemporary life, he might well have embraced this method. By the close of "Look Away, Look Away," after all, he suggests that any hopes for beneficial transformation—of which he seems, by this time, in short supply—will face "staggering difficulties," largely because of the intensity, in that era, of globalization.[38] Contemplating "The Next Phase of Cultural Work in the South" one year before Woodward's essay appeared, folklorist David E. Whisnant suggested that in a period of "multidimensional . . . and structural" change, exploring the myriad connections to and paths through the region might provide forms of understanding more applicable to contemporary life than "cultural isolationism."[39] But could these more diffuse approaches to southern history yield the insight into national difficulties that Woodward sought in a distinctive, bounded South, which might—he could never definitively confirm or deny—have learned from its experience?

Sam Tanenhaus, of course, demonstrates another reason that this moment is auspicious for reconsidering Woodward's argument: although the United States has been arguing vigorously about the meaning of its history since its very beginnings, that activity has recently been reenergized by the development of a political faction defining itself in part through its originalist stance toward the Constitution. In a remarkable coincidence, the nation has also been commemorating the 150th anniversary of a great struggle over that document: the Civil War. Of course, describing the war in this way could prove euphemistic. Allen Tate, in his biography of Jefferson Davis, for example, explained that views of secession as "treason" reflected "the naïve belief that loyalty to the Washington government was loyalty," whereas "the Southerners . . . conceive[d] the government . . . simply as the Constitution"; he went on to proclaim "profoundly wrong" the idea that the war was fought over slavery. But even if one retains Tate's phrasing, the "constitutional liberty" for which southern slaveholders argued was the right to hold human property and to maintain that property right across state lines. As is often noted, the rather popular refrain that the Confederacy seceded in order to preserve "states' rights" is incomplete; more fundamentally, it was concerned that the property rights of one group, as established up to that time, might be abridged at a future time if the movement to emancipate slaves—and thus honor what we now call human rights—succeeded. Accordingly, these constitutional questions were simultaneously legalistic and profoundly human, and writers on the subject emphasized those aspects of the question that seemed most strategic given their audience. Jefferson Davis himself, upon being inaugurated president of the Confederacy, proclaimed the South a society of constitutional originalists who had provided the document "framed by our fathers . . . the light that reveals its true meaning."[40]

Thus this chronological coincidence—the simultaneous emergence of the Tea Party and the commemoration of the Confederacy—has intensified a subtle but remarkable rhetorical resonance between the two. Bruce Collins notes that this fascination with "states' rights," so familiar from the battle over desegregation, has been associated with attacks on liberalism more broadly since the 1970s. Although such rhetoric is often described as the Republicans' "Southern Strategy" and understood specifically as veiled race-baiting, Lassiter describes it as a "suburban strategy" that "tak[es] advantage of the convergence of southern and national politics" by "accept[ing] the principle of equal opportunity under the law but refus[ing] to countenance affirmative action [and other] policies designed to overcome metropolitan structures of inequality."[41] For Collins, writing in 2003, this fascination with "states' rights" is one dynamic through which "the interest in the Confederacy as a Lost Cause has been rekindled,"[42] and it continues to appear prominently in political debate. To be clear, I know of no specific overlap between Tea Party members and those who look upon the Confederacy fondly; when reading a discussion board, for example, it is impossible to tell whether persons complaining about past and present federal tyranny both feel strongly about the justness of the Confederacy's aims and oppose contemporary regulation and taxation, or whether they draw these comparisons solely in order to encourage readers' attention to their more particular passion.[43] Further, although each group encounters the question of slavery in gesturing backward toward an idealized era, responses to that issue vary.[44] In their shared insistence that individual control of private property trumps federal plans to better the lives of citizens or residents more broadly, however, each of these groups reveals Woodward's insight concerning how education about history's cycles might help the nation understand its present.

Most usefully, by describing political efforts toward structural economic change as a Third Reconstruction, Woodward links this potential process to two previous phases in national history during which the parameters of citizenship changed, such that neither race nor the property claims of a slaveholder could limit a resident's (or would-be citizen's) rights. Each of these changes was seen as denying other citizens the privileges they had come to expect: private property, in the case of slaveholders, but also, in the midtwentieth century, the expanded political power that accrued to white southerners more generally. Woodward imagined that the Third Reconstruction would benefit poor Americans of all races (232), but his usage indicates his expectation that persons of the middle and upper classes would see such change as a theft of the privileges they had previously experienced, echoing the response of many white southerners to post–Civil War Reconstruction and the civil rights movement. I do not mean to suggest that anything like Woodward's Third Reconstruction has been deeply considered by the U.S. government, but the fact that a law mandating health insurance for almost everyone—and including subsidies for many—has been accused of imposing tyranny suggests the aptness of Woodward's linkage. Further, Woodward's skepticism concerning the "national myth of innocence" leads him to emphasize the difficulty of the nation's moves toward what we now consider democratic citizenship; as he explains in "Equality: The Deferred Commitment" (1958), a historian writing amid social change incurs "a special obligation of sobriety and fidelity to the record," including those moments when the federal government and its founding documents have not measured up to the values later generations may expect of the nation (87). By refusing to pander to "self-righteousness," the historian reveals the depth of the struggle over what have been central—and are perhaps still unsettled—questions within a polity.

In contrast, Woodward's friend Robert Penn Warren, in his own later work, continued to pursue the question of how regional history might affect personal memory and identity, and the effect is instructive. Although Warren is famous for his "conversion" from paternalist white supremacy to desire for racial reconciliation (which is not to say understanding of how he might contribute to such a project),[45] his rarely discussed essay *Jefferson Davis Gets His Citizenship Back* (1980) presents his early attraction to white southern hagiography as one he never thoroughly overcomes. The essay is specifically concerned with the process of how one gains knowledge of a collective history: Warren explains that as a small child, he slowly gathered his understanding of who Jefferson Davis was both "from a vaguely soaked-in popular notion of . . . the justice of the Southern cause (whatever it was; I didn't know)" and also from his grandfather, a Confederate veteran "who *was* history, [and] often a shock to my fuddled preoccupations."[46] This grandfather proclaimed himself for the Union in sympathy, if not action, and criticized "Jeff" for his conduct of the war, but Warren describes himself, as a teenager, as increasingly fascinated with the phallic memorial being constructed to Davis down the road; in his context, legendary accomplishment contrasts with both a town in decline and the threat of mortality, as "young men, some from the neighborhood, were dying far away" in World War I.[47] Implicitly, then, Warren admits that in forging "some meaning, however hard to define, on the relation of past and present," he is less interested in debate about history—of the kind he could have observed through his idiosyncratic elderly grandfather, for example—than in a model for heroic identity, the possibility that "the mystery of the pain, vision, valor, human weakness, and error of the past [could be] somehow transformed into, glorified into, the immobile thrust of concrete . . . rising from thistle, mullein, poverty grass, and broken timbers."[48]

Warren's essay effectively illustrates Maurice Halbwachs's influential model of collective memory: focused on his own development, it reveals how contemporary social frameworks accord import to narratives about the past. For Warren, Davis's history had become "news" because of economic uncertainty: the building of the cement monument created jobs, and, ironically, the threat of poverty was simultaneously signified by the "walking monument" of "Old Jeff Davis," a poor local resident and "the lowest of the low, insofar as a white man could reach that point."[49] Connected to this economic uncertainty, then, was the threat of lost status—both that of class and, more ambiguously, that of race: on the one hand, Old Jeff provides an opportunity to point to the status division between white and black during the era of Jim Crow (such that a white man couldn't be "the lowest of the low"), but on the other, he demonstrates the *need* to point to that division (since this white man seems possibly "the lowest of the low"). Such threat is also relevant to Halbwachs's model: the social frameworks of memory allow a group "to reconstruct an image of the past which is in accord, in each epoch, with the predominant thoughts of the society"—to address, for example, anxieties in the present.[50] Halbwachs's theory has been duly criticized for its "emphasis on community, consensus and cohesion,"[51] but we can ascertain with some confidence that status was a concern for at least one self-defined group with which Warren was associated: as Michael Kreyling argues, the writers at Vanderbilt who identified themselves as Agrarians were determined to establish their authority as southern and conservative intellectuals.[52] Writing in 1980, Warren describes his young self in a way that highlights the Agrarian quest to transform into a heroic mission their association with a region notorious for poverty and discredited beliefs.

But in illustrating how a hagiographic view of the southern past helped him produce a distinct identity, Warren also reveals how vigorously such views of history resist critical inquiry. Warren's version of Davis turns out to differ little from that of his colleague Allen Tate, published a half century earlier. Each praises Davis's benevolence as a slaveholder, and Warren accentuates Davis's devotion to the Constitution even more adamantly: "Both Calhoun and Davis (with thousands of others) saw the Constitution as equivalent to the tablets that Moses delivered from Sinai, in contrast to Lincoln, who . . . obviously did believe . . . that law and the Constitution depended ultimately on need, preference, and cold-blooded power."[53] Warren's complaint that Lincoln overstepped his constitutional role concerns not the Emancipation Proclamation but rather the suspension of habeas corpus; this focus of attention, however, serves not to support Lincoln's stance on the constitutional question of slavery but rather to evade the significance of that question. Although he has since been celebrated as "the Southerner forever demonstrating in art and argument how the issue of slavery and race was the fundamental question at the heart" of the Civil War, Warren here describes slavery as a "necessary, if not sufficient, reason," concentrating instead on differences between the regions' "state[s] of mind . . . [the South] embracing antique values, and the [North] in the process of developing new ones," including relativism, "total war," and "worship of wealth."[54] One cannot overstate how far he is, here, from the ideals for which Woodward lauded him: Warren challenges those "national myths of innocence" that worried Woodward, but he does so only through recycling myths of regional glory and national guilt.

Warren's career cannot be encapsulated by one relatively obscure essay, but this work does illustrate the great variety that his particular approach to the southern past could yield: always embedded in desire, anxiety, and the project of crafting a habitable self, Warren's work provides endless opportunity for exploration and insight but cannot be relied upon for historical clarity or accuracy. These virtues, better exemplified by Woodward's critical historian, seem simply necessary in discussing a figure like Davis, who continues to be promoted as a national, as well as regional, icon. Described as "remote and uncompromising" even by Tate, Davis might seem an unlikely figure for such recuperation, but the bill that led to his reinstatement as citizen proclaimed him, after all, "an outstanding American." Warren, whose essay first appeared in the *New Yorker,* notes that the proposal was introduced by the Republican senator from Oregon, Mark Hatfield; he does not add that, of the group cosponsoring the bill in the House and the Senate, five—including the former Dixiecrat Strom Thurmond—hailed from states of the former Confederacy.[55] Still, the support from the North and the West merits notice and also yields a Woodwardian irony: faced with unanimous congressional support for this bill, the president—Georgia Democrat Jimmy Carter—signed it with apparent discomfort.[56] Nor has Davis's star faded from the nation's horizon. Before his commemorative inauguration ceremony in Montgomery, Alabama,[57] he was incorporated into the Texas State Board of Education school curriculum revisions as Lincoln's ideological foil: the standards for eighth grade history, as of school year 2011–12, require students to "analyze Abraham Lincoln's ideas about liberty, equality, union, and government as contained in his first and second inaugural addresses and the Gettysburg Address and contrast them with the ideas contained in Jefferson Davis's inaugural address."[58] More liberal members of the board objected, noting that this pairing—Davis's singular and rather aggrieved claim to constitutional fidelity, versus Lincoln's shifting thoughts on the relationship between constitutional obligation and democratic ethics—could seem to justify the board's previous decision to describe the causes of the Civil War as "sectionalism, states' rights, and slavery—in that order."[59] In the end, although the board voted to reduce Davis's semantic parity with Lincoln in the standard, the task of explaining how political language can function either to negotiate or to obscure ethical questions—and how constitutional precepts, though binding, merit continued debate—will fall to the teachers of young teens.

These anecdotes suggest that, in the half century since Woodward wrote "The Search for Southern Identity," political ideologies in the United States have shifted in ways that Woodward could not—and perhaps willfully would not—have foreseen. For Woodward, slavery was a "great social evil," and any acceptance of "Lost Cause" mythology constituted a failure both intellectual and ethical; further, he hoped that this vexing past would help southerners develop a greater moral sense in their approach to politics and policy (20, 38). Although he acknowledged that he could find no evidence of such a regional distinction, he hoped rather desperately that he might because the United States as a whole seemed beset by a zealous conviction that the nation (unlike the morally recalcitrant region) could do no wrong. What seems to have happened in intervening decades is that—although this shift is not absolute—many more people from across the United States recognize that the nation's history involves a number of terrible acts and oppressive social arrangements, many of them—but not all—in the South. This shift came about in part because of movements since the 1960s that Woodward found off-putting: as Sheldon Hackney explains, "he felt the Left indulged in excesses of action and rhetoric that cost it public support, [and] Woodward likely came to see those tactics and that rhetoric as counterproductive."[60] But Woodward's sense of "public," as demonstrated above, was not always sufficiently attuned to diversity: those critiques of racism, imperialism, and unquestioning nationalism had lasting ideological influence that cannot be mapped by sectional lines. Meanwhile, however, political groups who continue to promote the old national myths of innocence and success no longer cast the South as an exception: on the contrary, as Nancy MacLean argues, a libertarian (as opposed to Agrarian) ideal of the "Old South" serves as "The Regional Utopia of the Modern American Right."[61] In this view, Jefferson Davis was correct about the Constitution, and the contemporary United States should be moving closer to his political vision of broad influence for extensive property-holders; conveniently for proponents, then as now, this platform omits mention of slavery.

Had Woodward imagined that, 150 years after the Confederacy lost the Civil War, the nation would still be debating that entity's merits, he might not have suggested that a specifically "southern" identity might constitute the best hope for promoting the values of modesty, caution, and justice in national politics. As Joyner's essay suggests, some liberal southerners may find Woodward's theory of regional identity inspiring, but little can be gained by mistaking this specific and often carefully developed political philosophy for a broader and inherent social dynamic. To be sure, there are political projects for which a concept of the local, more specifically, remains cogent, and for southern sites, this idea necessarily interacts with tropes from southern history. Edward L. Ayers, for example, in his whimsically apocalyptic "The Inevitable Future of the South," describes the disempowerment of rural districts and their complete takeover by agribusiness; here, "The Great Consolidation" eradicates not only racial tensions but also democratic governance, and the implication is that some impetus toward local control, although such movements have often tended toward exclusionary politics, may be necessary to prevent an unstoppable descent into corporate rule. In a very different style, W. Fitzhugh Brundage explores the possibility that "healthy exchange" concerning the southern past may help "Southerners . . . crea[te] a public culture that fully and appropriately acknowledges the South's contested past"; this project also involves transforming local environments, such that the past venerated by local and often tax-supported institutions is not one that many local residents justly find oppressive and inhumane. But neither of these political goals needs to rely on a specifically "southern" identity for its success; on the contrary, Brundage argues against any "idealized historical identity," and Ayers's experimental style seems intended to demonstrate the potential and the need for disassociating contemporary anticapitalist ideologies from the Agrarian manifesto *I'll Take My Stand.*[62] Rather than recycling a myth of southern identity, these projects benefit from the kind of careful and honest historiography that Woodward often advocated.[63]

NOTES

1. Interviewing representatives from the textbook publishing industry, one reporter found this perception of Texas's influence to be outdated. See Brian Thevenot, "Texas Textbooks' National Influence Is a Myth," *Texas Tribune* (Austin), March 26, 2010, www.texastribune.org (accessed December 21, 2010).

2. Russell Shorto, "How Christian Were the Founders?" *New York Times,* February 11, 2010, nytimes.com (accessed February 11, 2010); Abby Rapoport, "Former Texas State Board of Education Challenged," *Texas Tribune* (Austin), November 3, 2009, www.texastribune.org (accessed December 21, 2010); Sam Tanenhaus, "In Texas Curriculum Fight, Identity Politics Leans Right," *New York Times,* March 19, 2010, nytimes.com (accessed March 22, 2010).

3. C. Vann Woodward, *Thinking Back: The Perils of Writing History* (Baton Rouge: Louisiana State University Press, 1986), 116, 103.

4. C. Vann Woodward, *The Burden of Southern History,* 3rd ed. (Baton Rouge: Louisiana State University Press, 1993), 25. Subsequent references to this volume are cited parenthetically.

5. Woodward clarifies and extends this critique in "The Fall of the American Adam" (1981), in *The Future of the Past,* by Woodward (New York: Oxford University Press, 1989), 122, where he argues that previous generations of Americans have attributed social injustice to "individuals, groups, classes, sections."

6. Woodward, *Thinking Back,* 103.

7. Woodward, "The Search for Southern Identity," in *Burden of Southern History,* 25; Woodward, *Thinking Back,* 103.

8. Tanenhaus, "Texas Curriculum Fight"; Matthew D. Lassiter and Joseph Crespino, "Introduction: The End of Southern History," in *The Myth of Southern Exceptionalism,* ed. Matthew D. Lassiter and Joseph Crespino (New York: Oxford University Press, 2010), 8–12.

9. See, for example, Michael O'Brien, "C. Vann Woodward and the Burden of Southern Liberalism," *American Historical Review* 78, no. 3 (1973): 596–99; and Richard H. King, *A Southern Renaissance: The Cultural Awakening of the American South, 1930–1955* (Oxford: Oxford University Press, 1980), 274–75.

10. Gavriel D. Rosenfeld, "A Looming Crash or a Soft Landing? Forecasting the Future of the Memory 'Industry,'" *Journal of Modern History* 81 (March 2009): 122.

11. Because studies of collective memory often contemplate the changes that mnemonic practices undergo during processes of modernization, they vary in their ideas of whether the term "collective memory" is applicable across time. Thus, for historian Pierre Nora in 1984, the "quintessential repository of collective memory" is "peasant culture"; he suggests that "churches or schools" were once capable of the "transmission and conservation of collectively remembered values" but argues that contemporary society no longer experiences "the intimacy of a collective heritage." In contrast, for sociologist Maurice Halbwachs, writing in 1925, social change occurs in part through shifts in the social frameworks of memory: as certain traditions, and ways of conveying tradition, are perceived as increasingly useful (by the purveyors of "memory") or attractive (by its consumers), the dominant understanding of the past and its importance changes also. See Pierre Nora, "Between Memory and History: Les Lieux de Mémoire," trans. Marc Roudebush, *Representations* 26 (1989): 78; Maurice Halbwachs, *On Collective Memory,* trans. Lewis A. Coser (Chicago: University of Chicago Press, 1992), 182–90. For the foundational impact of Nora and Halbwachs on contemporary scholarship concerning collective memory, see David Scott, "Introduction: On the Archaeologies of Black Memory," *Small Axe* 26 (2008): ix–xi, xiv.

12. Kerwin Lee Klein, "On the Emergence of Memory in Historical Discourse," *Representations* 69 (2000): 130; Brian Thevenot, "Colbert Report Satirizes Texas History Textbooks," *Texas Tribune* (Austin), March 17, 2010, www.texastribune.org (accessed November 14, 2010); Rosenfeld, "A Looming Crash," 126–27.

13. Robert Penn Warren, *All the King's Men* (1946; reprint, New York: Harcourt, 2005), 656. Woodward attributes his inspiration to this line in *Thinking Back,* 109.

14. C. Vann Woodward, "The Future of the Past" (1970); "The Antislavery Myth" (1962); "The Fall of the American Adam" (1981), all in *The Future of the Past,* 23, 278, 125–26.

15. Woodward, *Thinking Back,* 117; C. Vann Woodward, "Preface to the First Edition" (1955), in *The Strange Career of Jim Crow,* 3rd rev. ed. (New York: Oxford University Press, 1974), xv; Woodward, "The Declining Years of Jim Crow" (1966), in *Strange Career,* 165.

16. O'Brien, "C. Vann Woodward," 596–97.

17. Scott Romine, *The Real South: Southern Narrative in the Age of Cultural Reproduction* (Baton Rouge: Louisiana State University Press, 2008), 25.

18. Laura F. Edwards, "Southern History as U.S. History," *Journal of Southern History* 75, no. 3 (2009): 534.

19. Bruce Collins, "Confederate Identity and the Southern Myth since the Civil War," in *Legacy of Disunion: The Enduring Significance of the American Civil War,* ed. Susan-Mary Grant and Peter J. Parish (Baton Rouge: Louisiana State University Press, 2003), 42–46.

20. O'Brien, "C. Vann Woodward," 599, 596; Nora, "Between Memory and History," 8.

21. Irving Howe, *William Faulkner: A Critical Study* (New York: Random House, 1951), xii, 20–24, 53–56, 202; R. W. B. Lewis, *The American Adam* (Chicago: University of Chicago Press, 1955), 198–99; Richard Chase, "The Fate of the Avant-Garde" (1957), in *The Partisan Review Anthology,* ed. William Phillips and Phillip Rahv (New York: Holt, Rinehart, and Winston, 1962), 219; Malcolm Cowley, "Introduction," in *The Portable Faulkner,* ed. Malcolm Cowley (1946; reprint, New York: Viking, 1954), 22–23.

22. Michael Kreyling, *Inventing Southern Literature* (Jackson: University Press of Mississippi, 1998), xii; Twelve Southerners, "Introduction: A Statement of Principles," in *I'll Take My Stand: The South and the Agrarian Tradition* (1930; reprint, Baton Rouge: Louisiana State University Press, 1977), xlvii.

23. Rosenfeld, "A Looming Crash," 122–23; Edward W. Said, "Invention, Memory, and Place," *Critical Inquiry* 26, no. 2 (2000): 185; W. E. B. Du Bois, *Black Reconstruction: An Essay toward a History of the Part Which Black Folk Played in the Attempt to Reconstruct Democracy in America, 1860–1880* (New York: Harcourt, Brace, 1935), 723.

24. James C. Cobb, *Away Down South: A History of Southern Identity* (New York: Oxford University Press, 2005), 204.

25. Allen Tate, "Remarks on the Southern Religion," in Twelve Southerners, *I'll Take My Stand,* 175; Susan V. Donaldson, "Gender, Race, and Allen Tate's Profession of Letters in the South," in *Haunted Bodies: Gender and Southern Texts,* ed. Anne Goodwyn Jones and Susan V. Donaldson (Charlottesville: University of Virginia Press, 1997), 492–518; Allen Tate, "The Profession of Letters in the South" (1935), in *Essays of Four Decades* (Chicago: Swallow Press, 1968), 525.

26. For the full version of this argument, see Leigh Anne Duck, *The Nation's Region: Southern Modernism, Segregation, and U.S. Nationalism* (Athens: University of Georgia Press, 2006), 146–72.

27. William Faulkner, *Requiem for a Nun* (1951; reprint, New York: Vintage, 1975), 80. See Barack Obama, "Barack Obama's Speech on Race" (transcript), *New York Times,* March 18, 2008, www.nytimes.com (accessed March 25, 2008). Woodward cites this line in "The Historical Dimension," in *Burden of Southern History,* 36.

28. Noel Polk, *Faulkner's Requiem for a Nun: A Critical Study* (Bloomington: Indiana University Press, 1981), 89–90; Faulkner, *Requiem for a Nun,* 133.

29. Ralph Ellison, *Invisible Man* (1952; reprint, New York: Vintage International, 1980), 164, 178, 313, 264–5.

30. Kreyling, *Inventing Southern Literature,* 76–125.

31. W. Fitzhugh Brundage, *The Southern Past: A Clash over Race and Memory* (Cambridge, MA: Harvard University Press, 2005), 6, 54, 229.

32. Madhu Dubey, "Postmodern Geographies of the U.S. South," *Nepantla* 3, no. 2 (2002): 363, 366, 365.

33. Ibid., 366.

34. Arlene R. Keizer, *Black Subjects: Identity Formation in the Contemporary Narrative of Slavery* (Ithaca, NY: Cornell University Press, 2004), 12; A. Timothy Spaulding, *Re-Forming the Past: History, the Fantastic, and the Postmodern Slave Narrative* (Athens: Ohio State University Press, 2005), 2.

35. Kenneth W. Warren, *So Black and Blue: Ralph Ellison and the Occasion of Criticism* (Chicago: University of Chicago Press, 2003), 56–82.

36. In some of Woodward's passages on the "underclass"—such as when he writes of "deteriorating school and family, delinquency, and riots" (248, 177)—he can, as Albert Murray writes, turn "into a social-welfare polemicist right before your scandalized eyes . . . jolly good Big Daddy Moynihan nonviolent war on poverty jive." Other formulations, however, are based in social struggle and structural change. See Murray, *South to a Very Old Place* (New York: McGraw-Hill, 1971), 19.

37. Charles Joyner, "'Forget, Hell!': The Civil War in Southern Memory," in *Legacies of Disunion: The Enduring Significance of the American Civil War,* ed. Susan-Mary Grant and Peter J. Parish (Baton Rouge: Louisiana State University Press, 2003), 19; Cobb, *Away Down South,* 329; Lassiter and Crespino, "Introduction," 12; Jon Smith and Deborah Cohn, "Introduction: Uncanny Hybridities," in *Look Away! The U.S. South in New World Studies,* ed. Jon Smith and Deborah Cohn (Durham, NC: Duke University Press, 2004). Historical contributions to this aspect of southern studies often incorporate attention to Atlantic studies, studies of the African Diaspora, hemispheric studies, U.S. imperialism, and globalization; the latter focus has also inspired new approaches to the U.S. South in anthropology and sociology.

38. He references globalization only obliquely, by citing Paul Kennedy's *Preparing for the Twenty-First Century* (New York: Vintage Books, 1994), 258.

39. David E. Whisnant, "The Next Phase of Cultural Work in the South: Where We Are, What We Have to Work With, Where We Are Going," *Southern Folklore* 49, no. 3 (1992): 189–90.

40. Allen Tate, *Jefferson Davis: His Rise and Fall, a Biographical Narrative* (New York: Minton, Balch, 1929), 4, 300; Robert E. Bonner discusses the development of "proslavery constitutionalism" during the decades and months before the Civil War in *Mastering America: Southern Slaveholders and the Crisis of American Nationhood* (New York: Cambridge University Press, 2009), 40–78, 220–40; Jefferson Davis, "Inaugural Address as Provisional President" (1861), in *Jefferson Davis: The Essential Writings,* ed. William J. Cooper (New York: Random House: 2004), 202.

41. Collins, "Confederate Identity," 38–40; Matthew D. Lassiter, *The Silent Majority: Suburban Politics in the Sunbelt South* (Princeton, NJ: Princeton University Press, 2006), 4–5.

42. Collins, "Confederate Identity," 47.

43. For the sesquicentennial of the Civil War, the *New York Times* has established a blog, *Disunion,* and an associated Facebook page, *Civil War / The New York Times.* Open discussion

forums are available at www.facebook.com/nytimescivilwar (accessed November 27, 2010). Newspapers covering commemorative activities also often offer accompanying discussion threads; see, for example, the "Comments" section to "Civil War's 150th Anniversary Stirs Debate on Race," *New Orleans Times Picayune,* December 11, 2010, www.nola.com/news/index.ssf/2010/12/civil_wars_150th_anniversary_s.html (accessed December 11, 2010).

44. When the 112th Congress began its session with a reading of the Constitution—a rule mandated by the new Republican majority, many of whom were supported by Tea Parties—it omitted sections of the original document later changed by amendments, including the passage designating each slave as 3/5 of a person for the purposes of the census; Representative Jesse Jackson Jr. argued that this approach occluded the history of oppressive inequity and political struggle that has led to the contemporary document. Several events commemorating secession have included "barely a nod to the role of slavery," but the state of Georgia is erecting a series of markers clarifying that the war was fought to defend that institution. See Jennifer Steinhauer, "Constitution Has Its Day (More or Less) in House," *New York Times,* January 6, 2011, www.nytimes.com (accessed January 12, 2011); Katharine Q. Seelye, "Celebrating Secession without the Slaves," *New York Times,* November 29, 2010, www.nytimes.com (accessed December 1, 2010); Katharine Q. Seelye, "One State Takes a New Look at Causes of War," *New York Times,* November 29, 2010, www.nytimes.com (accessed December 1, 2010).

45. See Michael Kreyling, *The South that Wasn't There: Postsouthern Memory and History* (Baton Rouge: Louisiana State University Press, 2010), 49-75; Anthony Szczwsiul, *Racial Politics and Robert Penn Warren's Poetry* (Gainesville: University of Florida Press, 2002).

46. Robert Penn Warren, *Jefferson Davis Gets His Citizenship Back* (Lexington: University Press of Kentucky, 1980), 9–10.

47. Ibid., 10, 11, 23. See Halbwachs, *On Collective Memory,* 53.

48. Warren, *Jefferson Davis,* 25, 23.

49. Ibid., 20, 11.

50. Halbwachs, *On Collective Memory,* 40.

51. Peter Burke, "History as Social Memory" (1989), in *Varieties of Cultural History* (Ithaca, NY: Cornell University Press, 1997), 55.

52. Kreyling, *Inventing Southern Literature,* 3–18.

53. Tate, *Jefferson Davis,* 71–72; Warren, *Jefferson Davis,* 40–41, 61–62. Incidentally, in describing the home-town ceremonies for Davis's return to citizenship, Warren pauses for a moment of unabashed minstrel humor; one could almost argue that this essay marches backward through the history of white southern fiction, from modernist introspection and philosophical contemplation, through Confederate hagiography, to the racial caricatures of Augustus Longstreet.

54. David W. Blight, *American Oracle: The Civil War in the Civil Rights Era* (Cambridge, MA: Belknap / Harvard University Press, 2011), 25; Warren, *Jefferson Davis,* 58, 61–62, 66, 67.

55. Tate, *Jefferson Davis,* 8. H. J. Res. 1040 summary and status (95th Congress, 1977–78), Thomas, Library of Congress, http://thomas.loc.gov (accessed January 14, 2011); S. J. Res. 16 summary and status (95th Congress, 1977–78), Thomas, Library of Congress, http://thomas.loc.gov (accessed January 14, 2011).

56. Congratulating Congress for "officially complet[ing] the long process of reconciliation . . . following the tragic conflict between the States," Carter noted, given the earlier restoration of Robert E. Lee's citizenship, "It is fitting that Jefferson Davis should no longer be singled out for punishment." He did claim, however, that "the divisions that threatened to destroy our Nation" also worked "to discredit the principles on which it was founded," implicitly, it would seem, indicting slavery as both national failure and cause of the war. See Jimmy Carter, "Restoration of Citizenship Rights to Jefferson F. Davis Statement on Signing S. J. Res. 16 into Law" (1978), in *The American Presidency Project,* www.presidency.ucsb.edu/ws/?pid=29993 (accessed January 14, 2011).

57. Seelye, "Celebrating."

58. "Texas Essential Knowledge and Skills for Social Studies, Subchapter B. Middle School" (August 23, 2010), *Texas Administrative Code (TAC), Title 19, Part II,* 34 (113.24, b) 8.C, http://ritter.tea.state.tx.us/rules/tac/chapter113/index.html (accessed November 14, 2010).

59. Brian Thevenot, "Texas Board of Education Fights over History," *Texas Tribune* (Austin), May 21, 2010, www.texastribune.org (accessed November 14, 2010). See also "Blogging the Social Studies Debate II," *TFN Insider,* Texas Freedom Network, May 20, 2010, http://tfninsider.org/2010/05/20/blogging-the-social-studies-debate-ii-2/ (accessed January 19, 2011).

60. Sheldon Hackney, "C. Vann Woodward, Dissenter," *Historically Speaking* 10, no. 1 (2009): 33.

61. Nancy MacLean, "Neo-Confederacy versus the New Deal: The Regional Utopia of the Modern American Right," in Lassiter and Crespino, *The Myth of Southern Exceptionalism,* 308–29.

62. Edward L. Ayers, "The Inevitable Future of the South," in *South to the Future: An American Region in the Twenty-First Century,* ed. Fred Hobson (Athens: University of Georgia Press, 2002), 95–97; Brundage, *The Southern Past,* 332. Brundage is not overly sanguine that changes in the heritage industry will alter political culture, and it is certainly the case that persons and institutions seeking to avoid meaningful debate have demonstrated the ease of doing so. When the state of Georgia instituted its Confederate Heritage and History Month in 2009, for example, it simultaneously pronounced the Ralph Mark Gilbert Civil Rights Museum "an official state historical civil rights museum," without any discussion concerning the relationship between these two decisions. See Senate Bill 27 AP, Georgia General Assembly, April 29, 2009, www1.legis.ga.gov/legis/2009_10/versions/sb27_AP_8.htm (accessed November 4, 2009).

63. Woodward, "The Antislavery Myth" (1962), 278–79.

3

A Lighter Burden?

Southern Political Identity in the Shrinking South

WAYNE PARENT

> Is there nothing about the South that is immune from the disintegrating effect of nationalism and the pressure for conformity? Is there not something that has not changed? There is only one thing that I can think of, and that is its history.
>
> —C. Vann Woodward, *The Burden of Southern History* (1970)

In this chapter, Wayne Parent, the Russell B. Long Professor of Political Science at Louisiana State University, explores Woodward's premise of a distinctive southern identity. Woodward argued that the original southern identity was based on both racial segregation and agrarian economic values, which not only made the original southern identity unique but provided a sense of identity for both wealthy and poor Caucasians. Following the civil rights movement and the industrialization that continues to transform the once rural South, Woodward also argued that the original southern identity would be transformed as a result of these societal changes. In addition, Woodward claimed that if a southern identity survived, it would be based on a "shared history" among southern whites and not on racial supremacy or an agrarian economy. He expected that this new southern identity would be shared and passed down from older generations to new generations. Given the dramatic partisan transformation of the South during the past few decades, from the solidly Democratic constituency to the stronghold of the GOP, many scholars have looked at the changing southern political identity to understand such dramatic political realignment. Some have argued that personal economic concerns, rather than racial animosity or rural values, are now driving southern attitudes and behaviors, much as personal economic concerns drive political attitudes and behaviors across the rest of the country. If these arguments are correct, then we would have evidence suggesting the end of a distinctive southern identity. Parent reviews Woodward's arguments surrounding southern distinctiveness and identity, compares Woodward's theses to recent arguments, and then uses the 2008 presidential election as a testing ground for identifying a distinctive southern identity. The first nomination of an African American presidential candidate by one of the two major political parties provides a unique opportunity to explore the extent to which a distinct southern political identity continues to shape the South. Ultimately, Parent finds substantial evidence of a distinctive southern identity, albeit confined to a smaller number of people living in a few of the deep southern states. Further, he finds substantial variation both within specific states and across generational cohorts.

In *The Burden of Southern History*, C. Vann Woodward expressed a fundamental contradiction about the politics of the American South that five decades later continues to fascinate scholars and spur mountains of theoretical and empirical analysis: despite the apparent thorough Americanization of the eleven states of the Old Confederacy, the region's political dynamics are stubbornly exceptional. As each national election passes, however, there are indications that fragment by fragment, that distinctive South is shrinking. By no means, however, has it disappeared.

In several of his works, Woodward recounts the roots of the solid political South. In the opening chapter on southern identity in *The Burden of Southern History*, Woodward describes how urbanization and industrialization caused the South to become indistinguishable from the rest of America by most measures. Therefore, southern identity rests in a desperate need for a sense of distinctiveness: "The threat of becoming 'indistinguishable,' of being submerged under a national steamroller, has haunted the South for a long time." And then in one of Woodward's most influential passages, he explains how southern identity is forged on a history of contrasts to the broader American experience. According to Woodward, America is a land of prosperity, while the South is a land of poverty. Success is a hallmark of the American character, while defeat is a stamp of the South after the Civil War. In addition, "American opulence and American success have combined to foster a legend of American innocence," while "the South's pre-occupation was with guilt, not with innocence, with the reality of evil, not with the dream of perfection."[1] Finally, America, "the land of the free," is a stark contrast to the South, where for generations a substantial majority of its citizens were not born free. Thus, even though by almost all concrete measures of society, the South began to resemble the rest of

America, the southerner's identity remained steadfastly distinct. This might surprise Woodward, were he still writing, but the distinct southern identity is most easily seen in the southern *political* identity. Continuity and change in southern political identity is the subject of this discussion. Highlighting Woodward's compelling deduction that southern identity is at its essence a psychological or emotional one is a valuable way to begin that discussion.

SOUTHERN POLITICAL IDENTITY AND RACIAL IDENTITY

The significance of this emotional—rather than concrete economic or demographic— distinctiveness to the *political* identity of the region was imprinted on the characterization of the southerner a few decades earlier by W. J. Cash, in the widely cited *The Mind of the South* (1941). Cash argued that the southern elite successfully manipulated a psychological bond between themselves and the poor white masses and, in doing so, broke the bond of economic condition and circumstance between the poor black and poor white masses. It is that emotional bond, which Cash eccentrically calls the "proto Dorian convention," that allowed a solid white South of rich and poor to dominate the political South throughout the century between the Civil War and the civil rights movement.[2]

Woodward suggested a similar sentiment about the political implications of southern identity a few years earlier as he explained the evolution of the political career of Tom Watson in *Tom Watson: Agrarian Rebel* (1938). Here he recounts the early agrarian economic populist promise of Watson and then how Watson transformed into a fierce racial demagogue. Woodward uses Watson's own words in dramatically surmising the frustration of the economic populists in trying to become independent of the established political elite: "The argument against the independent political movement in the South," wrote Watson in 1892, "may be boiled down to one word—nigger." Then Woodward laments: "With those words, Watson abandoned his old dream of uniting both races against the enemy and took the first step to the opposite extreme in racial views."[3] The ramifications of the politics of distinctly emotional and racial southern white male identity were clear.

Woodward was obviously distraught that his beloved South's political identity was expressed and defined as white supremacy. In a revealing and searing comment in *The Burden of Southern History,* Woodward puts part of the blame on progressives who were unable to stop it: "The liberal's feelings of guilt and impotence were reflected in the interest that the writings of Soren Kierkegaard and Reinhold Niebuhr aroused, and the mood of self-flagellation was expressed in the vogue of the novels of Franz Kafka and George Orwell."[4] The expressions of racial identity in racial populist politics at the time were raw and unapologetic. The masses expressing those sentiments were difficult objects of sympathy or concern for intellectuals.

Today those raw public expressions of racial superiority are rare in the South. If gauged by its public social acceptability, southern identity, simply defined as racial identity or white racism, certainly appears to have waned significantly over the years throughout the South. If the defining feature of southern identity is a strong sense of racial identity, it is expressed more as protecting an Old South status quo, a "good ole days" that was dominated by whites.

THE SOLID DEMOCRATIC SOUTH

The mechanism for harnessing this racial identity was the Democratic Party. V. O. Key's *Southern Politics in State and Nation* (1949) and Daniel Elazar's *American Federalism: A View From the States* (1966) provided an explanation for a uniquely southern political behavior that was almost universally accepted.[5] Elazar explains that the American South was settled by a landed gentry who governed the South as a paternalistic elite determined to maintain the social order. As the Civil War erupted and ended, the old order was stubbornly maintained as much as possible. The ideology of white supremacy did not end with slavery. The political vehicle for that continuity was the white-only Democratic Party. The white-only Democratic primary was used, challenged, and upheld in 1935 in *Grovey v. Townsend,* until this political vehicle for white supremacy was eventually overturned in *Smith v. Allwright* in 1944. During the time between the Civil War and World War II, the white-only Democratic Party dominated the South. Between 1865 and 1944, the national Democratic ticket won all but three elections in the eleven states of the Old Confederacy and dominated the congressional delegations by overwhelming numbers and in most states completely. In addition, only a handful of non-Democratic governors were elected and not a single Republican was elected to the U.S. Senate from these states until Texas elected John Tower to replace Lyndon Johnson in 1960.

During the period between the Civil War and World War II, the dominant Democratic Party did not always represent the landed gentry in these states. And while the occasional economic populist, such as Huey Long in Louisiana or Big Jim Folsom in Alabama, made quite a name for himself, again, as Woodward explained in *Tom Watson,* racial populism otherwise often overwhelmed the economic populism. When this racial populism stirred the white working classes as it fanned the flames of racism, it satisfied the old white elite, as well as diverting the political anger away from them.

SOUTHERN POLITICAL IDENTITY BEYOND RACE

The Democratic president Lyndon Johnson famously predicted that with the Democratic Party so closely associated with the passage of the Voting Rights Act in 1965, white southerners would convert in droves to loyal Republican voters. Indeed, it is easy to argue that the Old South Dixie Democrats, the Dixiecrats who dominated the South from Reconstruction until the 1970s, have simply been transformed into a significant and perhaps dominant part of a Republican majority in most national elections since that time. There is ample evidence to support the case. White southerners voted overwhelmingly against the staunchly civil rights ticket of Lyndon Johnson and Hubert Humphrey, which allowed Republican Barry Goldwater to carry five southern states, and in all but Louisiana, it was the first Republican win. No Republican presidential candidate had ever carried Mississippi, Alabama, Georgia, or South Carolina, but in 1964 Barry Goldwater carried them all. And in particularly racially charged Mississippi and Alabama, the Republican's first presidential electoral victory was breathtaking, amounting to 87 percent of the vote in Mississippi and 69 percent in Alabama.

The Voting Rights Act was a political shock to the makeup of the electorate of the Deep South. In Mississippi, Alabama, Louisiana, Georgia, and South Carolina, roughly one-quarter to one-third of each state's population, African Americans whose voting rights had been repressed, were now voting for the first time. A complete realignment in voting patterns emerged, with a racially integrated Democratic Party winning most state elections and an almost exclusively white Republican Party winning most national elections and eventually elections for representation in Washington.

Throughout the 1960s and 1970s, the voting patterns based on race and racial attitudes were well documented in studies like *Issue Evolution: Race and the Transformation of American Politics,* by Edward Carmines and James Stimson (1989).[6] However, racial political identity served to mask a broader southern political identity that also had firm roots in southern history. Republican Ronald Reagan's 1980 presidential campaign and resounding victory in the South tapped into these broader cultural identifiers and successfully bonded southern whites to the Republican Party in some fundamental ways. His campaign awakened the strong socially conservative strain in southern culture.

Since that time, when President Reagan brought southern-friendly social conservatives to the forefront of the Republican agenda in 1980, only the all-southern Democratic ticket of Bill Clinton and Al Gore was able to break up the rock-solid eleven states of the Old Confederacy. By 2004, the domination of the Republican Party in the South and even the southernization of the Republican Party were assumed. Indeed, the very solid Republican South was no more evident than in the 2000 and 2004 presidential elections. The most common narrative for this transformation was southern racial identity: the "Dixiecrat to Republican" explanation was the conventional southern party system realignment narrative. The old Dixiecrats had become Republicans. In the 1970s the Dixiecrat-to-Republican strategy was revived in the form of Nixon's Southern Strategy of "law and order" issues and later the connection of social programs to race. A complementary explanation was that the Republican Party had changed and had broadened its appeal to other parts of southern identity. With Ronald Reagan as its messenger, the GOP transformed into a party with a central, social-issue message that appealed directly to these Dixiecrats and their descendents. And these new social issues, such as abortion, prayer in public schools, and later gay rights issues, were distinctly different from the racial issues of the Dixiecrats. Thomas Frank popularized this explanation in 2004 in a political best-seller, *What's the Matter with Kansas,* where he made the case that working-class Kansans, like southerners, were not voting their economic interests with the Democrats but rather were voting for the Republicans because of cultural issues.[7]

The contention that a broader southern political identity is more significant than southern racial identity to the conversion of southern whites from overwhelmingly Democratic to solidly Republican voters is controversial. Larry Bartels slapped back with a fairly convincing argument in his review "What's the Matter with What's the Matter with Kansas," pointing out that the white working-class conversion from Democrat to Republican was primarily a southern phenomenon and implying that the social conservatives had clear racial underpinnings. Bartels's argument has roots in an extensive body of scholarship best represented by Dan Carter, whose *The Politics of Rage* and *From Wallace to Gingrich* detail the direct relation of the appeal of racial populism of politicians like George Wallace to the appeals of more contemporary southern Republicans.[8]

Standing in stark contrast to these southern-identity-based explanations for the Democratic-to-Republican conversion of most southern whites, whether racial or cultural, is an argument that, with the changing demographics of the South in the 1960s, 1970s, and 1980s, economics finally trumps emotions (and therefore identity) in southern political behavior. This explanation, put forward by Shafer and Johnston, posits that the new southern Republicans were an outgrowth of economic prosperity in the South. By the late 1980s, southerners had become in their occupational structure, according to Merle and Earl Black in *Politics and Society in the South* (1987), virtually indistinguishable from nonsouthern Americans.[9] In addition, the South had experienced dramatic growth in the latter twentieth century, and newcomers to the South were changing the political climate. The growing business classes of the South, both insiders and outsiders, were attracted to the economic messages of the national Republicans, and the Dixiecrat racial appeals were not relevant.

Together these analyses all seek to explain the conversion of southern whites from Democrats to Republicans in terms of southern identity. Two of them assert that southern identity is paramount but define the hallmark of southern identity in different ways, one as racial and the other as cultural. The work of Byron Shafer and Richard Johnston (and others) contends that the role of southern identity in southern politics is overstated. These authors agree with Woodward that racial identity would lessen, but they contend even that Woodward's southern emotional attachment to history is no longer a valid point. Rather, southern voting patterns, and specifically the conversion from Democratic to Republican patterns, simply reflected economic growth in the region.

THE FRACTURED SOUTH

By 2008 it became clear that all of these arguments could be clarified if "the South" was defined less generally as the entire region and more specifically as the parts of the region. In 2008 Democrats fielded a distinctly nonsouthern ticket with, dramatically, an African American as the standard-bearer. "Southernness" or, more precisely, the politics of a southern culture should have summarily rejected it. The initial electoral shock in that election was that the home of the capital of the Confederacy, Virginia, and the state that made Jesse Helms a southern conservative icon, North Carolina, embraced the ticket. It was a tentative embrace, but an embrace nonetheless. Many parts of the Old Confederacy, however, rejected the ticket summarily, even more emphatically than they had rejected the ticket headed by New Englander John Kerry in the previous election.

The election is therefore instructive. Obama should be weakest in the parts of the white South where southern identity, racial or otherwise, is strongest. He should fare better among those voters in the parts of the South where voting is not as firmly connected to traditional notions of southern political identity.

IDENTIFYING SOUTHERN POLITICAL CULTURE

Again, C. Vann Woodward's *The Burden of Southern History* rests on the notion that by 1960 there was only one remaining cause of an enduring southern identity, and that was an emotional attachment to southern history. He argues that two of the main pillars of southern identity, the agrarian lifestyle and racial identity, will wither away as a result of the urbanization and industrialization of the South and of the inevitable civil rights revolution.

He begins his discussion of southern identity with a description of southern agrarian values described in *I'll Take My Stand: The South and the Agrarian Tradition* (2006), the series of essays by twelve southern academics originally published in 1930. Their unwavering commitment to agrarian versus industrial values suggests that southerners should be more concerned with the quality of relationships with God and family than with gaining material goods. And while Woodward says that the commitment to God and family remains a part of the accepted southern character, he notes that the "dominant whites," at least, didn't want to reject "the fleshpots of the American living standard."[10] As the South evolves, southerners will adopt the American goal of economic prosperity.

Woodward then turns to U. B. Phillips and race. The "Phillipsian doctrine," as Woodward calls it, is one in which southern heritage and identity are tied directly to and defined by the conviction that the South must remain a "white man's country." In discussing Phillips and race, Woodward is particularly relevant to the present southern predicament: "If Southernism is allowed to become identified with a last-ditch effort to protect segregation, it will increasingly lose its appeal among the younger generation."[11]

Woodward considers and rejects notions that southern identity is tied primarily to a lack of material ambition or to adherence to white racial superiority. He then concludes that a unique southern identity must be the product of a shared history and a unique southern political culture based on this memory. Here is where the identity as a southerner, especially among whites, is of paramount importance.

Therefore, racial identity and upward mobility are characteristics that Woodward rejects as logical, enduring components of a southern character. He proposes that these will wither away as distinctions of southerners, leaving only a shared sense of history as a bond. He also notes the logical point that southern identity must be passed on to the next generation if it is to survive and suggests that it will survive through socialization of memory and history.

Woodward's 1960 discussion of the permanence of southern identity in *The Burden of Southern History* sets up a nice contrast and comparison to the conclusions of other studies, carried out much later, which benefit from decades of post-civil-rights observations. Several twenty-first-century scholars, including Dan Carter and Larry Bartels, insist that racial identity endures as a signifying characteristic of southern political culture. Byron Shafer and Richard Johnston, in contrast, agree with Woodward that southerners have embraced the American material-ambition ideal and that agrarian values are no longer relevant to southern identity. They extend their point and argue that southern economic-based voting was a better explanation than racial voting after the 1960s. Finally, if Woodward's sense that southern history passed on through generations is a clear indication of southern identity, younger southerners should exhibit the same unique southern political tendencies as their older counterparts.

These three points raised by Woodward about southern identity can be examined in the voting patterns in the 2008 elections by comparing southerners to the nation as a whole. Are racial voting patterns and, therefore, racial political identity the same both in and outside the South? Woodward and economic-based voting studies such as that of Shafer and Johnston would suggest that by now racial voting patterns should be the same inside and outside the South. Racial-identity scholars, represented by Carter and Bartels, would argue that racial identity plays a much larger role in southern voting patterns than in nonsouthern voting patterns.

Finally, Woodward's analysis would suggest that if a sense of southern identity is being passed on from one generation to the next, younger voters inside the South should vote similarly to their older counterparts. Outside the South, this may not be true. If young southerners are voting like their parents in uniquely southern voting patterns, and their parents are not voting in economic voting patterns, then these younger southern voters are very likely voting on the basis of either racial identity or Woodward's sense of southern identity.

The 2008 elections are fascinating in that they indicate that Woodward's argument is supported in certain regions of the South but not in others. The older southern racial-identity argument, which Woodward assumed would fade, remains sturdy in some of these same regions as well.

SOUTHERN CULTURAL IDENTITY AND THE 2008 ELECTIONS

This analysis uses a comparison of groups of voters in southern states to those in the nation as a whole in terms of their voting patterns. CNN state and national exit polls are used to examine these breakdowns. Extensive polling for this groundbreaking election provides a wealth of information to examine. The CNN exit polls were administered as voters left their voting place immediately after they voted. While exit polls released in waves during Election Day are notoriously off base, the complete results released after all voting is complete are consistent with actual returns nationally and across states. The CNN results are similar to those of other organizations and are particularly useful since CNN makes the poll results readily accessible to anyone and breaks them down by state.

For each of the characteristics, the national proportions are compared first with North Carolina and Virginia, the two southern states that showed the most change in partisanship, some of it due perhaps to temporary spikes in the youth and the black vote, but some of it due to longer-term trends. Next the national proportions and the North Carolina and Virginia numbers are compared to those for Alabama, Louisiana, and Mississippi, three states in the South that demonstrated a noticeable aversion to the Democrat. In fact, in Louisiana the Obama vote was even weaker than Democrat Kerry's losing total in the state four years earlier. Table 3.1 displays these results, which are also discussed in subsequent sections. Other states in the South showed patterns somewhere between these two sets of states. Those results, while not discussed below, are presented in table 3.2.

TABLE 3.1. Percent Obama vote by group in five states and the United States

	Alabama	*Louisiana*	*Mississippi*	*North Carolina*	*Virginia*	*United States*
Black	98	98	94	95	92	95
White	10	11	14	35	39	43
White >$50,000	9	8	13	31	39	43
White college graduates	13	12	18	38	44	47
White 18–24	13	18	17	56	42	54

Source: CNN 2008 Presidential Exit Polls, www.cnn.com/ELECTION/2008/results/polls.main.

TABLE 3.2. Percent Obama vote by group in four states and the United States

	Georgia	*South Carolina*	*Tennessee*	*Arkansas*	*United States*
Black	98	96	94	95	95
White	23	26	34	30	43
White >$50,000	25	25	32	28	43
White college graduates	25	32	37	31	47
White 18–24	20	24	45	34	54

Source: CNN 2008 Presidential Exit Polls, www.cnn.com/ELECTION/2008/results/polls.main.

RACIAL IDENTITY AND SOUTHERN POLITICAL CULTURE

The one area where the 2008 election will not provide particularly useful insight into southern identity is the area of black southern identity. This election is instructive in understanding the white South, but not the black South. All black Americans, including black southerners, fairly uniformly voted for the first black nominee of a major political party. The unprecedented unity among black voters precludes analysis of differences among them, which may come into focus as black presidential candidates become more common.

The results for black southerners are exactly as expected. Black voting behavior was essentially the same inside and outside the South, with 95% of African Americans nationally voting for Obama and 92% to 98% of black southerners reporting similar behavior across the southern states (see table 3.1).

The variation in white support for President Obama is enlightening. Among all voters nationwide, Barack Obama received 43% of white votes. In Virginia and North Carolina, his white support was somewhat lower, at 39% in Virginia and 35% in North Carolina. The contrast to the national vote is striking, however, in Alabama, Louisiana, and Mississippi, where he received only 10%, 11%, and 14% of white votes. Clearly, a key to understanding the southern political character is an acknowledgment that the political dynamic even within the white electorate may vary dramatically.

UPWARD MOBILITY AND SOUTHERN POLITICAL CULTURE

Next is a comparison of voting patterns in relation to upward mobility, measured by income and by college graduation. If white southerners who have demonstrated and experienced upward social and economic mobility vote the same as nonsouthern whites, southern political culture is irrelevant. Again, the results decidedly demonstrate that there is not a solid South.

Nationally, almost half (43%) of the higher-income voters supported the Democrat, while slightly more, 47% of whites making under $50,000 a year, were Obama supporters. Again, in North Carolina and Virginia the levels of support are somewhat lower and the proportions are similar. In North Carolina, 31% of wealthier and 42% of less wealthy whites voted for Obama. In Virginia, higher incomes supported Obama at a higher rate (39%) than in North Carolina; a similar 42% of lower incomes supported him. The contrast with the nation as a whole in the states of the deepest South, however, is conspicuous. Lower-income whites in these states, historically the old populist Democrats whose ancestors presumably supported the likes of Big Jim Folsom and Huey Long, gave almost no support to the 2008 Democratic presidential standard bearer. In Alabama support was at 11% and in Louisiana and Mississippi it was 16%. In all three states, support among higher-income whites was predictably even lower.

Although Obama fared better among college-educated voters than among those with higher income across the board, college education shows a similar pattern in voter preferences. Nationally, he gained the support of 47% of those who reported a college degree. In North Carolina and Virginia, his support was 38% and 44%, respectively, and in the three deep South states of Alabama, Louisiana, and Mississippi, again the drop was substantial. The support among those with a college degree in these three states was 13, 12, and 18%.

YOUTH AND SOUTHERN POLITICAL CULTURE

While Woodward specifically mentions what he sees as the waning significance of racial identity and the endurance of upward mobility, he makes the point that for a strong sense of southern culture to last, it must be passed on to future generations. This is especially true of young adults in the contemporary South, since even their grandparents did not likely have firsthand experience of the history that binds southerners. The Obama candidacy would have no obvious connection to a uniquely southern white culture. His region, race, and heritage were an abrupt affront to the Democratic tickets since the civil rights movement, which had all contained at least one southerner, and except in 1988 that person had been at the top of the ticket. Barack Obama's nomination by the Democratic Party was the first in this era that did not make a direct cultural appeal to this white dominant southern heritage that Woodward describes.

Support for Barack Obama nationally among voters of ages 18 to 24, only 11% of the national electorate, was a solid base of his support; fully 54% of these young white voters supported him. Nationally his support dropped more than ten points to roughly 41% in older groups.

In North Carolina, the youth-for-Obama phenomenon is at its most evident, with 56% of those young people surveyed supporting him and a drop to the low thirties for older groups. In Virginia the pattern was not as dramatic, with 42% of younger voters indicating support for the Democrat and an average of 38% among the older age groupings.

There are no indications of any substantial deviation from a traditional southern pattern of voting against the distinctly nonsouthern Democrat even among this fairly small group of young voters. In Mississippi 17% of young white voters preferred Obama and in Louisiana, 18%. In Alabama, only 13% of these voters supported the Democrat. As in the remaining states, Obama's support weakened even more among older groups.

TRADITIONAL SOUTH AND TRANSITIONAL SOUTH

This examination of southern voting patterns, with a closer inspection of five southern states, reveals an unmistakable trend. Two states, North Carolina and Virginia, exhibit political dynamics that would indicate that any uniquely southern political identity is not closely tied to racial identity and is certainly not being transmitted to the younger generation. The three states of Alabama, Mississippi, and Louisiana, however, have striking patterns of racial identity and unique southern patterns that are almost as strong with younger voters as with older ones. These five states well represent the ends of the spectrum in the South and best illustrate the differences within the region. Woodward would certainly conclude that southern identity, including southern racial identity, is alive and well in these three states in the Deep South. However, that identity, both racial and otherwise, has faded noticeably in North Carolina and Virginia. Other states in the South, as table 3.2 indicates, fall between these two sets of states.

Southern political identity, therefore, varies from state to state in the South. The identity of the states where southern political uniqueness is most pronounced would hardly surprise even the most casual follower of American and southern politics. Alabama, Mississippi, and Louisiana are states with demographic characteristics that are concentrated most heavily in the American South. These states have generally lower incomes and lower levels of higher education, are somewhat more rural, and have higher black populations. All of these characteristics are deeply rooted in the South that C. Vann Woodward describes in *The Burden of Southern History.* Southern states have a history of the ramifications of a social system that began with a plantation economy and slavery. While eleven southern states were home to this history, the states that continue to exhibit its effects also continue to exhibit uniquely southern tendencies in their voting patterns and, by implication, in their sense of identity. These are states where continuity in southern culture has trumped change.

DELVING DEEPER: VARIATION IN SOUTHERN POLITICAL IDENTITY WITHIN THE STATES

The study of racial identity as a paramount southern political identity has been extensive, and C. Vann Woodward's work has served a pivotal role in that scholarship. In fact, Martin Luther King praised Woodward's *The Strange Career of Jim Crow* as the historical bible of the civil rights movement.[12] In areas of the South where a significant presence of both races exists, the relationship between them is likely to remain a significant part of political identity and political dynamics. Therefore, areas of the South where both races are present in large proportions are places where we would expect a strong sense of racial identity. And, indeed, Alabama, Mississippi, and Louisiana meet that expectation.

With black and white relations in the South at center stage for most of its history, it is not surprising that other features of a unique southern identity have received less attention. It is those features that may add to the strong, perhaps complementary, sense of southern history that created an identity. The scholarship on southern political culture in the academic disciplines of history, sociology, and political science suggest several other aspects of the South that help create unique regional culture.

As Woodward notes in referencing *I'll Take My Stand,* the agrarian rural lifestyle may well have produced a less materialistic and more religious society in the South. In addition, the broad southern plantation economy and subsequent tenant-farming economy, concentrated mostly in Louisiana, Mississippi, Alabama, Georgia, and South Carolina, might be seen as a reason for the stratified social structure in the South and the need for large families and a family-oriented society. This economic structure may have produced less demand for higher education and certainly may explain the lower income levels of the masses.

Some historians focus on the much larger proportions of settlements from Celtic rather than English areas during much of the great European immigration waves of the 1800s. Grady McWhiney's classic 1988 work *Cracker Culture: Celtic Ways of the Old South* surmises that the propensity toward violence as a means of settling disputes among southerners is derived from their ancestors, who were primarily herders intent on preserving their sheep.[13]

Finally, the proportion of native southerners in an area would logically produce a political culture where the population has a greater sense of southern identity. States in the original Old Confederacy that have high concentrations of nonsoutherners, like Florida, are naturally less likely to exhibit characteristics of a southern culture than states like Louisiana, which has the highest concentration of state natives in the United States.

The scholarly literature on southern culture found in history, sociology, and political science suggests that several aspects of an area in the South might lead to a stronger sense of southern identity. First among these is a largely racially integrated area with significant proportions of both black and white citizens. Second, rural and agricultural areas can be expected to exhibit more southern tendencies. Third, lower income and lower concentrations of persons pursuing higher education should accompany more signs of southern political identity. Some historians would argue that areas with a significant Celtic population should show the same trend. Finally, higher proportions of nonsoutherners in the population might well lead to less evidence of southern political identity. These characteristics vary both by state and within states. Therefore, higher instances of southern identity within the South might be traced to higher instances of those features that produced a unique southern culture in the first place.

Some of these associations were examined in relation to the 2008 Obama vote at the county level in three states in a study conducted by this author and some colleagues.[14] While the results were mixed, there was clear evidence that racially integrated and rural counties were more likely to exhibit a uniquely southern political tendency in that election within these states than those less integrated and more urban or suburban. Some of the other characteristics showed some correlation in some of the states as well. These variations support the general observation that southern identity varies widely across the South, both between and within states.

CONCLUSIONS

In *The Burden of Southern History,* C. Vann Woodward directly addressed southern identity. He recognized that even though the South had undergone demographic changes that made it resemble the rest of the nation, a distinct identity rested in the minds of southerners. Woodward attempted to show that southern identity was more than racial identity. While the root of that identity remains in question today, there is evidence that a distinct southern way of thinking remains. Politics presents a useful setting to gauge the present existence of that identity. If voting patterns of southerners are demonstrably different from voting patterns of similarly situated nonsoutherners, a distinct southern mind-set must be at play.

The 2008 presidential election presented a particularly useful set of circumstances in which to explore the differences. For the first time since the Voting Rights Act in 1965, which transformed southern politics, a nonsouthern Democrat, Barack Obama, carried some southern states. Given the South's history of legal and normative racial discrimination, the fact that the Democratic candidate was the first viable African American candidate in history made the breakthrough all the more fascinating.

An analysis of the voting patterns in that election clearly showed that white Virginia and North Carolina voters most resembled their similarly situated nonsouthern counterparts. White voters in Alabama, Mississippi, and Louisiana, in contrast, did not; they displayed strikingly distinct voting patterns. The significance of Woodward's somewhat ethereal memory-based southern identity appears to be surprisingly resilient in these three Deep South states. In North Carolina, Virginia, and, to a lesser extent, other states in the South, that distinctiveness is fading away. Southernness as a political identity remains strong, but in less and less of the South.

NOTES

1. C. Vann Woodward, *The Burden of Southern History,* 2nd ed. (Baton Rouge: Louisiana State University Press, 1970), 8, 19, 21.

2. W. J. Cash, *The Mind of The South* (New York: Alfred A. Knopf, 1941).

3. C. Vann Woodward, *Tom Watson: Agrarian Rebel,* 2nd ed. (orig. published 1938; New York: Oxford University Press, 1963), 370, 372.

4. Woodward, *Burden of Southern History,* 143.

5. V. O. Key Jr., *Southern Politics in State and Nation,* new ed. (orig. published 1949; Knoxville: University of Tennessee Press, 1984); Daniel Elazar. *American Federalism: A View from the States* (New York: Thomas Crowell, 1966).

6. Edward Carmines and James Stimson, *Issue Evolution: Race and the Transformation of American Politics* (Princeton, NJ: Princeton University Press, 1989).

7. Thomas Frank, *What's the Matter with Kansas? How Conservatives Won the Heart of America* (New York: Henry Holt, 2004).

8. Larry M. Bartels, "What's the Matter with What's the Matter with Kansas?" *Quarterly Journal of Political Science* 1 (2006): 201–26; Dan T. Carter. *The Politics of Rage: George Wallace, the Origins of the New Conservatism, and the Transformation of American Politics* (New York: Simon and Schuster, 2005).

9. Byron E. Shafer and Richard Johnston, *The End of Southern Exceptionalism: Class, Race, and Partisan Change in the Postwar South* (Cambridge, MA: Harvard University Press, 2006); Earl Black and Merle Black, *Politics and Society in the South* (Cambridge, MA: Harvard University Press, 1987).

10. Twelve Southerners, *I'll Take My Stand: The South and the Agrarian Tradition,* new ed. (orig. published 1930; Baton Rouge: Louisiana State University Press, 2006), 10.

11. Woodward, *Burden of Southern History,* 10, 12.

12. C. Vann Woodward, *The Strange Career of Jim Crow* (New York: Oxford University Press, 1955).

13. Grady McWhiney, *Cracker Culture: Celtic Ways in the Old South* (Tuscaloosa: University of Alabama Press, 1988).

14. Wayne Parent, Matthew Fowler, and Peter Petrakis, "When White Goes Right: The Old South in the 2008 Presidential Election," paper presented at the 2009 annual meeting of the Midwest Political Science Association, April 2–4, Chicago.

4

The History of the Present

ROBERT C. MCMATH

> [The intellectual of today] will learn all he can from the new criticism about the irrational side of Populism and other reform movements, but he cannot afford to repudiate the heritage.
>
> —C. Vann Woodward, *The Burden of Southern History* (1968)

In this chapter, historian Robert C. McMath takes on the task of probing two of Woodward's essays: "The Irony of Southern History" and "The Populist Heritage and the Intellectual." In his analysis of the first essay, McMath explores Woodward's argument about the usefulness of irony as a means of throwing light on a complicated historical event: the liberal consensus that arose in the post–World War II era that envisioned unlimited prosperity in the context of a global struggle for power with the Soviet Union, a struggle for power that resulted in the birth of a "new American right," a rejection of New Deal liberalism, and a crippling xenophobia that was followed by repression and reactionary policies on the domestic front. Woodward, as McMath points out, believed that the southern experience could instruct his contemporaries about the hubris of such thinking and the cataclysmic consequences that could result. McMath finds a similar concern informing Woodward's essay "The Populist Heritage and the Intellectual." McMath argues that Woodward was not simply defending the Populists against an attack launched by certain of the authors in Daniel Bell's The New American Right *and by Richard Hofstadter in the 1950s. Although Woodward was certainly determined to establish that his Populists were not xenophobic, Jew-baiting racists and not the predecessors of the reactionaries of the 1950s, he also wanted his readers to appreciate the historical Populists properly, and he believed that, so understood, they could provide a tradition of revolt for those of his ilk concerned about the trajectory of American society in the 1950s. In the best tradition of Woodward, McMath then draws from both essays to suggest that irony, the southern experience, and the Populist tradition, properly informed by the new "social movement theory," can offer a useful way of understanding the current Tea*

Party phenomenon. The Tea Party adherents are part of a long tradition of social movements that do not necessarily share much in common outside of the fact that they cohere, more or less, as groups seeking a specific set of reforms at a particular point in history. Such groups are energized by a sense of some grievance, informed by media, and oriented in a certain way toward government. Unable to fully grasp the irony of their situation, they are certainly not the successors—nor would they mean to be—of the historical Populists of the 1890s.

In summing up an autobiographical essay in 1986, C. Vann Woodward demonstrated his mastery of rhetorical self-deprecation in a way that helps us understand what kind of scholar he really was. Then in his seventy-eighth year, Woodward feigned embarrassment while acknowledging the truth of charges leveled against him by some unnamed fellow historians. Yes, Woodward admitted, he was "a presentist, a moralist, an ironist, and a one-time activist . . . a chronicler with a weakness for history-with-a purpose, and one influenced by a theologian."[1] To a historian, being singled out as "a presentist" or "a chronicler with a weakness for history-with-a-purpose" is not, generally speaking, to be taken as a compliment. But Woodward was just that, a writer who, in the words of Howard Zinn, wished the past to speak wisely to our present needs.[2] Regardless of the subject at hand, Woodward understood himself to be a historian of the present.

In this chapter I show how Woodward practiced "the history of the present" in two essays republished in *The Burden of Southern History.* In one, he brings the ancient concept of irony to bear on southern history in order to raise big questions about the United States in the early years of the cold war, adapting for his own purposes the work of theologian Reinhold Niebuhr, specifically Niebuhr's recently published book *The Irony of American History.* In another essay, he jumps into a debate about the presumed relationship between potent neoconservative movements in postwar America and the historical Populist movement, about which Woodward had written sympathetically and well. Here he locked horns with leading social theorists of the day, and in particular with historian Richard Hofstadter, whose treatment of the Populists in his prize-winning book *The Age of Reform* translated social theory into a compelling narrative about the Populists and their place in the American political tradition. In these essays, one originally published in 1953 and the other in 1959, Woodward grappled with the ideas of two leading public intellectuals of the mid-twentieth century. Niebuhr and Hofstadter, like Woodward himself, viewed contemporary affairs and the human condition through the lens of history, and ideas that both men advanced a half century ago are very much part of public discourse in America today.

Believing that historians of the present are still needed if we are to comprehend the political culture of our own time, I offer a modest proposal for how they might proceed, employing a way of explaining the ironic situation that Woodward learned from Niebuhr and a historically grounded method of analyzing protest movements that emerged after the theory employed by Hofstadter collapsed. In the end, I argue, Woodward's use of irony in the first essay and his basic argument about the Populist tradition may still have value.

C. Vann Woodward saw two ways in which his own scholarly interests could invoke the past to instruct post–World War II Americans. First, he believed that the historical experiences of the American South, experiences that he characterized as "ironic," could be instructive for the nation that emerged from World War II as internationally dominant and domestically prosperous, but oblivious to the unintended consequences of its actions. Second, he was convinced that the political tradition that shaped him as a young man in the 1920s and 1930s (left-wing liberalism) and the historical political movement that this orientation had led him to study (late-nineteenth-century Populism) could speak wisely to the nation in the 1950s.

This "presentism" shows through in his earlier publications in southern history, beginning with *Tom Watson, Agrarian Rebel* (1938) and his magisterial *Origins of the New South, 1877–1913* (1951). Woodward later said of his biography of the Populist leader Watson: "It was a book *for* the 1930s and *of* the 1930s, a book for hard times and hard scrabble. . . . It was a time when mutinous voices were heard in the land, voices that seemed echoes of the 1890s."[3] Woodward's account of race relations in the post-Reconstruction South, excerpted from *Origins* and augmented with fresh insights, formed the basis of *The Strange Career of Jim Crow,* which bolstered the case for the civil rights movement. Woodward wrote about people facing seemingly insurmountable barriers, but his graceful and empathetic prose had about it an air of hopeful contingency and conveyed the sense that his protagonists just might prevail.

The essays published as *The Burden of Southern History* in 1960 show Woodward the presentist as a mature public intellectual, confident that his credentials as a *southern* historian gave him standing to speak to *national* audiences about important issues of the day. Nowhere does he claim that role more forcefully than in two essays from that collection, "The Irony of Southern History" and "The Populist Heritage and the Intellectual." In both, Woodward invoked history to shed light on public issues of the 1950s, issues that still resonate today.

IRONY, SOUTHERN STYLE

Woodward wrote "The Irony of Southern History" at a moment not unlike that of the early twenty-first century, when the United States' newfound power and global reach, combined with a naive belief in national innocence and virtue, created a precarious situation in which wise counsel was desperately needed. In that moment one of the nation's leading Protestant theologians and two giants of southern literature helped Woodward find the voice to say that such counsel could come from the American South, perhaps even from Woodward himself.

By 1951 Woodward had emerged as the dominant voice among a new generation of southern historians who rejected the ancestor worship of their predecessors. The publication of Woodward's *Origins of the New South* that year signaled this new attitude like no other event. Within the defensive and ancestor-worshiping Southern Historical Association, Woodward emerged as the leader of the young Turks, many of them World War II veterans like himself. When the war was over, they had come home to college and graduate school changed by their experiences. They all believed it was time for southerners, and southern historians, to stop refighting the Civil War and defending slavery, time instead to help build a new progressive America. For this group, the new America included a desegregated South and a desegregated Southern Historical Association. They elected Woodward as president of the SHA and worked with him and the young John Hope Franklin to ensure that African American scholars could not only join the association and present their research findings at meetings but also participate in its supreme ritual, the annual banquet and presidential address, Jim Crow laws be damned.

And so it was that in November 1952, Franklin and a handful of other

African American historians heard Woodward deliver the presidential address that was published in the association's journal as "The Irony of Southern History."[4] Woodward viewed with alarm the mood of postwar America, which was both celebratory of the nation's newfound status as a world power and fearful of the Red Menace. Domestically, the nation was turning away from the Populist / New Deal brand of reform toward "self-righteousness, complacency, and humorless idealism."[5] Woodward believed that the South had something instructive to tell the nation, a cautionary tale of ironic outcomes, and that he could be the one to express it. He signaled as much with the quotation from Arnold Toynbee that served as the epigraph for *Origins:*

> I remember watching [Queen Victoria's] Diamond Jubilee procession myself as a small boy. I remember the atmosphere. It was: Well, here we are on the top of the world, and we have arrived at this peak to stay there—forever! There is, of course, a thing called history, but history is something unpleasant that happens to other people. . . . I am sure, if I had been a small boy in New York in 1897 I should have felt the same. Of course, if I had been a small boy in 1897 in the Southern part of the United States, I should not have felt the same; I should then have known from my parents that history had happened to my people in my part of the world."[6]

In his concern about the triumphalist drift of national opinion, Woodward discovered a kindred spirit in theologian and ethicist Reinhold Niebuhr, then at the height of his powers as a public intellectual. In Niebuhr's ideas about irony the young Woodward found food for thought, and in his oratory, the equal of Tom Watson himself. "He spoke," Woodward recalled later, "with the tongue of a prophet and words of fire." Niebuhr gave voice to Woodward's alarm over the volatile combination of unprecedented global power and "illusions of innocence and virtue" in the United States and, in the latter case, in its rival the Soviet Union as well.[7] For Niebuhr, as quoted by Woodward, the onset of the cold war and the United States' sense of a life-and-death struggle against Communism created a dangerous situation in which Americans were "involved in ironic perils which compounded the experience of Babylon and Israel."[8]

Although Woodward later feigned surprise at having been influenced by a theologian, he and Niebuhr had much in common, and Woodward was by no means the only secular-minded historian to be influenced by the pastor turned seminary professor who stood in the nineteenth-century tradition of great pulpit orators who were also public intellectuals. Like Woodward in the impoverished South of the 1920s and 1930s, Niebuhr embraced left-wing politics during his years as a pastor and community leader in Henry Ford's Detroit. Niebuhr became a card-carrying Socialist in 1929 and did not leave the party until 1940.[9] Like Woodward, who settled on history as the discipline through which to understand the world he lived in, Niebuhr came to understand that "history is the stage upon which the drama of our human nature is played out. . . . In the end Niebuhr's analysis of the twists and turns of history attracted as many historians as it repelled. Foremost among admirers was the late Arthur Schlesinger, Jr., who supplied a page of helpful comments on the typescript of *The Irony of American History* and dedicated the first volume of his magisterial *The Age of Roosevelt* to the Protestant theologian."[10]

By the 1930s and 1940s, Reinhold Niebuhr was a highly visible public speaker and author whose books were widely noted and whose essays, reviews, and editorials seemed to appear everywhere. In 1948 his picture was the cover of *Time* magazine. He was a self-styled "circuit rider" to American colleges and universities and spoke frequently on campuses across the nation, and Woodward had heard him speak in his prime. Woodward may well have known that in the 1930s Niebuhr encouraged southern churchmen in organizing for social justice and even championed the causes of the Delta Cooperative Farm in Mississippi and the Southern Tenant Farmers' Union in Woodward's native Arkansas.[11]

In the postwar era, Woodward and Niebuhr shared a profound distrust for the political and cultural consensus that went by the name of "liberalism." This liberal consensus combined the optimism of transatlantic nineteenth-century liberalism with Americans' postwar confidence in their ability to master not only global enemies but also the vagaries of the business cycle and even nature itself, as evidenced by the harnessing of nuclear energy. This confidence gave rise to a political ideology widely supported by most Democrats and many Republicans; it included among its core tenets faith in (1) America's "reformed" capitalism as an engine of abundance and social justice, (2) the "natural harmony of interests in society" and the rapid abolition of social class, (3) the ability of *government* to solve pressing social problems through the application of scientific expertise and tax dollars, and (4) eventual victory in the nation's struggle to save the world from Communism.[12] As Niebuhr put it in *The Irony of American History*, published just months before Woodward delivered his presidential address: "We have dreamed of a purely rational adjustment of interests in human society; and we are involved in 'total' wars. We have dreamed of a 'scientific' approach to all human problems; and we find that the tensions of a world-wide conflict release individual and collective emotions not easily brought under rational control. We had hoped to make sharp distinctions between justice and injustice; and we discover that even the best human actions involved some guilt."[13]

The term *irony,* grounded in ancient Greek drama, has many layers of meaning. While southern writers Robert Penn Warren and Cleanth Brooks helped Woodward develop an ironic rhetorical style, it was Niebuhr who got him thinking about the "what" and the "how" of ironic explication. Niebuhr developed an understanding of the word that reflected his own historical, classical, and theological perspectives. Niebuhr wrote, "If virtue becomes vice through some hidden defect in the virtue . . . if wisdom becomes folly because it does not know its own limits . . . the situation is ironic." A careful student of Niebuhr's use of irony explained it this way: "We perceive a human action as ironic . . . when we see the consequences of that action as contrary to the original intention of the actor and can locate a significant part of the reason for the discrepancy in the actor himself or his intention." For Niebuhr, "ironic" actions carried a sense of personal or collective responsibility for wrongdoing, even if unconsciously so.[14]

While Woodward did not share Niebuhr's theological way of understanding the world, his own outlook was profoundly moral, and he embraced the theologian's application of irony to the American myth of innocence and power, to which the southern experience stood in sharp contrast. Equally important, he recognized a valuable tool for his own work in the *technique* of Niebuhr's ironic analysis. In "The Irony of Southern History" Woodward paraphrased Niebuhr to show how "the scholar" could explicate the ironic situation for a wide audience:

> In the nature of things the participants in an ironic situation are rarely conscious of the irony, else they would not become its victims. Awareness must ordinarily be contributed by an observer, a nonparticipant, and the observer must have an unusual combination of detachment and sympathy. He must be able to appreciate both elements in the incongruity that go to make up the ironic situation, both the virtue and the vice to which pretensions of virtue lead. He must not be so hostile as to deny the element of virtue or

strength on the one side, nor so sympathetic as to ignore the vanity and weakness to which the virtue and strength have contributed.[15]

Woodward applied this ironic technique to two episodes from southern history, the first from the 1830s, when the Jeffersonian tradition of open debate was overwhelmed by proslavery orthodoxy. In that decade, Woodward explained, "the South concentrated its energies upon the repression of heresy and raised intellectual barricades against the ideas of a critical and unfriendly world."[16] The irony of this situation derives from the self-confidence of proslavery intellectuals, who, having read the Greek and Roman classics in the original, believed they were recreating Greek democracy on a grander scale. Woodward quotes from a speech by Robert Barnwell Rhett, delivered when South Carolina seceded, in which that young fire-eater imagines what a historian in the year 2000 would write about the expansion of the South's new "democratic empire" to the Pacific and into Mexico. Rhett's imaginary historian praises the secessionists for creating "a civilization which has never been equaled or surpassed . . . teeming with orators, poets, philosophers, statesmen, and historians equal to those of Greece and Rome" and celebrates "the glorious spectacle of a free, prosperous, and illustrious people."[17]

Woodward the moralist, influenced by a theologian, combined irony and analogy to instruct his fellow countrymen on the lessons that southern experience offered postwar America. The open southern society prior to 1830 was like the United States in the 1930s, when the country experienced "the most thoroughgoing inquest of self-criticism that our national economy had ever undergone." But in the mid-1940s, as in the mid-1830s, "the floodstream of criticism dwindled to a trickle and very nearly ceased altogether."[18] "Both these revolutions in public attitudes," Woodward observed, "were reactions to contests for power in which the two societies found themselves involved . . . each party to the conflict, of course, contended that the other practiced the more immoral, wicked, and shameless type of exploitation and that its own system was benevolent, idealistic, and sound."[19]

Woodward's second example, discussed only briefly, seemed apt for a nation that had recently taken upon itself the responsibility of reconstructing its defeated foes. Thinking of the reconstructions of Japan and Germany as well as that of the defeated South, Woodward noted that "ironic contrasts between idealistic aims and pragmatic consequences are characteristics of reconstruction periods as well as war crises."[20]

Implicit in Woodward's application of irony to southern history was a belief that, if rightly interpreted by southern intellectuals, these stories might influence public opinion and even public policy. But the irony of history could not be confined to the dead past. Only eight years after "Irony" was republished in *The Burden of Southern History,* Woodward brought out a revised edition of the book that included a new essay entitled "A Second Look at the Theme of Irony." In it Woodward acknowledged, "Revolutionary changes in the last two decades have blurred the distinctiveness of the South." He admitted that history had at last caught up with the United States in the form of an intractable war and failed attempts at reconstruction in Vietnam, with American policy set by a southern president, supported by a southern secretary of state, and executed by a southern general. "But if history had caught up with America," Woodward conceded, "it would seem that the irony of history has caught up with the ironist—or gone him one better."[21]

Following the collapse of the Soviet empire and after the horrific attack on the United States on September 11, 2001, public outpourings of patriotism and calls for retaliation were matched by a vision of America's place in the world that was reminiscent of the vision and popular outbursts that had alarmed Woodward and Niebuhr a half century before. Articulated in speeches by President George W. Bush and members of his administration, this vision was stated succinctly in "National Security Strategy of the United States" (September 2002): "The great struggles of the twentieth century between liberty and totalitarianism ended with a decisive victory for the forces of freedom—and a *single sustainable model for national success:* freedom, democracy, and free enterprise. . . . The United States will use this moment of opportunity to extend the benefits of freedom across the globe. We will actively work to bring the hope of democracy, development, free markets, and free trade to every corner of the world."[22] The most important foreign policy outcome of this vision has been the invasion, occupation, and attempted reconstruction of Iraq and Afghanistan. Domestically, the new-old mix of power and illusions of virtue contributed to the return of culture wars that called to mind the suppression of dissent in the 1830s and 1950s that had so troubled Woodward.

An assessment of this new-old vision of America's role in the world could engage the skills of a new practitioner of the ironic interpretation of history, a young public intellectual in the tradition of Woodward and Niebuhr.

Renewed interest in Niebuhr's writings in the past several years has focused in particular on his use of irony and cuts across the political spectrum from George Gilder and Michael Novak (who claimed him as the original neo-conservative, based on his strong anti-Stalinism in the postwar era) to David Brooks and Barack Obama.[23] But today the revived interest in Niebuhr and irony includes no mention of Woodward. Why not? Perhaps because Woodward merely suggested the value of an ironic interpretation of history but did not flesh it out. Or perhaps because southern history, once replete with instructive ironies, has lost its distinctiveness and thus its power to instruct.

Woodward said as much when he began his autobiographical essay by quoting Justice Oliver Wendell Holmes quoting Henrik Ibsen: "'Truths,' said the playwright, 'are by no means the wiry Methuselahs some people think them. A normally constituted truth lives—let us say—as a rule, seventeen or eighteen years; at the outside, twenty, seldom longer.'"[24] This was probably not just another of those rhetorical feints for which Professor Woodward was famous, although one can never be sure. It is still true, as Woodward noted, that a distinctive southern history now confined to books *may* still have the power to persuade, but the likelihood of that happening is far greater among the members of the historians' guild than among American citizens at large, even those who still call themselves southerners.

What remains fresh and vital in the essay and in Woodward's later reflections on ironic history is his account of the epiphany he experienced when applying Niebuhr's *technique* of ironic analysis, or perhaps more accurately, Niebuhr's appeal for an empathetic frame of mind when seeking to explain an ironic situation: since "participants in ironic situation are rarely conscious of the irony," it is up to "an observer, a nonparticipant . . . [with] an unusual combination of detachment and sympathy. He must be able to appreciate both elements in the incongruity that go to make up the ironic situation, both the virtue and the vice to which pretentions of virtue lead."[25] Thanks to Professor Woodward for pointing the way.

WOODWARD'S POPULISTS

The same dramatic swing in public opinion toward "the repression of heresies" that troubled Woodward after World War II also produced scholarly criticism of the subject of Woodward's early research, late-nineteenth-century Populism, which some of the critics conflated with post–World

War II movements on the far right, including McCarthyism. "The Populist Heritage and the Intellectual" was Woodward's rejoinder, not in defense of the new radical right, in which he professed to have no interest, but of *his* southern Populists and, by extension, of progressive liberalism.[26] Woodward vigorously defends historical American Populism, and in a broader sense he also challenges the view of some liberal intellectuals—already in transition to neoconservatism—that in the postwar era of prosperity, populistic New Deal liberalism was an outmoded and exhausted ideology. To speak of "populistic New Deal liberalism" is to invite an argument about continuities of reform traditions in America, but for Woodward, a common bond of struggle against economic distress in the 1890s and the 1930s created a Populist *heritage* that transcended specific policies and parties.

The Populists whose battles Woodward had first chronicled in *Tom Watson, Agrarian Rebel* (1938) were mostly hardworking farmers trapped in a terrible economic depression and enslaved by predatory banks and railroads.[27] Drawing upon two decades of farmer-labor political platforms, the Populists cobbled together a list of demands that revolved around governmental intervention in economic life to address the structural problems they and other hardworking Americans faced every day. Populist organizations, both voluntary associations like the Farmers Alliance and the People's (Populist) Party itself, were overwhelmingly white. But in an effort to turn their demands into law, and in the face of ferocious and violent opposition from Democrats, white Populists in the South attempted to forge political alliances across racial lines. Those alliances, and their movement itself, could not withstand the onslaught of intimidation, terror, and massive election fraud on the part of Democrats, and they collapsed almost as quickly as they had sprung up. But American Populism had left a democratic legacy and economic vision that Woodward believed was still worth fighting for. I am part of a generation of scholars who, inspired by Woodward's writings and by the civil rights movement that unfolded before our eyes,[28] confirmed through our research many of his basic conclusions about Populism and its program while sometimes disagreeing with him on details about who the Populists were and how they came to be mobilized. At a time when the term *populism* is associated almost entirely with movements that proclaim the government to be the enemy of the people, it is important to understand that the Populists of the 1890s believed otherwise. For them it was the giant, uncontrolled conglomerates in banking, transportation, and commerce that threatened the livelihoods and liberty of ordinary Americans, not the government. They believed that only the federal government could rein in these greedy giants and restore a level playing field where ordinary producers could compete.

Far from hoping to shrink government to a size where it could be drowned in a bathtub, as antitax advocate Grover Norquist famously proposed, Populists advocated a sweeping expansion of the federal government's role in the economy, including governmental regulation or even ownership of railroad and telegraph systems, sweeping national currency reforms, a progressive income tax, protection of the rights of labor, and a massive system of credit and marketing support for producers of agricultural commodities. It is all there in the Populists' Omaha Platform of 1892, a document that had taken shape in the local gatherings of organized farmers and workers across the country over the course of two decades.

ANOTHER VIEW: THE IRRATIONAL POPULISTS

For Woodward, the Populists were, in the main, humane, democratic, and economically progressive—rational actors in the marketplace and New Dealers before their time—and Woodward firmly believed that Populism was strongest and most radical in the South.[29] Woodward was moved to defend the Populists by the publication in 1955 of two books that portrayed them as backward-looking agrarian fundamentalists who yearned for a lost Golden Age, downwardly mobile provincials driven to irrational outbursts by status anxiety, and even anti-Semitic forebears of American fascism. One was *The New American Right,* a collection of essays edited by Daniel Bell, eleven years Woodward's junior but already emerging as a leading sociologist and public intellectual. Other contributors to the volume included prominent sociologists Talcott Parsons, David Riesman, Nathan Glazer, and Seymour Martin Lipset, along with historian Richard Hofstadter, whose own work made use of an emerging theory in social psychology, status anxiety, to explain movements like Populism.

In the opening essay, Daniel Bell announced (perhaps a little too fervently) that *The New American Right* was not fundamentally concerned with what might be the "passing phenomenon" of McCarthyism, but rather with the "deeper-running social currents of a turbulent mid-century America," born "not of depression but of prosperity." The book, Bell explained, offered a new framework for understanding these turbulent times, "derived from an analysis of the exhaustion of liberal and left-wing political ideology, and [from] an examination of the new, prosperity-created 'status groups' which in their drive for recognition and respectability, [had] sought to impose older conformities on the American body politic."[30]

Bell and his coauthors were part of a school of thought among postwar American social scientists influenced by the writings of, among others, Max Weber, Karl Mannheim, and Theodor Adorno on the role of authoritarianism and social status in politics. They labored in the very shadow of fascism, totalitarianism, and the Holocaust, which heightened the urgency of their efforts to explain contemporary mass movements. They would have known about the toxic mixture of overheated nationalism and scientific racism that, in the second half of the nineteenth century, fermented into the stuff of virulent anti-Semitism. Some of these scholars had themselves escaped from Hitler's deadly rule to find refuge in American universities, especially at Columbia, where in 1953–54 as part of a campuswide seminar they and others developed a powerful new set of social constructs grounded in social psychology that they believed would replace Marxian class analysis in explaining mass behavior. As historian William Leuchtenburg later recalled of those days at Columbia, "We were all thinking in that direction, it was in the water."[31]

Hofstadter's contribution to *The New American Right,* "The Pseudo-Conservative Revolt," was a hard-hitting critique of the emergent conservative movement, which, though smaller than the forces of the New Deal at high tide, possessed the energy and focus that liberalism had seemingly lost. Hofstadter concluded, "The ideology of pseudo-conservatism can be characterized but not defined, because the pseudo-conservative tends to be more than ordinarily incoherent about politics." His first example was a woman who, when Eisenhower defeated Taft for the Republican presidential nomination in 1952, declared, "This means eight more years of socialism."[32] Other examples included McCarthyites, proponents of a preemptive nuclear attack on the Russians, and authoritarian personalities of all sorts. (Hofstadter readily acknowledged his debt to Adorno's recently published book *The Authoritarian Personality.*) The pseudocons offered nothing more than their anger to a nation that seemed to have largely accepted at least a watered-down version of cold war liberalism of the type described above. In general, Hofstadter attributed the rise of this pseudoconservatism to "the rootlessness and heterogeneity of American life, and above all, of its peculiar scramble for status and its peculiar search for secure identity."[33]

The closest Hofstadter came to mentioning Woodward's Populists was a passing, nonspecific reference to the "populistic culture" of the United States.[34] Other authors were more direct, but without Hofstadter's caution. Among other claims, as Woodward later recounted in "The Populist Heritage and the Intellectual," Peter Viereck asserted that "beneath the sane economic demands of the populists of 1880–1900 seethed a mania of xenophobia, Jew-baiting, intellectual baiting, and thought-control lynch spirit." Talcott Parsons found "elements of continuity between western agrarian populism and McCarthyism." And Victor C. Ferkiss (not a contributor to *the New American Right*) said flatly that "American fascism had its roots in American populism."[35] One sometimes hears these claims associated with Hofstadter's name even today, but he never made them, perhaps for a reason to which we now turn.

THE ODD COUPLE: WOODWARD AND HOFSTADTER

Despite the credentials of its authors and the boldness of their pronouncements, *The New American Right* was not the greatest threat to Woodward's interpretation of Populism and progressive reform in America. A greater challenge came from Hofstadter's *The Age of Reform: From Bryan to FDR* (1955), which received the Pulitzer Prize in 1956.[36] Thirty years after its publication, historian Alan Brinkley declared *The Age of Reform* to be "the most influential book ever published on the history of twentieth-century America,"[37] and he may well have been right. It was "a book for the times and of the times," as Woodward said of *Tom Watson* and the 1930s.[38] The social theories that were "in the water" at Columbia in the early 1950s were soon in the air among academicians and the reading public, and "status anxiety" provided for many a persuasive explanation of all the unreasonableness. Even today, many journalistic accounts of the Tea Party movement and other manifestations of the newest New American Right echo *The Age of Reform,* sometimes without knowing the source of their interpretation.

Furthermore, Hofstadter's book was a work of literary craftsmanship of the highest order, with an argument that was easy to grasp and a narrative buttressed by compelling anecdotes. *The Age of Reform* mirrored the best work in the new field of American studies, which "set out to analyze the abiding myths of the American past: agrarianism, the self-made man, the virtuous folk."[39] Like Smith in *Virgin Land,* Hofstadter wove together statements from a relative handful of writerly participants in the movement to create what seemed to be a persuasive analysis of the Populist mind, while also, like Smith, largely ignoring the role of partisan politics in shaping culture, and then he did the same with Progressivism. Neither movement, in Hofstadter's telling, had much to do with the New Deal and modern liberalism. Hofstadter had mastered the existing literature on agriculture, agrarian thought, and farm movements in America, and consequently his treatment of Populism was more balanced than the work of his fellow authors in *The New American Right.* But he did offer a novel explanation of why men and women chose to participate in the Populist movement.

Hofstadter's conclusion about the Populists, in a nutshell, was this: "Rank in society! That was close to the heart of the matter, for the farmer was beginning to realize acutely not merely that the best of the world's goods were to be had in the cities and that the urban middle and upper classes had so much more of them than he did but also that he was losing in status and respect as compared to them."[40] Woodward's earnest Populists and their radical program of reform largely disappear in Hofstadter's well-crafted narrative and in selected examples of conspiracy theories, nostalgia, and anti-Semitism.

For some social scientists, Hofstadter's book was a historical vindication of their own theorizing, but the author was more concerned with its standing among his fellow historians. Hofstadter's work criticized the two giants of the preceding generation, Charles A. Beard (who popularized an economic interpretation of history) and Frederick Jackson Turner (whose frontier thesis Hofstadter believed to be profoundly wrongheaded).[41] But in a more specific sense, Hofstadter was taking aim at John D. Hicks and C. Vann Woodward, the leading historians of Populism, both of whom were associated with the Progressive or economic school of interpretation. Beard and Turner were dead, and thus not able to defend themselves, but Hicks wrote a positive review, much to Hofstadter's surprise.[42] Woodward waited until 1959 before responding in print to *The New American Right* and *The Age of Reform,* when he published "the Populist Heritage and the Intellectual" in *The American Scholar.*

To understand why Woodward held his fire for four years, it is useful to know that by 1955 Richard Hofstadter and C. Vann Woodward had been close friends for almost a decade and would remain so until Hofstadter's untimely death of leukemia in 1970. They had met just after the war while both were doing research at the National Archives and quickly became friends. One can imagine conversations over coffee in which the two scholars commiserated about the drudgery of archival research, which for both was something to be endured before getting on with the writing, which they loved. Despite their professional differences, they stayed in close touch, and their families shared vacations. Woodward later recalled that their friendship "was never threatened by our differences, either of origin [one born on the Lower East Side of Manhattan and the other in eastern Arkansas] or of views."[43]

A letter from Woodward to John D. Hicks in 1960 confirms the supposition that his friendship with Hofstadter had caused him to delay a reply: "I . . . have long felt that an answer was required. I hesitated a long time to do it, because so many of our critics were long-time friends and historians with whom I have much in common in the way of tastes and sympathies. Had this not been the case, I doubtless would have been somewhat harsher in my strictures."[44] That said, when reading some of the more cautious and respectful passages on farmers' worldviews in *The Age of Reform* with the knowledge of this great friendship in mind, it is easy to imagine that we are hearing Hofstadter's side of a conversation with Woodward. And in reading "The Populist Heritage and the Intellectual," the reverse is also true.

Woodward's 1959 essay was carefully constructed to win support from liberal intellectuals for the "neo-Populist" New Deal tradition, which Woodward himself had embraced since the late 1930s. To do that, he had to attack what he believed was the substitution of a new stereotype for an old one—replacing the romantic 1930s view of Populism as "the root of all good in democracy" with an opposite maxim in the 1950s: "*Radix malorum est Populismus.*"[45] The shift, Woodward noted, occurred when critics of McCarthyism applied the label "populist" to groups in the United States whose values seemed dangerously close to those of the Nazis. Woodward argued on historical and geographical grounds that the linkage of historical Populism with the contemporary radical right was simply inaccurate. Critics mistakenly situated the heartland of historical Populism in the Midwest (home to Senator McCarthy), while in fact, as even Hofstadter had pointed out, the strength of the movement was in the southern and Great Plains states and in the Rocky Mountain West. The South, Woodward noted, had not strongly supported McCarthyism. Reprising the theme of southern distinctiveness from "The Irony of Southern history," Woodward said of the Populist era: "Thirty years after Secession and Civil War, the South suffered a second alienation from the dominant national spirit," when grinding poverty gave rise to a political movement that blamed eastern capitalists and their southern agents for the ills of southern farmers.[46]

Quoting Seymour Martin Lipset as claiming that movements spurred by status anxiety occurred in "periods of prosperity, especially when full employment is accompanied by inflation," Woodward asked how this social theory could possibly apply to impoverished Populists in the deflationary 1890s, and then he gave his own explanation for the rise of their movement: "Populism was hardly 'status politics.' And I would hesitate to call it 'class politics." It was more nearly 'interest politics,' and more specifically 'agricultural interest politics.'"[47]

Woodward conceded troubling qualities among the Populists but introduced evidence that placed those thoughts and actions in context, calling as his witness none other than Professor Hofstadter.[48] Having acknowledged that Populists did sometimes exhibit "irrational or retrograde traits," he thanked Hofstadter for "the spirit of civility and forbearance," in contrast to others who seem eager for the job of "heaping upon Populism, as upon an historical scapegoat, all the ills to which democracy is heir."[49] After enumerating the accusations of populist-fascist associations, Woodward brushed them aside by demonstrating the critics' ignorance of what he called "the genuine article" of Populism and by placing the Populists' "irrational or retrograde traits" in the context of similar excesses among the elites of their day, noting, for example, the statements of New York Police Commissioner Theodore Roosevelt in 1896 "that the Populists were 'plotting a social revolution and subversion of the American Republic' and proposing to make an example of twelve of their leaders by 'shooting them dead' against a wall."[50]

While noting that some Populists expressed anti-Semitic views, he again called Hofstadter as witness for the defense, citing his qualifying statement in *The Age of Reform* that "Populist anti-Semitism was entirely verbal and rhetorical."[51] By this neither Woodward nor Hofstadter meant to deny the significance of words, but with the Holocaust still fresh in mind, both were making an important distinction, developed more fully in the years to come by Holocaust scholars, between folk stereotypes and episodic pogroms in Europe and the lethal form of racism, abetted by modern science and technology, that emerged between the 1870s and 1920s, first in France and then in Germany, out of a witches' brew of pseudoscience, romantic myths of the *Volk,* war-induced hypernationalism, and economic depression.[52]

In "The Populist Heritage and the Intellectual," Woodward's tone in responding to Populism's critics was often restrained, and with regard to Hofstadter, it was almost deferential. We may never know whether this was another of his canny stratagems for disarming his reader or a gentleman's public reply to a dear friend with whom he disagreed. Woodward was not so much trying to convince Populism's academic critics that they were wrong on the facts as he was trying to persuade what was still a large and vital community of progressive intellectuals to join him in embracing a "Populist heritage," despite its faults, and even to provide that community with a new generation of thought leaders. Woodward ends his appeal with a heartfelt plea: "[The intellectual] will learn all he can from the new criticism about the irrational and illiberal side of Populism and other reform movements, but he cannot afford to repudiate the heritage."[53]

Not long after the publication of *The Age of Reform,* challenges to Hofstadter's reading of the Populists began to appear from scholars who had done extensive archival research on the subject, and by the 1970s and 1980s, Woodward's view of historical Populism, or something like it, largely prevailed over Hofstadter's in the battle of interpretations among American historians.[54] Furthermore, as we shall see, the theoretical underpinning of Hofstadter's work was swept away by advances in the social scientific study of social movements. Nevertheless, in the decades that followed, Woodward the presentist, who "wished the past to speak wisely to our present needs," lost the war over the use of the term. Today, those who mold public opinion, for better or for worse, know little of Woodward's Populism and care less about its potential import for a revived liberalism. But they profess great interest and claim expertise in the revival of conservatism in America and have anointed one or another of its branches as the true and only Populism, even though most contemporary conservatives groups, including the Tea Party, avoid the term. For many of these pundits, regardless of whether they have read *The Age of Reform,* "populism" works as a label for any number of what they view as irrational mass movements.

A half century and more after scholars first argued over who in American politics should be called a populist, one wonders if this is an issue worth fighting about. Should we care who inherits the populist mantle if the term has become devoid of any meaning at all? It is difficult, even for historians with a vested interest in the outcome, to work up any enthusiasm for another fight over who owns the brand, particularly if the debate now has little to do with historical American Populism. *However,* the debate in which Woodward, Hofstadter, and the authors of *The New American Right* participated all those years ago might help frame another question: how are historical Populism, New Deal populism (Woodward's "Populist Legacy"), and conservative movements of the past forty years alike, and how are they different *as social movements*?

EXPLAINING AND COMPARING SOCIAL MOVEMENTS

1890s Populism and various strands of conservatism in postwar America are movements organized in opposition to prevailing political institutions and ideologies, and both lived in a state of *dynamic contention* with established parties and political ideologies. The term *contentious politics* applied equally well to late-nineteenth-century Populists and to anticommunists and social or economic conservatives of the twentieth and early twenty-first centuries.[55] Despite profound differences on policies, these, and a host of other movements that have flourished over the past two centuries, are similar in their use of available cultural and technological resources and in the choices they face in trying to get a foothold in politics. Late-nineteenth-century Populism and some manifestations of early-twenty-first-century conservatism can be usefully compared as *movements* with histories of their own. Unfortunately, neither Woodward nor Hofstadter offered useful guides for this kind of comparison.

Woodward's explanation of *his* Populism was grounded in the economic self-interest of American farmers. Fair enough as far as it goes, but beyond that, his explanation of the Populist movement required only four things: "great financial distress and inequality; an ideology and program that interpret this distress to the sufferers and offer remedies; charismatic leaders like Tom Watson . . . to do the explaining; and just enough instability or competition in the political system to give agrarian radicalism a chance of electoral success."[56] Hofstadter's explanation was even thinner: provincial and backward-looking farmers distressed by their loss of status were stirred to act collectively by a handful of second-rate literary figures and conspiracy theorists like Ignatius Donnelly and "Coin" Harvey. In their different ways, both Woodward and Hofstadter tended "to see isolated, deprived individuals as the main actors in collective action,"[57] rather than considering the ways in which social networks drew people into movements, helped determine who would join and who would not, and engaged in "dynamic contention" with the prevailing political forces and institutions of the day.

Since the 1960s social theorists and historians of collective behavior have developed more useful ways of understanding social movements, including Populism and other contentious movements in American politics, and also for comparing popular mobilization across time and space. These approaches begin by taking seriously the history and culture within which movements emerge. Students of social movements now seek to understand the whole range of cultural resources that movement participants have at their disposal for conceptualizing, articulating, and acting on their grievances. These resources include not only popular visions of a rightly ordered political economy (often expressed through national historical narratives), but also popular religion and value systems, ethnic and other group identities, and dense networks of voluntary associations.

Social movements involve the organized effort of people to achieve goals that are, in some sense of the word, political. Movements are a form of "contentious politics" engaged in sustained interaction with governments and political institutions.[58] Social movements as we know them first emerged in the early nineteenth century, primarily in Great Britain, Western Europe, and the United States. They have followed broadly recognizable patterns and careers since then, with variations of the historical pattern now being exported to many other parts of the world.[59]

Social movements were made possible by the diffusion of printing/literacy and voluntary associations in the West that, particularly in Great Britain, converged to form what Sidney Tarrow called "communities of print and association." These communities appeared simultaneously with the growth of national electoral politics and gave ordinary citizens the tools to influence emerging democratic systems in ways they had never experienced before. Easily available printed material and "federated" issue-oriented associations (local chapters affiliated with a national organization) became part of a "repertoire of contention" that, like repertoires in music or drama, comprised a set of learned behaviors with which people could create new movements. Furthermore, much of this repertoire became "modular," meaning it could be learned in one setting and then applied to another.

Think, for example, of farmers' clubs' adaptation of the Methodist circuit-rider system as an organizing tool in the 1880s or the John Birch Society's use of Tupperware party–style coffee klatches to win suburban recruits in the 1950s. As this pair of examples demonstrates, the *forms* of communication and community have changed radically over time. Think of Google and Facebook as compared to mass-produced newspapers and pamphlets. But their centrality to social movements remains unchanged.

People join social movements because they have a sense of grievance about something, and movements give meaning and direction to those grievances, not just by means of a superimposed global ideology, but more commonly by a set of "frames" that shape grievances into more resonant claims. Framing not only generalizes specific grievances but also defines the "us" and "them" of a movement, both individually and organizationally. Historically, as Sidney Tarrow and others suggest, movements typically involve more than a single organization; they consist of "cycles of contention," in which "early risers" are joined by later waves of citizens in organizations and episodes that cover considerable territory. Such movements are often perceived as unified forces even though they may contain many disparate organizations and agendas. Think of the various organizations, messages, and tactics that converged in the American civil rights movement.

Finally, movements exist in relation to governments and other power centers, and the response of governments to them plays a major role in their success or failure. That is to say, certain government actions open up opportunities for movements, while others increase the constraints that movement participants face. Government, in other words, can lower or raise the "cost" of participation. Compare, for example, the "velvet revolutions" in Poland, Czechoslovakia, and East Germany in 1989–90, which were actually aided by uncertainty and compromise on the part of the Soviet Union, with the Chinese student rebellion occurring at the same time, which was brutally suppressed by the authorities. (Chinese authorities watched and learned from the velvet revolution.) Think also of the relative successes of the American Populist Party in states where one or both of the two major parties suppressed or co-opted the third-party movement.[60]

Social movements are "modern," sustained efforts of people who consider themselves powerless to alter power relationships. They draw people into voluntary associations but are larger than any single organization. They are political, but not coterminous with parties. They are embedded in familiar social institutions but often at odds with them. Rather than viewing movements as static forms of mass behavior and asking only why people join them in the first place, this approach calls for study of the *careers* of movements over time. Unlike the authors of *The New American Right*, practitioners of this approach follow the suggestion of Tilly to "treat the social movement as an established way of doing political business, rather than as a set of deviant individuals."[61] This approach, used judiciously, allows for true comparison of movements across time and political boundaries by analyzing in relation to each other the differing but comparable elements of two or more movements—their modular repertories, frames, and dynamic contention with the holders of power.

CODA: SOCIAL MOVEMENTS AND THE HISTORY OF *THIS* PRESENT

For those today who, like Woodward, are drawn to "the history of the present,"[62] this is a moment filled with opportunities. In recent years social movements have reshaped the political landscape, or attempted to do so, in Asia and Africa as well as in Europe and the Western Hemisphere.[63] Contentious politics has become the norm, and opportunities for analysis and comparison abound. In the United States, recent monographs have applied the techniques of Tarrow, Tilly, McAdam, and others to historical movements ranging from antislavery to civil rights.[64] The various strains of conservative political movements that have attracted large followings in the past few decades could be next. The point of such comparisons would not be to say who is or is not a populist, but rather to treat movements historically and analytically and to contextualize, categorize, and explain movement-based politics in *this* present. This is not the place for a rigorous application of these methods to contemporary conservatism, but these movements of the early twenty-first century clearly belong to the class of "modern" collective behavior as it has developed over the past two centuries and are ripe for such a treatment.

Every beginning in recorded history has antecedents, but the appropriate beginning for comparisons involving "contemporary" conservatism in the United States is the 1970s, the history of which, as Eric Hobsbawm wrote, "is that of a world which lost its bearings and slid into instability and crisis."[65] When Woodward revised *The Burden of Southern History* in 1968, the West was on the verge of a crisis in the postwar economic order that, in the United States, led to the collapse of the liberal consensus (see p. 85). That consensus, and the social contract that it inspired, had rested on the presumption that postwar prosperity was here to stay: the economic security of most Americans could last indefinitely based on high employment rates, expansion of retirement and medical benefits, and opportunities for home ownership, if only experts in government and business were allowed to continue fine-tuning the economy.

In "The Irony of Southern History," Woodward had criticized the "self-righteousness, complacency, and humorless idealism" of millions of postwar Americans who thought this way, and he held up the experience of the impoverished South as a corrective. (Compare Niebuhr in *The Irony of American History:* "Our difficulty as a nation is that we must now learn that prosperity is not simply coordinated to virtue, and that virtue is not simply coordinated to historic destiny.")[66] But many Americans saw what was happening as nothing less than the fulfillment of the American dream, and they believed it could last forever. Soon, however, Americans had reason to affirm Arnold Toynbee's realization after the fall of Britain from its lofty Victorian perch, "that history had happened to my people in my part of the world."

The 1970s witnessed a major energy crisis, economic "stagflation" (simultaneous high unemployment and high inflation), job-killing globalization, the collapse of the postwar social contract between management and labor, and the fruition of rights revolutions based on race and gender. On the economic front, while multinational corporations flourished, national economies could no longer sustain job growth, real wages shrank, and job security diminished, triggering a loss of security in job-related health and retirement benefits.

The political outcome of this economic crisis was not, as some predicted, a triumph of the left or of left-leaning Populism, but a loss of confidence in "the grand ideologies of modernization,"[67] which translated in the United States into the collapse of the Keynsian-liberal consensus of Democrats and moderate Republicans, and in Western Europe into regime crises that destroyed most of the major center right and center left parties.

Whereas Woodward's Populists and their heirs had looked to government to solve economic problems, emergent political movements in the 1970s believed that government *was* the problem and blamed it for economic decline. In the United States this antigovernment shift overlapped with a sense that the country had lost its moral compass and was degenerating into godless hedonism and also with a backlash against movements for racial and gender equality. The conservative movements that mushroomed in the 1970s had roots in the 1950s and even in pre–New Deal economic thought. But they have had a greater impact on national politics than the movements against which the authors of *The New American Right* railed.

Contemporary American conservatism is rife with divisions and contradictions (libertarianism versus social conservatism, for example). The agendas of its various strands include lowering taxes and shrinking government (in particular its regulatory apparatus and the taxes it collects), promoting religious values through public policy, reversing federal policies on desegregation and affirmative action, and restricting immigration.[68] But the internal divisions of contemporary conservatism are no deeper than those of other major movements of the past two centuries, and despite its lack of unanimity, the movement has cohered well enough to shift the center of political gravity well to the right. This family of movements is "political but not coterminous with parties," as Tilly would have it, even though since Ronald Reagan won the presidency in 1980, movement participants have mainly aligned themselves with the Republican Party, sometimes warily. The Tea Party movement is among the wary. According to an April 2010 poll, 43 percent of Tea Party supporters held an "unfavorable" opinion of the GOP, and 52 percent agreed with the statement that the country needs a third party to complete with the Democratic and Republican parties.[69]

Some elements of contemporary conservativism openly espouse racist ideologies and conspiracy theories. The rise of paramilitary movements in the 1990s was widely noted at the time, but their recent resurgence has gone largely unremarked in the mainstream media.[70] Some movement organizations have adopted the theology of "Christian Identity" (which is alien to any orthodox Christian belief system and denies the full humanity of Jews) or a militant strain of libertarianism popularized by *The Turner Diaries* (1979), which, in the heroic style of Ayn Rand, is cast as the rediscovered diary of a foot soldier in the "Great Revolution" against ZOG (the Zionist Occupation Government).[71] Today, more than in the 1950s, conspiratorial thinking that previously put adherents "off the grid" is finding its way into "mainstream" politics.

Unlike extremist groups, which avoid electoral politics altogether and are sometimes literally off the grid, most strands of contemporary American conservatism fit the pattern of social movements outlined above. Their ideologies or "frames" energize millions of movement participants, while movement champions in the media disseminate their ideas to a wide audience. The repertoires of modern movements on the right often look like "communities of print and association," updated to include technologies of the Internet age, partisan reporting of cable TV, and richly endowed foundations and political action committees skilled in the art of funneling resources to like-minded movements. The new conservatism is unquestionably a type of "contentious politics."

The new conservatism began as a self-conscious minority battling the powers, but its success in helping bring about Ronald Reagan's presidential victory brought it close to the centers of power. During and after the Reagan years, conservatives of various stripes found themselves discomfited when their representatives were thrust into positions of forming coalitions with nonpurists and governing through institutions where compromise with unbelievers was necessary. It has always been so with movements. The squabbles during the 2010 election cycle between mainstream Republican leaders (many of them yesterday's movement firebrands) and Tea Party adherents, along with the divisions among Republicans in the 112th Congress, echo the wars of maneuver between movements and parties that have gone on in America since the expansion of the franchise and the beginning of the party system in the early nineteenth century.

The Tea Party phenomenon emerged in the early months of 2009 as a decentralized and seemingly spontaneous grassroots movement in the aftermath of the near collapse of housing and financial markets. Massive infusions of federal support for financial institutions that were pushed through Congress by the Bush and Obama administrations added fuel to the movement in a moment of extreme economic peril and the beginning of a major recession.

Early reports of the Tea Party movement's "going viral" suggested a spontaneous outpouring of support by millions of enthusiasts. In the 1880s and 1890s, journalists observing the rise of Populism made the same point with a (then) familiar figure of speech from *Uncle Tom's Cabin:* "It just growed like Topsy." Then as now, suggestions that movements appear out of nowhere should be taken with a grain of salt, for both of these mobilizing efforts drew heavily upon frames and repertories of earlier movement organizations. That said, the Tea Party movement did attract a huge following in a short time, probably a larger percentage of American voters than Populism enlisted in its heyday. A *New York Times*–CBS poll taken in April 2010 indicated that 18 percent of Americans supported the Tea Party, most of them Republican, white, male, over the age of forty-five, and of above-average income.[72] A subsequent CBS poll, taken in August 2010, suggested that almost 30 percent favored the Tea Party, although the amorphous nature of the movement made it difficult to verify those figures. If the Tea Party was the vanguard of a conservative Republican army in 2010, the independent voters who switched in massive numbers from the party of Obama to the GOP became its main force. Together, they registered a resounding protest against the Democratic Party, but one that did not necessarily represent long-term support for the GOP.

Whatever the size and staying power of this Tea Party–led movement, it has been aided by forces rarely seen on the side of social movements. Few if any have had the financial support from extremely wealthy individuals and well-endowed organizations that the Tea Party movement has enjoyed. Have any other movements garnered the support from established news media that the Tea Party gets from Fox News? In the 1890s, the forebears of Fox News were busy branding the old-time Populists as socialists, anarchists, and gullible hayseeds.

While generalizing about the agendas of a movement as diffuse as the Tea Party is risky, most observers agree that the movement initially drew most heavily from the libertarian, small-government tradition and less so from social conservatism, although that may be changing. It draws upon conservative ideologies from the 1970s on, as well as the John Birch Society, which spread rapidly in the 1960s. As its name suggests, the movement defines itself in relation to a certain perspective of our national history. Tea Party advocates identify themselves with the patriots of 1776, not with the Populists of 1896.[73] Their particular reading of the revolutionary moment is not shared by most historians of that era,[74] but, with the help of Glen Beck, Rush Limbaugh, and other Tea Party champions, it resonates with a great many Americans.

The Republican landslide of 2010, led by the Tea Party movement and angry independents, was a continuation of that wave of dissatisfaction with government and politics as usual that began in the 1970s. Once again, as in the administration of Jimmy Carter, a Democratic president faced a movement-led opposition fueled by widespread distrust of government and by discontent over its ineffectiveness in the face of crises ranging from the crash and the recession to the Gulf oil spill and—beneath it all—a sense that the nation was losing its place as the world's preeminent power.

In the months leading up to and following the 2010 elections, anti–Tea Party polemics multiplied. So far, relatively little sober *analysis* of this movement has appeared in print, although more is under way. Perhaps this much-needed analysis could begin with the simple act of *listening* carefully to what these angry people are saying. Recall the lesson Woodward learned from Niebuhr about assessing the ironic situation: "The observer must have an unusual combination of detachment and sympathy. He must be able to appreciate both elements in the incongruity that goes to make up the ironic situation, both the virtue and the vice to which pretensions of virtue lead. He must not be so hostile as to deny the element of virtue or strength on the one side, nor so sympathetic as to ignore the vanity and weakness to which the virtue and strength have contributed." Recall also Charles Tilly's advice to "treat the social movement as an established way of doing political business, rather than as a set of deviant individuals."

The contemporary conservative movement, in its various manifestations, is a major force in politics. It is not going away, and even those who may wish for a revival of Woodward's Populist legacy cannot afford the luxury of sitting back and calling its participants paranoid, or victims of false consciousness, or racist. Tilly and others who have thought deeply about social movements offer us tools for crafting a more useful kind of public commentary.

But what of the historical Populists and their legacy in the Progressive Era and the New Deal? Is *that* Populism dead? Is the Tea Party its reincarnation? The Tea Party is *not* part of the historical Populist legacy in America, nor does it claim to be, despite being labeled as populistic by many pundits. As Charles Postel has written, after followers of Ronald Reagan sought to repeal the New Deal, "the tea parties have launched a campaign to repeal the Progressive Era. The Progressive reforms they most object to are the ones that farmers and Populists first put on the political agenda."[75] An enumeration of Populist/Progressive policies that they seek to overturn reads like a cross between the Populist Platform of 1892 and Theodore Roosevelt's "Bull Moose" platform of 1912.[76] If the Populists of the 1890s could see the full program of the Tea Party movement of today, they would, as Postel observed, recognize it immediately as the program of their archenemies the monopolists and "Gold Bugs." In fact, a major objective of many Tea Party activists is a return to the gold standard.

But is the Populist legacy dead, or maybe just attenuated, misconstrued? Not dead, perhaps, but not invoked by Democratic leaders or other national figures amid what can only be called a "populist moment." The opening salvo of the People's Party platform of 1892, which was ratified "upon the 116th anniversary of the Declaration of Independence," resonates today : "[We] meet in the midst of a nation brought to the verge of moral, political, and material ruin. Corruption dominates the ballot-box, the Legislatures, the Congress, and touches even the ermine of the bench. The people are demoralized. . . . The newspapers are largely subsidized or muzzled, public opinion silenced, business prostrated, homes covered with mortgages, labor impoverished, and the land concentrating in the hands of capitalists."[77]

Consider another "populist moment" when, in May 1933 J. P. Morgan Jr. was called to testify before the Senate Committee on Banking and Currency to explain the debacle in the financial industry that helped trigger the Great Depression, much as his father had been compelled to testify in 1912 before a subcommittee of the House Committee on Banking and Currency investigating the major banks' role in the Panic of 1907. The elder Morgan, with his son in attendance, had been humiliated by that experience, and in 1913 the committee, chaired by Congressman Arsène Pujo of Louisiana, found that a cartel of companies headed by the Morgan and Rockefeller interests exercised near-monopolistic control of the banking, securities, and insurance industries in America to the detriment of the whole financial system.[78]

The actions of Congress and president in 2009 were quite different in the face of the near collapse of the financial system. Perhaps an American president simply cannot talk that way today, but one could certainly articulate a basic Populist principle that might appeal to many of the independents who have deserted him, if not to the Tea Party's true believers. When the old Populists spoke in "producerist" language about the economy (the person who produces should reap the reward for his labor, not the parasitic middleman or financier), they were articulating the basic principle of *fairness.* Conversely, the preamble to the Populists' Omaha platform cataloged the fundamental *unfairness* of the system at that moment: government and business, they believed, had conspired to rig the system against ordinary farmers and workers. Perhaps Tea Partyites, in the tradition of Ayn Rand, have no use for terms like "fairness," but many of those independents who have made common cause with them do.

That said, *both* major parties in their turn have helped create economic and regulatory policies that are, in many respects, unfair. The Tea Party movement exists today partly because of that fact. The original Populists, faced with a similar set of circumstances, believed it was their duty to create a humane political alternative, and they did so, sometimes at great personal risk. Could this be the moment when contentious politics, involving multiple parties and multiple movements, brings about a humane reordering of American politics?

NOTES

1. C. Vann Woodward, *Thinking Back: The Perils of Writing History* (Baton Rouge: Louisiana State University Press, 1986), 146.

2. "When we compel the past to speak, we want neither the gibberish of total recall nor the nostalgia of fond memories; we would like the past to speak wisely to our present needs." Howard Zinn, *New Deal Thought* (Indianapolis: Bobbs-Merrill, 1966), vi.

3. Woodward, *Thinking Back,* 42.

4. C. Vann Woodward, "The Irony of Southern History," *Journal of Southern History* 19 (February 1953): 3–19. Leading participants in the group of insurgents, in addition to Woodward, included Howard Zinn, August Meier, and John Bell Williams. All of them pressed for the integration of the SHA's annual convention in 1949, resulting in John Hope Franklin's invitation to present a paper (but not to attend the still-segregated banquet in the Williamsburg Inn). By 1952 Franklin had been joined by several other African American scholars as members of the SHA, but the manager of the convention hotel in Knoxville went back on a commitment to allow integrated dining. With the support of SHA secretary Ben Wall and program chair LeRoy Graf, the banquet and presidential address were moved to an integrated restaurant outside of Knoxville. But the excitement of this jab at Jim Crow, combined with Woodward's mumbling delivery, probably meant that few in the audience caught the drift of Woodward's address. This episode is well described in John Herbert Roper, *C. Vann Woodward, Southerner* (Athens: University of Georgia Press, 1987), 165–69.

5. C. Vann Woodward, *The Burden of Southern History* (Baton Rouge: Louisiana State University Press, 1968), 193. All quotations from Woodward's essays "The Irony of Southern History" and "The Populist Heritage and the Intellectual" are from the 1968 edition, rather than the 1960 edition or the original essays.

6. The quotation is repeated in C. Vann Woodward, "The Irony of Southern History," in *Burden of Southern History,* 189.

7. Woodward, *Thinking Back,* 105, 106. It was said of Tom Watson that "he talked like the thrust of a Bowie knife."

8. Ibid., 105. Expanding the quotation fleshes out Niebuhr's ironic analogy between Israel-Babylon and the United States–Soviet Union and helps explain why Woodward was so drawn to Niebuhr's analysis: "Israel is undoubtedly a 'good' nation as compared to the great nations surrounding it. But the pretentions of virtue are as offensive to God as the pretensions of power. One has the uneasy feeling that America as both a powerful nation and as a 'virtuous' one is involved in ironic perils which compound the experiences of Babylon and Israel." Reinhold Niebuhr, *The Irony of American History* (New York: Scribner's, 1952), 160.

9. Richard Wightman Fox, *Reinhold Niebuhr: A Biography* (New York: Pantheon Books, 1985), 117, 193.

10. Richard Crouter, *Reinhold Niebuhr on Politics, Religion, and Christian Faith* (New York: Oxford University Press, 2010), 20, 23. Crouter argues that Niebuhr's thought was influenced more by the interplay of history and current affairs than by systematic theology. See also Schlesinger's insightful essay "Reinhold Niebuhr's Role in American Political Thought and Life," in *Reinhold Niebuhr: His Religious, Social, and Political Thought,* ed. Charles W. Kegley and Robert W. Bretall (New York: Macmillan, 1956), 189–222. Schlesinger's understanding of Niebuhr's place in American religious history far exceeded that of Woodward, who had little interest in that aspect of history.

11. Fox, *Reinhold Niebuhr,* 176.

12. Paraphrased from Godfrey Hodgson, *America in Our Time* (New York: Random House, 1976), 76. Hodgson call this set of ideas "the ideology of the liberal consensus." The extreme ideological polarization of the two major political parties that is now taken for granted did not develop for another decade.

13. Niebuhr, *Irony of American History,* 18–19.

14. Roper, *C. Vann Woodward,* 202, 205; Niebuhr, *Irony of American History,* viii; Richard Reinitz, *Irony and Consciousness: American Historiography and Reinhold Niebuhr's Vision* (Lewisburg, PA: Bucknell University Press, 1980), 19. Long before the publication of *Irony,* Niebuhr had broken with the optimistic, utopian liberalism of his youth and, along with Emil Brunner and several other theologians, reaffirmed the ancient doctrine of "original sin." That reaffirmation did not sit well with liberal theologians, let alone secular historians, and Niebuhr later conceded that using the term had been a "pedagogical mistake" even though the concept was sound. Crouter, *Reinhold Niebuhr,* 57. In the final chapter of *Irony* Niebuhr laid out in detail his theological/biblical understanding of the relationship between irony and sin, briefly summarized thusly: "The Biblical interpretation of the human situation is ironic, rather than tragic or pathetic, because of its unique formulation of the problem of human freedom. . . . The evil in human history is regarded as the consequence of man's wrong use of his unique capacities. The wrong use is always due to some failure to recognize the limits of his capacities of power, wisdom, and virtue. Man is an ironic creature because he forgets that he is not simply a creator but also a creature" (155, 56).

15. Woodward, *Burden of Southern History,* 193–94.

16. Ibid., 203.

17. Ibid., 195.

18. Ibid., 196, 197.

19. Ibid., 199–200.

20. Ibid., 207–8. Woodward harbored grave misgivings about FDR's idealistic and universal "Four Freedoms" as a basis for foreign policy. In the summer of 1953, Woodward observed reconstruction, Japanese style, during a teaching assignment in Tokyo.

21. Ibid., 229, 230.

22. White House, "National Security Strategy of the United States," September 2002, http://georgewbush-whitehouse.archives.gov/nsc/nss/2002/, italics added.

23. David Brooks, "Obama, Gospel and Verse," *New York Times,* April 26, 2007, national edition; Brooks, "Obama's Christian Realism," *New York Times,* December 14, 2009, national edition. Brooks first suggested Niebuhr as a guide for post-9-11 foreign policymaking in the *Weekly Standard* within two months of the terrorist attacks in New York and Washington.

24. Woodward, *Thinking Back,* 3.

25. Woodward, *Burden of Southern History,* 193–94.

26. C. Vann Woodward, "The Populist Heritage and the Intellectual," *American Scholar* 29 (Winter 1959): 55–72.

27. In many parts of the country, organized labor played a major role in the Populist movement, but this is not a point of emphasis in the Watson biography or in *Origins of the New South.* Two recent studies have added greatly to our understanding of the role played by the Knights of Labor and other unions in American Populism: Matthew Hild, *Greenbackers, Knights of Labor, and Populism: Farmer-Labor Insurgency in the Late-Nineteenth-Century South* (Athens: University of Georgia Press, 2007); and Michael Pierce, *Striking the Ballot: Ohio Labor and the Populist Party* (De Kalb: Northern Illinois University Press 2010).

28. The civil rights movement not only influenced students of Populism in the 1960s and 1970s but also shaped the development of social movement *theory.* See, in particular, Doug McAdam, *Political Process and the Development of Black Insurgence, 1930–1970* (Chicago: University of Chicago Press, 1982); and McAdam, *Freedom Summer* (New York: Oxford University Press, 1988).

29. The most formidable challenge to Woodward's claim that southern Populists were more radical than western ones is found in Norman Pollack, *The Just Polity: Populism, Law, and Human Welfare* (Urbana: University of Illinois Press, 1987), 189–217.

30. Daniel Bell, "Interpretations of American Politics," in *The New American Right,* ed. Daniel Bell (New York: Criterion Books, 1955), 3–4.

31. David S. Brown, *Richard Hofstadter: An Intellectual Biography* (Chicago: University of Chicago Press, 2006), 89–94, quotation on 92. Brown traces the origins of this construct to the Frankfort School, several of whose members found their way to Columbia.

32. Bell, *New American Right,* 36.

33. Ibid., 42.

34. Some of Hofstadter's coauthors, and perhaps Hofstadter himself, would have initially associated the term *populism* with antimodern, anti-industrial movements of artisans, shopkeepers, and farmers in late-nineteenth-century France and Germany, which often fanned the flames of anti-Semitism, though not in the deadly form of the Third Reich. See George L.

Mosse, *Toward the Final Solution: A History of European Racism* (New York: H. Fertig, 1978); and Shulamit Volkov, *Germans, Jews, and Antisemites: Trials in Emancipation* (New York: Cambridge University Press, 2006).

35. Quoted in C. Vann Woodward, "The Populist Heritage and the Intellectual," in Woodward, *Burden of Southern History,* 147–49.

36. Hofstadter's biographer states that as a member of the Pulitzer selection committee in 1956, Woodward supported the selection of *The Age of Reform* for the Prize. Brown, *Richard Hofstadter,* 112.

37. Alan Brinkley, "Richard Hofstadter's *The Age of Reform:* A Reconsideration," *Reviews in American History* 13 (September 1985): 462. See also Robert M. Collins, "The Originality Trap: Richard Hofstadter on Populism," *Journal of American History* 76 (June 1989): 150–67; and Michael Kazin, "Hofstadter Lives: Political Culture and Temperament in the Work of an American Historian," *Reviews in American History* 27 (June 1999): 334–48.

38. Woodward, *Thinking Back,* 42.

39. Brown, *Richard Hofstadter,* 107–8, quotation on 107. Brown notes that Hofstadter patterned *The Age of Reform* after the best remembered of the lot, Henry Nash Smith's *Virgin Land: The American West as Symbol and Myth* (1950), a work that Hofstadter greatly admired.

40. Richard Hofstadter, *The Age of Reform: From Bryan to FDR* (New York: Vintage Books, 1955), 33.

41. Brown, *Richard Hofstadter,* 74–76.

42. Ibid., 111 and 252n28.

43. Woodward, *Thinking Back,* 41. In a tribute delivered at a memorial service for Hofstadter in New York, Woodward said that their friendship "never seemed to be handicapped by the considerable differences in our backgrounds and points of view, and I am as certain as I am of anything that it was never interrupted or threatened by sharp disagreements over our common fields of scholarship, even those publically expressed." C. Vann Woodward, *The Future of the Past* (New York: Oxford University Press, 1989), 349–50. In addition to their shared love of history as literature, the two men shared a fleeting association with Communism in their youth. Hofstadter briefly belonged to the party while a graduate student at Columbia, and Woodward joined forces in Atlanta with party members in defense of a black Communist and traveled through the Carolinas with Communist organizer Don West during the general strike of 1934. In later years both men considered themselves to be political liberals.

44. Quoted in Brown, *Richard Hofstadter,* 116.

45. Woodward, "Populist Heritage," 147.

46. Ibid., 141.

47. Ibid., 152–53, quotation on 153.

48. The original *American Scholar* article and the version reprinted in *Burden of Southern History* have only one footnote, a lengthy listing of books and articles associated with the new critical view of Populism. *The New American Right* is listed first, and *The Age of Reform* is buried near the end. *The Age of Reform* is nowhere mentioned by name in the text of Woodward's article, but each of the four passages that refer to or quote Hofstadter are taken from it, not from his essay in *The New American Right.*

49. Woodward, "Populist Heritage," 146.

50. Ibid., 161.

51. Ibid., 154.

52. Mosse, *Toward the Final Solution,* chap. 4. Eric Hobsbawm summed up a discussion on this point thusly: "It is a mistake to confuse the racism of American Populists or the chauvinism of French Republicans with proto-Fascism." *The Age of Extremes: A History of the World, 1914–1991* (New York: Pantheon Books, 1994), 121.

53. Woodward, "Populist Heritage," 166.

54. One of the first challenges was among the most scathing. In "Hofstadter on Populism," Norman Pollack suggested that the preponderance of evidence from the historical record conflicted with all of Hofstadter's main conclusions about Populists' attitudes and motivation. *Journal of Southern History* 26 (November 1960): 478–500. Walter T. K. Nugent presented the most effective critique in *The Tolerant Populists: Kansas Populism and Nativism* (Chicago: University of Chicago Press, 1963). In a measured response to Hofstadter focusing on the bellwether state of western Populism, Nugent concluded that "Populism in Kansas was a political response to economic distress," not a mass outpouring of status anxiety. Nugent chided Hofstadter for failing to situate the Populists within the rough-and-tumble world of partisan politics and also noted, correctly, that the evidence simply does not exist to prove or disprove Hofstadter's claims about Populists' motivations: "Superficial resemblances between mid-twentieth-century psychological mechanisms and late-nineteenth-century group behavior does not prove anything about the latter" (31). The scholarly debate over Hofstadter's findings began even before publication of *The Age of Reform.* After reading a draft of the book, even two of Hofstadter's best graduate students, Stanley Elkins and Eric McKitrick, told him that his claims about Populist anti-Semitism overstated the case and were not based on evidence, while his Columbia colleague Peter Gay questioned him as to whether the book was "an a priori construction." Brown, *Richard Hofstadter,* 106–7, quotation on 107.

55. The terms *dynamic contention* and *contentious politics* and their meaning for contemporary students of social movements are addressed below.

56. Robert C. McMath, "C. Vann Woodward and the Burden of Southern Populism," *Journal of Southern History* 68 (November 2001): 752.

57. Sidney Tarrow, *Power in Movement: Social Movements and Contentious Politics,* 2nd ed. (New York: Cambridge University Press, 1998), 23. Tarrow was not speaking directly of Hofstadter or Woodward, but he was referring to the theoretical constructs within which both men framed their studies.

58. The characterization of social movements outlined here is drawn primarily from Tarrow, *Power in Movement;* Charles Tilly, "Social Movements and National Politics," in *Statemaking and Social Movements: Essays in History and Theory,* ed. Charles Bright and Susan Harding (Ann Arbor: University of Michigan Press, 1984); Charles Tilly, *Popular Contention in Great Britain, 1768–1834* (Cambridge, MA: Harvard University Press, 1995); McAdam, *Political Process;* Doug McAdam, Sidney Tarrow, and Charles Tilly, *Dynamics of Contention* (Cambridge: Cambridge University Press, 2001); and Donatella della Porta and Mario Diani, *Social Movements: An Introduction,* 2nd ed. (Malden, MA: Blackwell, 2006).

59. While one focuses on the recurring patterns and "repertoires" when comparing movements across time and space, it is also essential not to fall into yet another form of the ahistorical error of the status anxiety school. As historian and sociologist Charles Tilly once admonished his readers: "The recognition of the historical specificity of the forms of collective action is the beginning of wisdom." Tilly, "Social Movements," 305.

60. See, in particular, Jeffrey Ostler, *Prairie Populism: The Fate of Agrarian Radicalism in Kansas, Nebraska, and Iowa, 1880–1892* (Lawrence: University Press of Kansas, 1993).

61. Tilly, "Social Movements," 315. Tilly does not mean to imply, nor do I, that movements are always fully rational in their beliefs and actions.

62. The reporting / historical analysis of Timothy Garton Ash from Europe before, during, and after the collapse of the Soviet empire is among the best of the genre. Garton Ash borrowed the phrase from George Kennan, who had used it in a review of one of his earlier books. "It is for me, Garton Ash wrote, "the best possible description of what I have been trying to write for twenty years." *History of the Present: Essays, Sketches, and Dispatches from Europe in the 1990s* (New York, Random House, 1999), xii.

63. For a global survey, see Adam Roberts and Timothy Garton Ash, eds., *Civil Resistance and Power Politics: The Experience of Non-Violent Action from Ghandi to the Present* (Oxford: Oxford University Press, 2009). This volume includes a strong essay on the anti-apartheid movement in South Africa, and if updated it will do the same for Tunisia and Algeria.

64. See, for example, Michael P. Young, *Bearing Witness against Sin: The Evangelical Birth of the American Social Movement* (Chicago: University of Chicago Press, 2006); Elizabeth S. Clemens, *The People's Lobby: Organizational Innovation and the Rise of Interest Group Politics in the United States, 1890–1925* (Chicago: University of Chicago Press, 1997); Michael Lienesch, *In the Beginning: Fundamentalism, the Scopes Trial, and the Making of the Antievolution Movement* (Chapel Hill: University of North Carolina Press, 2007); and Edwin Amenta, *When Movements Matter: The Townsend Plan and the Rise of Social Security* (Princeton, NJ: Princeton University Press 2006). Earlier works grounded in this general perspective on social movements in its early stages, when it was known as "resource mobilization theory," include the previously cited McAdam, *Freedom Summer;* and Donna Barnes, *The Rise and Fall of the Southern Farmers Alliance and People's Party in Texas* (Austin: University of Texas Press, 1984), an important study that has been largely ignored by historians. All the works mentioned here were written by political scientists or sociologists.

65. Hobsbawm, *The Age of Extremes,* 403.

66. Niebuhr, *Irony of American History,* 54.

67. Hans-Georg Betz, *Radical Right Wing Populism in Western Europe* (New York: Palgrave Mcmillan, 1994), 1.

68. For an early but still useful dissection of these various strains, see Godfrey Hodgson, *The World Turned Right Side Up: A History of the Conservative Ascendancy in America* (Boston: Houghton Mifflin, 1996).

69. *New York Times,* April 14, 2010.

70. Southern Poverty Law Center, *The Second Wave: Return of the Militias* (Montgomery, AL: Southern Poverty Law Center, 2009). For the story of the "first wave" and its relation

to the Christian Identity movement, see James William Gibson, *Warrior Dreams: Violence and Manhood in Post-Vietnam America* (New York: Hill and Wang, 1994); Michael Barkun, *Religion and the Racist Right* (Chapel Hill: University of North Carolina Press, 1994); and Daniel Levitas, *The Terrorist Next Door: The Milita Movement and the Radical Right* (New York: Thomas Dunne Books / St. Martin's Press, 2002); Catherine McNicol Stock, *Rural Radicals: Righteous Rage in the American Grain* (Ithaca, NY: Cornell University Press, 1996).

71. *The Turner Diaries* was written under the pseudonym of Andrew MacDonald by William Pierce, an American Nazi who was a protégé and successor to Georgia Rockwell and a one-time physics professor at Ohio State University. In the book Turner is initiated into a secret inner circle of revolutionaries called "The Order" and then he blows up the FBI Building with a bomb made of fertilizer and fuel oil. The Oklahoma City bomber, Timothy McVey, had participated in the Posse Comitatus and other paramilitary groups. When he was arrested, he had several extremist publications in his possession, including excerpts from *The Turner Diaries.* Groups within this orbit included the Aryan Nation, which advocated formation of a separate white state in the Pacific Northwest; Posse Comitatus, which mixed extreme anti-Semitism with extreme antigovernment beliefs that led some to murder federal marshals; and The Covenant, the Sword, and the Arm of the Lord (CSA), which was headquartered on the Arkansas-Missouri border before its compound was seized and its leaders arrested by federal authorities in 1985. McVey had spent time with the CSA in Arkansas, and the bombing of the Murrah Federal Building in Oklahoma City occurred ten years to the day after the federal raid on its compound.

72. *New York Times,* April 15, 2010.

73. An American history textbook strongly endorsed by Glen Beck and popular among movement participants expressed some sympathy with the farmers who comprised the core of the Populist movement but found that their demands for government intervention in the economy were delusional. Defeats at the polls and in the marketplace, the authors contend, "produced an angst that exaggerated the plight of the agrarians, a phenomenon called psychic [*sic*] insecurity by historian Richard Hofstadter." "The Populists," they conclude, "bequeathed a disturbing legacy to American politics and economics." Larry Schweikart and Michael Allen, *A Patriot's History of the United States: From Columbus's Great Discovery to the War on Terror* (New York: Sentinel, 2004), 420, 421.

74. For a somewhat polemical treatment of this subject by one historian of the revolutionary era, see Jill Lepore, *The Whites of Their Eyes: The Tea Party's Revolution and the Battle over American History* (Princeton, NJ: Princeton University Press, 2010).

75. Charles Postel, "Populist Scholarship and the Crisis of the New Gilded Age," a paper presented at the Agricultural History Society annual meeting, Rollins College, Winter Park, FL, June 2010. See also Postel, "Sarah Palin a Populist?" *Politico,* March 3, 2010.

76. The progressive whom Tea Party activists most love to hate is not Theodore Roosevelt, but Woodrow Wilson, a somewhat reluctant convert to progressivism in midcareer who presided over a substantial expansion of the federal government's role in the economy, parts of which came into being through legislation championed by former Populists from the South and West. See, in particular, Elizabeth Sanders, *Roots of Reform: Farmers, Workers, and the American State, 1877–1917* (Chicago: University of Chicago Press, 1999).

77. *Omaha Morning World-Herald,* July 5, 1892.

78. For a comparison of what Congress did in 1933 and did not do in 2008–9, see Alan Brinkley, "When Washington Took on Wall Street," *Vanity Fair,* June 2010. The Pujo Committee hearings in 1912–13 set the stage for ratification of the Sixteenth Amendment to the Constitution and passage of the Federal Reserve Act and the Clayton Antitrust Act.

5

Woodward's Losers

Disappearing Democrats in Southern Political History

PATRICK G. WILLIAMS

The intellectual must not be alienated from the sources of revolt.

—C. Vann Woodward, *The Burden of Southern History* (2008)

In probing Woodward's "The Populist Heritage and the Intellectual," Patrick Williams challenges a basically one-dimensional understanding of southern Democrats. He argues that we have a much fuller understanding of the "losers," the Populists and the Radical Republicans, than we do of southern Democrats. We have been satisfied too easily with explanations that force, fraud, and racism played the major role in the Democrats' ability to solidify their control during an era when significant challenges arose in the form of third-party movements. He argues that scholars would be wise to examine the "dollars-and-cents" appeal the Democrats had for most white voters. Woodward is, in part and perhaps unwittingly, responsible for this scholarly oversight. Writing in a time when he and others were "spooked" by McCarthy-era excesses, Woodward was searching for a usable past and focusing on the rebels in southern politics, but the work he inspired was largely empty of any systematic examination of their opponents' multifaceted appeal. The debate over the nature of the Democrats of the late nineteenth century focused mainly on whether they were new men of the middle class, as Woodward would have it, or the old agrarians in new guise. Even here, there was little penetrating analysis of their white constituency. As Williams argues, however, these Democrats appealed to a wide spectrum of voters long before disenfranchisement statutes were passed. Rather than accepting racism, patriarchy, and stolen votes as the sole explanations for their success, scholars should understand that struggling small property owners had a profoundly different understanding of their economic interests and the role of government than they do. Specifically, Williams cites the example of Virginia Democrats who lost control when they departed from the party's low-tax doctrine. Rather than using history to understand the present, Williams suggests that we draw on more nuanced and thoughtful analysis of the new conservatism of the late twentieth century in reconsidering the Redeemer Democrats of the previous century.

Through three editions, C. Vann Woodward's *The Burden of Southern History* remained committed to the idea of southern distinctiveness—even as it had to surrender the first edition's notions of America's exceptionalism. In identifying constituents of that distinctiveness, Woodward listed "one-party politics" alongside "the one-horse farmer, one-crop agriculture . . . the sharecropper, the poll tax, the white primary, the Jim Crow car, the lynching bee."[1] But it is only a passing mention—which seems odd. Surely, the South shouldered few burdens weightier than the one-party rule of Democrats, unmatched elsewhere in the nation in either longevity or reach. The party's lawmakers could be held directly responsible for several other of the items on Woodward's list of distinctive things and, at the very least, tolerated most of the rest. Yet even though this one-party rule endured (albeit fraying at the edges) as the first edition went to press in 1960, Democrats are otherwise not much in evidence in *The Burden of Southern History*—except perhaps in the bruises and bullet wounds they left upon the body of southern Populism. Populism is the species of southern politics that is given spirited and lengthy attention in *Burden,* in one of its most cited essays, "The Populist Heritage and the Intellectual." If, as James C. Cobb suggests in chapter 1 of this volume, *The Burden of Southern History* "managed to move southern racial practices toward the periphery," the "therapist of the public mind" here left another noisome complex largely untreated.

It would be foolishness to suggest that this imbalance characterized Woodward's work more generally. *Origins of the New South*'s earlier treatment of the generation of Democrats who "redeemed" the South from Reconstruction rule was so wickedly revisionist as to shape study of the party for decades to come.[2] Still, the short shrift that *Burden* gives Democrats as compared to Populists does suggest something of Woodward's legacy in the twenty-first century. "The Populist Heritage and the Intellectual" spoke up for Populism in an era when Populists were out of fashion in the academy. It spoke up for southerners within that movement in an era when the South was generally associated in the public mind with reaction. It spoke up for rebels in an era when "consensus history" suggested that the most salient fact of the nation's political history was not conflict but Americans' shared commitment to private property and individual liberty. It spoke up in an era when many intellectuals might still be spooked by lingering McCarthyism. Woodward finished the essay with a ringing declaration that "the intellectual must not be alienated from the sources of revolt." Scholars, he said, could not afford to repudiate the Populist heritage.[3] Knowingly or not, several generations of historians followed Woodward's lead.[4] They made empathetic connection with Populists but also with other southern insurgents: those who struggled to establish biracial democracy in the wake of emancipation; those who struggled for a just return on their labor; those who struggled to be heard in civic dialogues from which they were formally excluded; and those who struggled for a modicum of respect, security, and self-governance in a world bristling with threat and insult.

The result was some of the finest scholarship of the second half of the twentieth century and the first tenth of the twenty-first. But a perhaps inevitable byproduct of Woodward's inspiration is the odd situation that southern political history seems to find itself in lately. At least when it comes to the period Woodward wrote most about, we know considerably more about the losers than the winners—in the sense that we have richer and more nuanced portraits of Radical Republicans, Readjusters, and Populists than of the Democrats who made sure Reconstruction remained an unfinished revolution and who, a generation later, knocked Populists into a cocked hat (or was it a wool hat?). The losers have been painted in dense and vivid color, while the winners are often sketched in black and white.

To say that our picture of Redeemer Democrats remains incomplete is *not* to suggest that little has been written about them in the last fifty years. Lots has, and largely at C. Vann Woodward's instigation. Many have tested the *Origins* proposition that "Redemption was not a return of an old system nor the restoration of an old ruling class." Redeemers, Woodward said, tended to be new men, or old Whigs, interested in commerce and industry and in league with northeastern capital—though typically as dogsbodies and cats paws rather than equal partners. "In the main, they were of middle-class, industrial, capitalistic outlook, with little but a nominal connection with the old planter regime."[5] A slew of studies in the 1960s and 1970s considered the relative importance of such developmentally oriented "New South" Democrats in the parties of individual states, as compared to "Bourbons" and "agrarians" with more deeply sunk roots. In some cases they found a leadership elite stuffed with Redeemers of the Woodward sort. Elsewhere, they found men more directly connected to the "old planter regime" or more attentive to assorted agricultural interests.[6] More broadly conceived challenges to Woodward's notion that the Civil War marked a decisive break in southern history also addressed the identity of the postbellum Democratic leadership. Scholars found planters as favorably situated in many communities in 1880 as they had been in 1860. Jonathan Wiener and Dwight Billings suggested that the old regime in fact guided Alabama and North Carolina's postbellum industrial development.[7]

But these inquiries into postbellum Democrats' antecedents and identities seemed to dead-end. To begin with, it became clear that persistence did not amount to continuity. Even where elites remained peopled by Democrats of the old sort, the revolutions wrought in class relations, labor arrangements, communal life, and even family structure by emancipation made nonsense of the notion that an ancien régime had survived—as did the expansion and reorientation of commerce wrought by railroads, the rise after 1880 of "business plantations" organized on a very different model from the slave-worked variety, and the stark decline in the influence that southern states exercised in national government (at least for a time).[8] Close inspection of the politics of individual southern states made it increasingly difficult to discern the sort of coherent bipartite or tripartite factionalism that terminology like "New South Democrat," "agrarian," and "Bourbon" seemed to imply—rendering it all the more difficult to say that any one of them held the reins. Members of these putative factions, it turned out, varied enormously among themselves in their understandings of government. They seemed to be pitted as frequently against one another as against members of what historians had identified as opposing factions. In Texas, for example, some "New South" Democrats adamantly believed that the goal of economic development would be best served by the state's nurturing private enterprise (such as through land grants and tax exemptions) while otherwise minimizing the burdens imposed on citizens. They slugged it out with others who wished the state both to nurture private enterprise and to tax and spend in the name of public education and population growth. Democrats who had traditionally been denominated "agrarians" included men who stood at opposite ends of the spectrum from one another when it came to political economy—those willing to concede to the state only the barest of police powers (with few responsibilities in nurturing either private enterprise or social welfare) and those who, like Greenbackers or Populists, embraced unprecedented extensions of federal power over the credit system and transportation infrastructure.[9] In short, the closer we looked, the less these southern Democratic parties looked like anything so simple as Woodward *or* his critics had described. Democrats' internal politics seemed to be about momentary, shifting coalitions rather than the long-term struggle of cohesive factions.[10]

As a portrait emerged of southern Democratic parties as sprawling, amorphous messes, rather than modular structures built from a few factional components, many historians seemed ready to throw up their hands or wash them entirely of Redeemer Democrats. An impressive seventy-fifth-anniversary issue of the *Journal of Southern History* that aspired to "address the state of the field and then suggest the future direction of southern history scholarship" had little to say about the several generations of Democrats who, as Woodward had written, "laid the lasting foundations in matters of race, politics, economics, and law for the modern South."[11] This crew also fared rather badly in another admirable historiographical revue, the Blackwell *Companion to the American South,* where Redeemers were visible only at the peripheries of discussions of Reconstruction politics, Populism and Progressivism, and the origins of disenfranchisement and Jim Crow.[12] When the time came to celebrate the fiftieth anniversary of *Origins of the New South* in 2001, an especially distinguished scholar pronounced Redeemers "dry bones," "the study of whom, as our colleagues in the sciences would say, is a 'mature field,' meaning 'nothing much left here, time to move on.'"[13]

But wait a minute. Should historians really toss out these dry bones—before postbellum Democrats find their Robert McMath, their Jane Dailey, their Eric Foner, their Charles Postel, their Steven Hahn? Should they move on before more of them have dirtied their hands—and perhaps soiled their souls—by making the same sort of empathetic connection with the Democratic rank and file that Woodward encouraged us to make with Populists, southern Republicans, Greenbackers, and Virginia's Readjusters? Historians have indeed spent more than enough time picking over the antebellum antecedents of the postbellum Democracy. They've spent more than enough time on fruitless factional taxonomy. But can the subject of the Redeemers be said to be exhausted until scholars have plumbed the extraordinary hold the Democratic Party had on many southern states even before the disenfranchisement of many black and white opposition voters? As courageous as Redeemers' opponents may have been—and as cogent as their critique may seem to us—the sad fact is that they usually lost.

To explain this sorry outcome, historians often resort to a familiar litany. Many people can reel it off even when they can't walk a straight line. Reconstruction collapsed and Populism failed amid storms of Democratic violence, fraud, and race-baiting. Persuasive cases can be made for the centrality of political violence in the creation and maintenance of Democrats' New South. Certainly, during Reconstruction, war was no mere extension but, instead, the *essence* of politics in the states with the largest African American populations and most vigorous Republican presences—Mississippi, Louisiana, South Carolina. In other states, violence and chicanery seem on occasion to have been essential to Democrats' meeting the challenges offered by disaffected whites teamed up with African American Republicans, such as in Arkansas in 1888 or a decade later in North Carolina.[14] Even in states where Democrats remained in comfortable control of the state house and the governor's mansion, we find skullduggery and shootouts decisively shaping developments in individual communities—no small thing, given how crucial local government was under many state constitutions in the South.[15]

Still, to pile up the majorities the party achieved in so many elections in so many places for so long a time by violence and fraud alone would seem to require Democrats to have possessed an administrative capacity for the black arts as extensive as that of modern authoritarian states—or, at least, skill in long-distance coordination that probably only railroads, steel companies, and the post office actually possessed in the late nineteenth century. In the likely absence of that, what question should scholars really be asking when confronted, for example, with the many counties in Texas and Arkansas where Democrats scored victories year after year? Should it be, "How did so many people have their votes so regularly stolen?" Or should the question instead be "Why are all these voters habitual Democrats?"

Many historians have a ready answer to this latter question, too: race. Certainly, they would be correct in citing its power. There is no denying the artfulness, vigor, and steadiness with which Democratic politicians and editors wielded the slogans of white supremacy. There is no denying the power of racial ideology among generations of white southerners—whether they harbored a racism that demanded that the African American working class remain subordinate and in place, a racism that could instead contemplate the expulsion of African Americans from a community, or a racism consisting of a more abstract (if still visceral) disdain for people rarely seen in any great number. There is no denying that racialism divided people who had common enemies at the country store and in the county courthouse. White southerners were reluctant to be seen acting in partnership with African Americans. African Americans, in turn, found it difficult to muster much fraternal feeling for neighbors who had previously offered them little but contempt, brutality, or a bare subsistence.

Some of the richest work in southern political history since the 1990s has deepened our understanding of postbellum Democrats' gendered politics of white identity (indeed this work offers much of what is new in the study of Redeemers). Scholars like Jane Dailey and Stephen Kantrowitz have offered sophisticated treatments of the racial appeals Democratic leaders and party activists made to white voters. White males' expectations of patriarchal authority allowed Democratic politicians and pundits to portray black uplift as necessarily eroding white men's privileges and African American empowerment as creating the prospect of black men's authority over and access to white women.[16]

But, in emphasizing Democratic leaders' application of force and fraud or the undeniable power of their rhetoric of white manhood, might we sometimes overlook the possibility that very many white southerners also felt themselves to be well governed by Democrats? Could historians do more to test the hypothesis that many voters liked what they got from the New South state—or, at least, liked the promises Democrats made with respect to taxes and services? Historians have no difficulty dealing with the fact that white southerners thought about race and gender in ways very alien to modern sensibilities. Do they always as readily acknowledge that many of those southerners thought about government in ways very different than many of us do? Scholars know how burdensome poll taxes could be to rural people who saw little cash money over the course of the year.[17] Have they taken seriously enough the burden property taxes might represent for those only a few steps higher on the agricultural ladder? Have they considered the possibility that localism's appeal might not have been grounded exclusively in race?

Rather than asking how white southerners were coerced or seduced away from voting their economic interests, historians might instead ask how their subjects' understanding of those interests may have differed from their own. Redeemer political economy was woeful, indeed, in its long-term consequences for the South. Offering little to the have-nots and demanding little of the haves, Democrats in the 1870s, 1880s, and 1890s helped assure that a region rich in natural and human resources continued, even a century later, to routinely rank toward the bottom of assorted indices of citizens' well-being. But, as John Maynard Keynes reminded us, "This *long run* is a misleading guide to current affairs. *In the long run,* we are all dead."[18] Living in the short term, many white southerners might well have thought it in their *material* interest to vote for Democrats year in and year out. In many states, the largest single source of government revenue was ad valorem taxes on land. While the proportion of white farmers who owned their land declined between 1870 and 1920, there remained many thousands who presumably had reason to reward a party that promised and, in many instances, delivered tangible reductions in property tax rates, a meaningful shift of property taxation away from rural real estate, or both, in the years following Reconstruction—as well as a repudiation or scaling of state debt that saved the public considerable expense. Democrats certainly made southern tax systems no less regressive, and their fiscal (and other) policies no doubt served planters and other large landholders best. In some states, the promised property tax relief may have been vitiated by reduced exemptions, increased capitation taxes, high rates of local taxation, and Redeemers' failure to tax corporate property at its full worth. But many small-time landowners seem either to have seen a doubtlessly appealing diminution in their property tax bill or at least to have welcomed the promise of such. Significantly, one of the rare losses Redeemers suffered in the post-Reconstruction years came in Virginia, whose Democrats—Jane Dailey notes—were atypical of their breed in raising taxes and honoring their state's debt.[19]

Retrenchment left Redeemer government relatively little money in the 1870s to spend on education, asylums, and other services. The example of Virginia is again useful in warning us away from the crude formulation that white farm families placed little value on such services, being unwilling or unable, for instance, to sacrifice their children's labor and send them off to school. Readjusters seemed to have scored points not only by calling for *less* spending on debt service but by calling for *more* spending on public education.[20] But long experience had likely kept many white southerners' expectations of the state low. And, by the 1880s, southern Democrats showed some improvement in serving citizens—spending more, for example, on schools and Confederate pensions (which might particularly have appealed to yeomen veterans of the "poor man's fight").[21] While clearly inadequate from a twenty-first-century perspective, this greater generosity, when combined with meaningful tax relief, might have seemed well worth endorsing at the polls. None of this means to suggest that the rural white landowners who seem to have represented the bulk of the Democratic constituency were either fat or happy in the postbellum decades—not as cotton and tobacco prices sank and stayed sunk, not with the crop lien and growing dispossession. But, evidently, a significant number of them did not blame Democrats for the credit or transportation infrastructure that oppressed them—although it certainly might seem that more of them *ought* to have found fault with Democrats for passing landlord-tenant laws, fence laws, and dog taxes in Reconstruction's aftermath. Such legislation had as its immediate target freed people but came to burden increasing numbers of whites as commercial agriculture spread through the backcountry and to the frontier.[22]

Happily, given the occasion of this volume, the most incisive treatment of the material basis of the Democratic appeal came in a Festschrift honoring none other than C. Vann Woodward. In "Fiscal Policy and the Failure of Radical Reconstruction in the Lower South," J. Mills Thornton III carefully demonstrated that white southern farmers had a dollars-and-cents reason to welcome Redemption, however susceptible they might also have been to the rhetoric of white supremacy. Emancipation had shifted the tax burden from slaveholders to landowners generally, and an activist Reconstruction state had sent their tax rates skyrocketing. Yet with emancipation having vastly increased the number of citizens requiring services, spending per individual, as least as far as whites were concerned, did not meaningfully increase over antebellum levels. White landowners owed more but did not get more. "However great the social needs apparent from the [state] capital may have been," Thornton writes, "it would not have been irrational for the small white farmer to have felt himself overtaxed and underserved by Republican policies."[23] Certainly, Texas Democrats felt that railing against Reconstruction's fiscal sins paid as many political dividends as ranting about white supremacy. Relatively few of their constituents faced much of a prospect of "Negro rule" in any case, since the proportion of African Americans in Texas's population was shrinking, even as its largely white frontier counties boomed. At the end of his essay, Thornton gently urged other scholars to follow up with careful study of fiscal politics in individual southern states. Not enough of that work has been done. To fully plumb the sources of Democratic allegiance, we need, most immediately, more detailed studies of what the Redeemer state demanded of and delivered to its citizens—such as has been carried out in the case of Georgia by Peter Wallenstein.[24]

Compared to the collapse of Reconstruction, the material basis for Democrats' victories over Populists must necessarily remain more obscure. Southerners had few examples of Populist government against which to measure the Democrats' appeal. But Carl Harris has made the case that rural southerners had reason to be pleased with their representatives in Congress through the 1880s and 1890s, what with Democrats' widespread and generally early embrace of corporate regulation and free silver. James Tice Moore has made a similar case for governors and state legislators, suggesting that Democrats earned their victories with the services they delivered to white farmers (including agricultural education and experiment stations) and the demands they did *not* make on them in terms of taxation or debt service.[25] In the case of Populism, historians might need to plumb white southerners' beliefs about government and not simply their understandings of their own material interests. As immobilized as many white southerners were by a partisanship that identified their section and race with the Democratic Party, it seems possible, too, that good Populist ideas like the subtreasury and railroad nationalization might have seemed like bad ideas to many voters. Democrats were offering them the alternatives of free silver and regulated private enterprise. What benefits the subtreasury and corporate expropriation might offer could, by their lights, have been outweighed by the prospects of more intrusive and expensive government. As much as it might pain scholars with New Deal sensibilities to think that suffering people could have reasoned this way, the possibility that they did at least warrants further investigation.

To suggest that white southerners might have soberly decided their material interests and principles of government could be served better by

Democrats than by Reconstruction Republicans—or as well by Democrats as by Populists—is by no means to carry a brief for Redeemers. They are hardly a prepossessing crew. One can come away from a session reading their newspapers or personal correspondence wishing nothing so much as to be scrubbed clean with a wire brush.[26] Still, as unsympathetic as modern observers might find them, and as essential as it is to compass the experience of "black southerners, white dissidents, and women of both races," scholars will not have a sufficiently complete picture if they move the winners from center stage and fail fully to account for their appeal to voters.[27]

It should not be so hard to do. Historians might look to the scholarship on *modern* conservatism to guide them in studying the nineteenth-century southern variety, particularly since much of it has been written by people apparently as out of sympathy with the New Right as many Woodward-inspired historians are with Redeemer Democracy. As the study of modern conservatism blossomed as a scholarly enterprise in the 1990s, Dan T. Carter highlighted the role race played in the growing appeal of the Right after 1964.[28] While few will dismiss the power of racial backlash in some quarters—and no scholars in their right minds would remove Carter's *The Politics of Rage* from their reading list—other historians have since given us a richer sense of the many ways the Right's appeal extended beyond race. The anticommunism of the suburbanites of Orange County, the galvanizing force of court decisions on school prayer and abortion, churchgoers' dismay at pornography and gay liberation, upset over the counterculture or "permissive" education, the increasing appeal of deregulation, the impact of the "stagflation" of the 1970s on homeowners of modest means, westerners' anger over federal governance of public land and resources, the United States' humiliation on the international stage—there seemed to be a lot more than racial animosity in the mix.[29] This scholarship has surely established that any picture of American political development since the 1970s would not be very complete should it focus exclusively on some conservatives' conjuring with white supremacy or males' expectations of mastery. That picture would be similarly incomplete should historians limit themselves to telling the stories of the losing side of the Reagan Revolution, vividly chronicling the hard times of organized labor or feminists while giving only a passing glance at those who broke the unions or sank the Equal Rights Amendment. Perhaps a lesson can be drawn from this newer scholarship in considering the South of Wade Hampton and Ben Tillman, one that would prompt scholars to wonder if those Redeemers, like modern conservatives, possessed a more multifaceted appeal.

The South of Joe Wilson and Mike Huckabee—this South of the twenty-first century—remains, of course, a bastion of modern conservatism. It would be difficult to argue that, in the 2008 presidential election, Barack Obama's abysmal showing in places like Arkansas had *nothing* to do with race. Pearl K. Ford, Angie Maxwell, and Todd Shields have produced carefully considered data demonstrating the significance of "symbolic racism" in presidential voting in Arkansas and Georgia in 2008.[30] A more seat-of-the-pants reckoning suggests that only race could explain why a white Arkansan would vote for the stony Yankee patrician John Kerry in 2004 but not for Obama, who, if nothing else, has a talent for the southern art of autobiographical storytelling. One of the nation's best-known white southerners, Jimmy Carter, has gone so far as to declare that "an overwhelming portion of the intensely demonstrated animosity toward President Barack Obama is based on the fact that he is a black man. . . . That racism inclination still exists. And I think it has bubbled up to the surface because of the belief among many white people, not just in the south but around the country, that African Americans are not qualified to lead this great country."[31]

Yet as much as race might have shaped the tone of attacks on the Obama administration—and as unhinged as opposition rhetoric has sometimes become—I wonder if thoughtful people can take the full measure of our political landscape if they fail to give respectful consideration to these conservatives' beliefs about government. Tea Party ideas about the Constitution have, it probably should be conceded, a credible intellectual heritage, for instance. No one can wish away the Tenth Amendment or certain founding fathers' fingerprints on the Virginia and Kentucky Resolutions.

When "The Populist Heritage and the Intellectual" first appeared in 1959, C. Vann Woodward was surely correct to worry about scholars' alienation from the sources of revolt. The appearance of "history from the bottom up" and New Left scholarship within a few short years ought to have soothed that concern. These days, Woodward might caution us instead against alienating ourselves from the sources of reaction and from the forces of order. For all the effort it might require, for all the brush scrubbings it might inspire, if we intend fully to plumb the South, past and present, we will need to make empathetic connection with those who voted for the winning side and those who vote for the other side.

NOTES

1. C. Vann Woodward, *The Burden of Southern History,* updated 3rd ed. (Baton Rouge: Louisiana State University Press, 2008), 5.

2. C. Vann Woodward, *Origins of the New South, 1877–1913* (Baton Rouge: Louisiana State University Press, 1951).

3. Woodward, *Burden of Southern History,* 166.

4. Robert C. McMath Jr. has testified to this inspiration: "Woodward told stories of long-forgotten southerners, black and white, who struggled to create better futures for themselves and their people. In Woodward's skillful telling, even their failures allowed modern-day Americans to imagine alternatives to the segregated status quo and to envision a biracial coalition of working people capable of reclaiming the democratic promise of Populism. No wonder that his writings inspired many of us to believe that '[t]heirs is a legacy waiting to be fulfilled.'" McMath, "C. Vann Woodward and the Burden of Southern Populism," in *Origins of the New South Fifty Years Later: The Continuing Influence of a Historical Classic,* ed. John B. Boles and Bethany L. Johnson (Baton Rouge: Louisiana State University Press, 2003), 190.

5. Woodward, *Origins,* 21–22, 20.

6. See, for example, Jack Maddex Jr., *The Virginia Conservatives, 1867–1879: A Study in Reconstruction Politics* (Chapel Hill: University of North Carolina Press, 1970); William J. Cooper Jr., *The Conservative Regime: South Carolina, 1877–1890* (Baltimore: Johns Hopkins Press, 1968); William Ivy Hair, *Bourbonism and Agrarian Protest: Louisiana Politics, 1877–1900* (Baton Rouge: Louisiana State University Press, 1969).

7. For studies emphasizing the persistence and power of antebellum elites in the postbellum world, see, for example, Randolph Campbell, "Population Persistence and Social Change in Nineteenth-Century Texas: Harrison County, 1850–1880," *Journal of Southern History* 48 (May 1982): 185–204; Jonathan Wiener, *Social Origins of the New South: Alabama, 1860–1885* (Baton Rouge: Louisiana State University Press, 1978); Dwight Billings, *Planters and the Making of a "New South": Class, Politics, and Development in North Carolina, 1865–1900* (Chapel Hill: University of North Carolina Press, 1979); Carl H. Moneyhon, *The Impact of the Civil War and Reconstruction on Arkansas: Persistence in the Midst of Ruin* (Baton Rouge: Louisiana State University Press, 1994).

8. See, for instance, Barbara Jeanne Fields, "The Advent of Capitalist Agriculture: The New South in a Bourgeois World," in *Essays on the Postbellum Southern Economy,* ed. Thavolia Glymph and John J. Kushma (College Station: Texas A&M University Press, 1985), 73–94; Harold Woodman, "The Reconstruction of the Cotton Plantation in the New South," ibid., 95–119; Steven Hahn, "Class and State in Postemancipation Societies: Southern Planters in Comparative Perspective," *American Historical Review* 95 (February 1990): 75–98.

9. These points are rehearsed at tiresome length in Patrick G. Williams, *Beyond Redemption: Texas Democrats after Reconstruction* (College Station: Texas A&M University Press, 2007); Patrick G. Williams, "Of Rutabagas and Redeemers: Rethinking the Texas Constitution of 1876," *Southwestern Historical Quarterly* 106 (October 2002): 231–53.

10. Thus, at the end of his unusually comprehensive study of southern Democrats in the 1870s—now more than twenty-five years old—Michael Perman, though continuing to

analyze the party in terms of its agrarian-Bourbon and New South wings, had to pronounce it "an expanding, diverse, and disaggregated coalition." Michael Perman, *The Road to Redemption: Southern Politics, 1869–1879* (Chapel Hill: University of North Carolina Press, 1984), 277.

11. "Commemorating Seventy-Five Years of the *Journal of Southern History*," *Journal of Southern History* 75 (August 2009): 531; Woodward, *Origins*, 22.

12. John Boles, ed. *A Companion to the American South* (Malden, MA: Blackwell, 2002), 284–347.

13. McMath, "C. Vann Woodward," 192.

14. See, for example, Kenneth C. Barnes, *Who Killed John Clayton? Political Violence and the Emergence of the New South, 1861–1893* (Durham, NC: Duke University Press, 1998); Matthew Hild, *Greenbackers, Knights of Labor, and Populists: Farmer-Labor Insurgency in the Late-Nineteenth-Century South* (Athens: University of Georgia Press, 2007), 218–21; Stephen Kantrowitz, *Ben Tillman and the Reconstruction of White Supremacy* (Chapel Hill: University of North Carolina Press, 2000); James Hogue, *Uncivil War: Five New Orleans Street Battles and the Rise and Fall of Radical Reconstruction* (Baton Rouge: Louisiana State University Press, 2006); Eric Foner, *Reconstruction: America's Unfinished Revolution, 1863–1877* (New York: Harper and Row, 1988), 558–63.

15. Worth Robert Miller, "Harrison County Methods: Election Fraud in Late Nineteenth-Century Texas," *Locus* 7 (Spring 1995): 111–28; Lawrence Goodwyn, "Populist Dreams and Negro Rights: East Texas as a Case Study," *American Historical Review* 76 (December 1971): 1435–56.

16. Kantrowitz, *Ben Tillman;* Jane Dailey, *Before Jim Crow: The Politics of Race in Postemancipation Virginia* (Chapel Hill: University of North Carolina Press, 2000). On the continuing salience of the defense of white manhood in Democratic politics, see Bryant Simon, "The Appeal of Cole Blease of South Carolina: Race, Class, and Sex in the New South," *Journal of Southern History* 62 (February 1996): 57–86.

17. J. Morgan Kousser, *The Shaping of Southern Politics: Suffrage Restriction and the Establishment of the One-Party South, 1880–1910* (New Haven, CT: Yale University Press, 1974), 64–65.

18. John Maynard Keynes, *Monetary Reform* (New York: Harcourt, Brace, 1924), 88 (emphasis in the original).

19. Dailey, *Before Jim Crow*, 29, 181n72; J. Mills Thornton III, "Fiscal Policy and the Failure of Radical Reconstruction in the Lower South," in *Region, Race, and Reconstruction: Essays in Honor of C. Vann Woodward*, ed. J. Morgan Kousser and James M. McPherson (New York: Oxford University Press, 1982), 386–87; James Tice Moore, "Redeemers Reconsidered: Change and Continuity in the Democratic South, 1870–1900," *Journal of Southern History* 44 (August 1978): 374; Williams, *Beyond Redemption*, 151, 158; Carl Moneyhon, *Arkansas and the New South, 1874–1929* (Fayetteville: University of Arkansas Press, 1997), 19; Allen Going, *Bourbon Democracy in Alabama, 1874–1890* (University: University of Alabama Press, 1951), 83–86; Edward Ayers, *The Promise of the New South: Life after Reconstruction* (New York: Oxford University Press, 1992), 44–45; Peter Wallenstein, *From Slave South to New South: Public Policy in Nineteenth-Century Georgia* (Chapel Hill: University of North Carolina Press, 1987), 187, 189; Perman, *Road to Redemption*, 229–31; Woodward, *Origins*, 59–60. Michael

Hyman has demonstrated that the southern yeomanry had reason to be dissatisfied with Democrats' tax policies. That such dissatisfaction was, in fact, widespread is not as clearly shown; Hyman, "Taxation, Public Policy, and Political Dissent: Yeoman Disaffection in the Post-Reconstruction Lower South," *Journal of Southern History* 55 (February 1989): 49–76.

20. Dailey, *Before Jim Crow,* 44–45.

21. Thornton, "Fiscal Policy," 387–88; Wallenstein, *From Slave South to New South,* 210–13; Williams, *Beyond Redemption,* 164–65; James Tice Moore, "Origins of the Solid South: Redeemer Democrats and the Popular Will, 1870–1900," *Southern Studies* 22 (Fall 1983): 297–98; Going, *Bourbon Democracy in Alabama,* 152, 205–6.

22. Williams, *Beyond Redemption,* 89–91.

23. Thornton, "Fiscal Policy," 351, 366 (quotation), 367, 378.

24. Wallenstein, *From Slave South to New South.*

25. Carl Harris, "Right Fork or Left Fork? The Section-Party Alignments of Southern Democrats in Congress, 1873–1897," *Journal of Southern History* 42 (November 1976): 471–506; Moore, "Redeemers Reconsidered," 357–78; Moore, "Origins of the Solid South," 285–301.

26. My thanks to Professor Janine Parry for this image, which I have unceremoniously swiped.

27. The quotation comes from the introduction to Jane Dailey, Glenda Elizabeth Gilmore, and Bryant Simon's signal collection of essays, *Jumpin' Jim Crow: Southern Politics from Civil War to Civil Rights* (Princeton, NJ: Princeton University Press, 2000), 5.

28. Dan T. Carter, *From George Wallace to Newt Gingrich: Race in the Conservative Counterrevolution, 1963–1994* (Baton Rouge: Louisiana State University Press, 1996); Dan T. Carter, *The Politics of Rage: George Wallace, the Origins of the New Conservatism, and the Transformation of American Politics* (New York: Simon and Schuster, 1995).

29. David Chappell picks a fight on this score in "What's Racism Got to Do with It? Orval Faubus, George Wallace, and the New Right: A Review Essay," *Arkansas Historical Quarterly* 57 (Winter 1998): 453–71. For a clear-eyed study of the varied constituents of modern conservatism, see Lisa McGirr, *Suburban Warriors: The Origins of the New American Right* (Princeton, NJ: Princeton University Press, 2001).

30. Pearl K. Ford, Angie Maxwell, and Todd Shields, "What's the Matter with Arkansas? Symbolic Racism and 2008 Presidential Candidate Support," *Presidential Studies Quarterly* 40 (June 2010): 286–302.

31. Ewen MacAskill, "Jimmy Carter: Animosity toward Barack Obama Is Due to Racism," *Guardian.co.uk,* September 16, 2009 (accessed March 24, 2010).

6

The End of Woodward's Second Reconstruction?

African American Political Participation in the South

CHARLES S. BULLOCK III

> And he will write of how conservatives of North and South, East and West came together regardless of party and called a halt, and how Negro leaders were divided in council and fell out with each other, and how their white allies withdrew in silence and confusion and timidity, and how some of them and some of their Negro friends tacitly acquiesced in the consensus of tokenism, and how a few took high office and endorsed it. Then, observing that since in the first instance the cycle ran from 1865 to 1877 and in the second from 1954 to 1966, our future historian may tentatively hypothesize that a baker's dozen years is par for the course.
>
> —C. Vann Woodward, *The Burden of Southern History* (1968)

In this chapter, Charles Bullock, the Richard B. Russell Professor of Political Science at the University of Georgia, argues that Woodward was premature when he argued that the "Second Reconstruction" had ended. When Woodward published The Burden of Southern History, *he saw similarities between the time following Civil War Reconstruction and the time following the civil rights movement in the late 1960s. Specifically, Woodward witnessed the congressional defeat of a civil rights bill in 1966, increased national attention focused on the Vietnam War, and young people across the nation showing greater concern for other issues instead of civil rights. Woodward believed that this growing indifference among citizens in the non-South would signify a halt in the progress of civil rights and equality among African Americans—similar to the halt in progress following the Civil War Reconstruction once the federal government became focused on other national concerns. Bullock argues that while Woodward may have been correct about the waning interest in civil rights among nonsouthern citizens and the federal government, he failed to foresee the significant influences, and long-term effects, that would be produced by the Voting Rights Act of 1965. Bullock argues that, in contrast to the post–Civil War*

Reconstruction era, the contemporary period has seen substantial progress for African Americans. He claims that Woodward, in his revised editions to Burden, *was too pessimistic regarding ongoing civil rights reforms. Bullock points to increased voter registration and voter turnout among African Americans following the Voting Rights Act, growing numbers of African American legislators, particularly at the state level, and the election of President Barack Obama as proof that Woodward was too pessimistic in his declaration that the Second Reconstruction period had ended.*

In one of the essays in Woodward's *The Burden of Southern History,* the noted southern historian rings down the curtain on what he has identified as the Second Reconstruction. As noted in James Cobb's essay (chapter 1), by the time Woodward added the passage cited in this chapter's epigraph to the revised edition of *The Burden of Southern History,* he had become less optimistic than when the collection originally appeared in 1960. The 1964 Civil Rights Act and the Voting Rights Act passed the following year had not ushered in an era of racial harmony. In this lament, initially published in *Harpers,* Woodward sees the previous twelve years as similar to the post–Civil War Reconstruction in terms of an expansion of opportunities for African Americans. But with the congressional defeat of a civil rights bill in 1966, which came after summers of urban riots and a growing concern, especially among young whites, about the expanding scope of war in Vietnam, Woodward concluded that the nation's interest in and support for expanding the rights and opportunities of African Americans had passed.

Woodward was not alone in believing that the federal effort to encourage and protect African American political participation had for a second time in history come apart on the Scylla and Charybdis of southern opposition and northern indifference. Woodward quotes Leslie Dunbar: "Everywhere you look with people in a position of power and authority, they have things they regard as more important."[1] The perception that the expansion of civil rights culminating with the 1965 Voting Rights Act served as a prelude to a massive federal retreat persisted in some quarters. Three decades later, Woodward's former doctoral student J. Morgan Kousser published a book with the title *Color Blind Justice: Minority Voting Rights and the Undoing of the Second Reconstruction.*[2]

While Woodward had a keen understanding of the past and its ability to influence the present, his assessment that the Second Reconstruction would last no longer than northern efforts to promote black opportunities after the Civil War has proven too pessimistic. Despite fluctuations in financial markets, the numbers of African Americans in the middle class have continued to expand. Equal access to public accommodations, the most controversial aspect of the 1964 Civil Rights Act, long ago achieved the status of almost universal acceptance, so that in the rare instance when an individual faces rejection because of race, it becomes a major news story. Institutions of higher education, both north and south, compete aggressively to attract minority students. African Americans long since broke through glass ceilings to become leaders of major corporations and foundations. Barack Obama's election as president shattered the ultimate glass ceiling.

Even the setback that sparked Woodward's gloomy assessment proved short-lived, as Congress adopted open-housing legislation two years later in the wake of Martin Luther King's assassination. The congressional motivation for the open-housing legislation may have been to create a memorial for the slain civil rights leader. However, that cannot explain the continued support for Section 5 of the Voting Rights Act, the most extraordinary selective curtailment of state autonomy ever enacted, which Congress expanded in 1975 to include language minorities, thereby extending preclearance requirements to Texas, Arizona, and parts of Florida and California to protect Latinos and to Alaska to protect that state's natives. Congress most recently extended Section 5 through 2031.

It is only fair to acknowledge that criticizing Woodward for his negative outlook involves a degree of Monday morning quarterbacking. He could not have known that the Supreme Court would dramatically expand the scope of the preclearance requirement of the Voting Rights Act or that Congress would extend the coverage of this portion of the legislation at least through 2031. And while the impact of the Voting Rights Act had begun to be felt by the time Woodward wrote, only the most optimistic would have predicted the political gains that African Americans have realized over the past two generations.

The objective of this essay is not to examine all of the dimensions in which Woodward's pessimistic assessment could be judged incorrect. My purpose is to review the continued progress of African Americans in the political realm. More specifically, I explore the expansion of black political participation and office-holding in the South.

SECTION 5 OF THE VOTING RIGHTS ACT

Part of Woodward's negative assessment must have stemmed from his failure to perceive the consequences of Section 5 of the Voting Rights Act. His inability to anticipate accurately the consequences of Section 5 is understandable, since a stunning expansion in its scope had not yet occurred when he wrote. The Supreme Court dramatically extended the reach of Section 5 in *Allen v. State Board of Elections,* handed down the year after publication of the revised edition of *The Burden of Southern History.* This unprecedented legislation sharply curbed state authority to regulate voter registration. Jurisdictions subject to Section 5 had to obtain approval either from the attorney general of the United States or from a panel of three judges on the district court of the District of Columbia before implementing changes in their laws affecting elections, and *Allen* defined the impact on elections very broadly, as is explained later. The requirement that jurisdictions obtain preapproval from federal authorities before implementing laws relating to elections applied to those entities that met two conditions. The initial trigger mechanism included in the 1965 act identified jurisdictions in which less than half of the voting-age population had registered or voted in the 1964 presidential election *and* which had a test or device as a prerequisite for registration. A literacy test was the most common suspect requirement. These two criteria singled out Alabama, Georgia, Louisiana, Mississippi, South Carolina, Virginia, and almost half of the counties in North Carolina.

Given the extraordinary nature of federal intervention into what had been a state or local responsibility, Section 5 carried a sunset provision limiting it to five years. The half-decade limitation may have fueled Woodward's bleak assessment. He recalled that legislation passed during Reconstruction had authorized federal litigation to protect the voting rights of former slaves. Initially this legislation resulted in hundreds of suits being filed.[3] However, the enthusiasm for enforcement by the attorney general soon waned, and a generation later, Congress repealed most of the provisions, which had already fallen into disuse.

EXPANDING THE RIGHT TO VOTE

The Voting Rights Act grew out of President Lyndon Johnson's frustration with the slow progress made in extending the right to vote to African Americans in the South. Despite legislation passed in 1957, 1960, and 1964 that sought to remove barriers to black registration, less than half of the South's black adults had enrolled to vote as of 1964.[4] In addition to economic and physical intimidation, prospective black registrants in much of the South had to demonstrate their literacy and, in some states, explain portions of the federal or state constitution. Some county registrars illegally rejected applications from African Americas who had no problems reading and writing.

Following passage of the 1965 legislation, President Johnson moved quickly to demonstrate the federal government's commitment to implementing this statute. Within days after Johnson signed the bill into law, the attorney general sent agents into southern states to begin registering qualified African Americans rejected by local officials. Federal registrars went into counties that had especially low rates of black registration and by 1967 had achieved impressive progress.[5] Within two years, more than 150,000 African Americans registered to vote with federal examiners. Approximately 40 percent of these were in Alabama, with slightly fewer being added to the voter rolls in Mississippi. Smaller numbers of registrants signed up with federal officials in Georgia, Louisiana, and South Carolina. The aggressiveness with which federal authorities implemented the Voting Rights Act (VRA) persuaded other registrars to come into compliance, so that procedural barriers to black registration quickly eroded. To prevent the erection of new obstacles, a strategy that the South had used to frustrate earlier efforts at school desegregation, Section 5 prevented the implementation of new requirements until reviewed and approved by federal authorities.

Table 6.1 reports the share of the adult black population registered in each southern state before and after passage of the VRA. Increases occurred in every state, but there was greater change in states subject to Section 5. In none of the seven Section 5 states had a majority of the adult black population registered prior to passage of the legislation. Within two years of enactment, a majority of the black adults had registered in each state. Monumental change transformed Alabama and Mississippi, where fewer than one in five adult African Americans had registered prior to adoption of the VRA. Black registration also increased in the four states not subject to Section 5; a substantial increase occurred in Arkansas, the one noncovered state in which less than a majority of the adult African Americans had registered prior to 1965. The states not covered continued to have larger shares of their adult black population signed up to vote than did the Section 5 states, but the gap narrowed dramatically. Prior to passage of the VRA, the median share of black adults registered in states subject to Section 5 stood at 31.6 percent, compared to the median of 54.4 percent for the remaining four states. Post-VRA, the median for the covered states had risen to 52.6 percent, compared to 63.2 percent in the other four states. The greatest increases came in the two states in which federal examiners signed up the largest numbers of registrants. Federal officials signed up approximately sixty thousand black voters in both Alabama and Mississippi.

TABLE 6.1. Share of the African American voting-age population registered to vote

	Pre-VRA	*Late 1960s*
States covered by Section 5 of the 1965 VRA		
Alabama	19.3	51.6
Georgia	27.4	52.6
Louisiana	31.6	58.9
Mississippi	6.7	59.8
North Carolina	46.8	51.3
South Carolina	37.3	51.2
Virginia	38.3	55.6
States not covered		
Arkansas	40.4	62.8
Florida	51.2	63.6
Tennessee	69.5	71.7
Texas	57.7	61.6

Sources: U.S. Commission on Civil Rights, *Political Participation,* (Washington, DC: U.S. Government Printing Office 1968), 12–13. The Texas pre-VRA figure comes from *VEP News* 4 (January–February 1970): 3.

While the VRA sought to facilitate black registration, the criteria for coverage by Section 5 (the level of registration and/or turnout in 1964) considered total participation figures, not simply those for African Americans. A condition for inclusion under Section 5 was that less than half the voting-age population had registered or voted in 1964. In addition to the registration increases reported in table 6.1, a second indicator of the impact of the VRA comes from a comparison of participation in the 1964 and 1968 presidential elections. As table 6.2 shows, turnout increased by less than 4 percent across the nation. However, in every southern state, participation increased by more than twice that rate, and most states experienced an increase many times greater than the national figure. While more voters turned out in each southern state in 1968 than four years earlier, the five states having the greatest increases were subject to Section 5. In the two states with the lowest rates of adult black registration prior to the VRA, turnout increased by more than 50 percent. The third-party presidential candidacy of Alabama governor George Wallace, who won these states' electors, probably inspired some of that increase, but it also undoubtedly reflects the reality that by 1968 more than half of the eligible black electorate had signed up to vote. As evidence of the likely impact of increased black registration, Hubert Humphrey attracted 150,644 votes in Mississippi, where Lyndon Johnson had polled only 52,618 four years earlier. Participation increased substantially in the covered states, so much so that had the 1968 turnout figures been used to determine coverage by Section 5 of the VRA, then in each of these states a majority of the voting-age population, as reported in the 1960 census, cast ballots. If estimates of the 1968 voting-age population had been used, then Georgia probably would have been the only state without a majority of its citizens going to the polls.

TABLE 6.2. Voter participation in the 1964 and 1968 presidential elections

	1964	1968	% Change
States covered by Section 5 of the 1965 VRA			
Alabama	689,818	1,049,922	52.2
Georgia	1,139,335	1,250,266	9.7
Louisiana	896,293	1,097,450	22.4
Mississippi	409,146	654,509	60.0
North Carolina	1,424,983	1,587,493	11.4
South Carolina	524,779	666,978	27.1
Virginia	1,042,267	1,361,491	30.6
States not covered			
Arkansas	560,426	619,969	10.6
Florida	1,854,481	2,187,805	18.0
Tennessee	1,143,946	1,248,617	9.1
Texas	2,626,811	3,079,216	17.2
United States	70,644,592	73,211,875	3.6

Source: Election returns taken from John L. Moore, Jon P. Preimesberger, and David R. Tarr, eds., *Congressional Quarterly's Guide to U.S. Elections,* vol. 1, 4th ed. (Washington, DC: Congressional Quarterly, 2001).

Estimates made by the Census Bureau in its biennial postelection surveys over the past decade have reported black registration and turnout rates in southern states very similar to those for whites. Indeed, in some recent years the participation rates for blacks have exceeded those for whites.[6] Comparisons with participation rates in states that maintain official tabulations by race show that the Census Bureau often overestimates African American turnout, but none have evidence of declining rates for blacks that would hint at resurgent efforts at discrimination. In the 2008 general election, the three states that report turnout by race (Georgia, Louisiana, and South Carolina) showed the share of the vote coming from African Americans rising to record levels.[7] With 30 percent of the vote coming from African Americans in each of these states, black turnout constituted a share of the electorate at least equal to the black share of the adult population. In each Section 5 state except Mississippi and Texas, exit polls show the black share of the turnout at least equal to the black eligible population as estimated by the Census Bureau for 2008.[8] In the two states not currently subject to Section 5, black turnout did not reach the black share of the adult population.

EXTENSION OF THE VRA

Despite the increases in black participation, Congress extended Section 5 for an additional five years in 1970. In 1975, Congress extended the legislation for another seven years in order to cover the redistricting that would follow the 1980 census. The 1975 extension also broadened the scope of Section 5 to cover jurisdictions having large numbers of language minorities, if the jurisdiction had failed to provide election materials in 1972 in the language the minority spoke and if less than half of the voting-age population had registered or voted in that presidential election. In the South the 1975 legislation extended coverage to Texas and five Florida counties. Congress has extended Section 5 twice more, in 1982 and then again in 2006, each time for a quarter century. These two most recent extensions did not make additional jurisdictions subject to Section 5 requirements. Thus, contrary to Woodward's fears, Congress has remained steadfast in maintaining federal oversight of registration procedures and elections in most of the South.

Section 5 sought to freeze existing requirements for registration and to ensure that covered jurisdictions would not adopt new standards that would make black registration and voting more difficult. The original version of the Voting Rights Act and the first two extensions did nothing to challenge existing practices that might have a discriminatory effect. In 1982, Congress expanded the reach of the VRA by rewriting Section 2. This provision had heretofore been interpreted as adding no protections but simply restating the constitutional guarantees.

Congress recast Section 2 in response to a Supreme Court decision stipulating that for plaintiffs to prevail when challenging an existing condition, they had to prove intent to discriminate by the government being sued. After extended debate, Congress reduced the evidentiary burden on plaintiffs. It amended Section 2 so that all plaintiffs needed to prove when challenging an existing electoral system was that minorities had less opportunity than whites to participate in the political process and to elect their preferences to office. Freedom from the burden of proving defendant jurisdictions guilty of intentional discrimination stimulated numerous challenges to at-large electoral formats at the local level. Section 2 also expanded the scope of the VRA, since it could be used to attack long-standing electoral practices, whereas Section 5 was restricted to instances in which a covered jurisdiction proposed a change from the status quo. Section 2 challenges, while widespread in the South, occurred in all parts of the nation, wherever the representation of minority groups on collegial bodies fell short of their share of the population. Section 5, even following the amendments in 1970 and 1975, impacted only sixteen states, and in almost half of these states, most of the counties escaped the need for preclearance.

Critical to getting the votes needed to adopt Section 2 had been the proviso inserted by Senate Minority Leader Bob Dole, which read: "Nothing in this section establishes a right to have members of a protected class elected in numbers equal to their proportion of the population." By the time Congress voted to extend the Voting Rights Act in 1982, most jurisdictions had completed the redistricting necessary to adjust for population shifts identified in the 1980 census. Therefore, the consequences of Section 2 for redistricting plans did not become fully apparent until the early 1990s. Despite the statement that the legislation did not require the proportional representation of minorities, the Department of Justice (DOJ) adopted a strategy of requiring the creation of majority-minority districts whenever possible. This strategy became known as the Max Black approach, short for "maximizing black representation." The DOJ rejected redistricting plans from Section 5 states in which additional majority-minority districts could be created. Even jurisdictions not subject to Section 5 felt pressure to increase the numbers of majority-minority districts, fearing that not doing so would leave them open to litigation. As is discussed later, the Max Black approach resulted in a substantial increase in majority-minority districts.

AFRICAN AMERICAN LEGISLATORS IN THE SOUTH

Beginning with 1968, enumerations of black officeholders became available from the Joint Center for Political Studies. The Joint Center, later renamed the Joint Center for Political and Economic Studies, continued to publish periodic counts of black officeholders through 2001. The first enumeration identified 464 black officeholders in the South.[9] By the time of the last enumeration, the number of southern black officeholders had swelled to 5,620.[10] While most black officeholders serve at the local level, the analysis in this essay is restricted to legislative and congressional offices. Focusing just on these higher offices makes it possible to extend the analysis to 2009.

After generations of having all-white legislatures, the first African American elected to a southern legislature in modern times won a seat in the Georgia Senate after a redistricting carried out in 1962. This initial gain was due less to civil rights legislation than to early skirmishes of the Redistricting Revolution. After the Supreme Court ruled in the Tennessee case *Baker v. Carr* that legislative districts must better reflect population variations, litigation was initiated in many states.[11] In Georgia, the legislature responded to a court order invalidating portions of its apportionment system by redrawing the Senate districts. Increasing the seats allocated to Fulton County from one to seven resulted in one district having a predominately black electorate, and it chose Leroy Johnson, an African American, to represent it.

Although Georgia had the third-lowest proportion of its African American adults registered to vote in the early 1960s, the large concentration of blacks in Atlanta made possible the election of a second African American senator, along with seven black representatives who were chosen in a special election late in 1965. These initial black representatives also owed their success to the effort to bring the distribution of seats in the lower chamber in line with population rather than county lines. Aside from the nine black legislators in Georgia, a century after the Civil War ended, only one other African American served in a southern legislature.

As table 6.3 shows, the substantial increase in the number of blacks serving in lower chambers of southern legislatures following the 1966 election apparently had little impact on Woodward's assessment. By 1967, the first African Americans had entered the lower chambers in Louisiana, Mississippi, Texas, and Virginia, along with the first black Texas senator of the twentieth century.

TABLE 6.3. African American legislators from the South, 1965–2009

	State Senate		*State House*		*Congress*	
	No.	*%*	*No.*	*%*	*No.*	*%*
1965	2	0.4	8	0.6	0	0
1967	3	0.7	22	1.7	0	0
1969	6	1.3	26	2.0	0	0
1971	7	1.5	34	2.6	0	0
1973	7	1.5	54	4.1	2	1.9
1975	11	2.2	85	6.5	3	2.8
1977	11	2.2	93	7.1	3	2.8
1979	13	2.8	108	8.2	2	1.9
1981	14	3.1	112	8.5	2	1.9
1983	22	4.8	133	10.1	2	1.7
1985	33	7.2	144	11.0	2	1.7
1987	34	7.4	151	11.5	4	3.4
1989	40	8.7	155	11.8	4	3.4
1991	45	9.8	166	12.7	5	4.3
1993	63	13.7	197	15.0	17	13.6
1995	67	14.6	209	15.9	17	13.6
1997	71	15.5	222	16.9	16	12.8
1999	70	15.3	224	17.1	16	12.8
2001	71	15.5	229	17.5	16	12.8
2003	72	15.7	239	18.2	17	13.0
2005	74	16.1	239	18.2	18	13.7
2007	6	16.6	246	18.8	17	13.0
2009	77	16.8	254	19.4	16	12.2

Source: Created by the author.

Elections held in 1968, the year in which an updated and expanded version of *The Burden of Southern History* appeared, brought still more blacks into southern legislatures. The number serving in lower chambers expanded to 26, which constituted 2 percent of all southern legislators, and the number of black senators doubled to 6. Tennessee elected 2 black senators and Virginia elected 1. The initial black representatives entered the Florida and North Carolina lower chambers. Following the 1968 elections, only Alabama, Arkansas, and South Carolina still had all-white legislatures.

Congress enacted the first extension of Section 5 in 1970. In the wake of the 1970 census, the Supreme Court ruled in a Georgia case that redistricting plans in states subject to Section 5 must be precleared by the federal government.[12] As a result of the uncertainty generated by more demanding standards for equalizing populations among districts and the newly found federal authority for reviewing redistricting plans, several states did not fully implement their plans until the 1974 election. Following that election, the number of black representatives across the region had grown to 85, and the number of black senators had risen to 11. By the middle of the 1970s, every lower chamber in the South had black members; Georgia led the way with 19, which constituted more than 10 percent of its total membership. Seven state senates also included black members, although none had more than a pair.

As a result of small chamber size (Texas), the use of multimember districts (South Carolina), and the combination of a relatively small black population in a very populous state (Florida), not until 1983 did every southern upper chamber have an African American senator. In that year the largest number of black senators (4) served in Georgia. By the beginning of the next decade, the number of black senators had doubled again, and every state had at least 2, while Georgia had 8. The redistricting in the early 1990s produced another increase in black senators, as their ranks expanded from 45 to 63, a 40 percent increase. The Black Max approach adopted by the DOJ in the nine southern states subject to Section 5 of the Voting Rights Act contributed to the drawing of new majority-black districts. The ranks of black senators doubled to 8 in Louisiana, increased from 2 to 5 in Florida, and jumped from 4 to 10 in Mississippi. Growth in the numbers of black senators has slowed since 1993 and as of 2009 stood at 77, which constituted about one-sixth of all southern senators.

From the beginning of the Second Reconstruction, the proportion of seats filled by blacks in southern lower chambers has exceeded the figure for the upper chamber. The number of black state representatives has increased in every election except the one held in 2004, when the number held constant at 239. The most dramatic gains came following redistricting. The legislatures elected after the first redistricting following the 1970 census showed an increase of 20 black representatives, with substantial growth occurring in Louisiana and Texas. Before the seating of a new legislature in 1975, Alabama, Georgia, and South Carolina developed new plans, and these, along with smaller increases in other states, added 31 black representatives. As in the upper chambers, the lower chambers had another large infusion of black members in the early 1990s when racial gerrymandering bumped up the numbers of black representatives in Georgia (4), Louisiana (9), Mississippi (9), and North Carolina (4), with gains of 1 or 2 seats in four other states. Almost one-third of the total number of black-held lower-house seats as of 2009 was added in the three elections of 1972, 1974, and 1992.[13]

African Americans' presence in lower chambers has grown more dramatically since 1993 than has the number of black senators. Currently more than 250 southern representatives are African Americans, and in 2009 blacks held almost 20 percent of the total membership in lower chambers.

CONGRESSIONAL REPRESENTATION

The third component of table 6.3 reports the presence of black members of Congress from the South. In 1972, following the first decennial congressional redistrictings after passage of the Voting Rights Act, districts in Atlanta and Houston sent the first southern African Americans to Congress in the twentieth century. Barbara Jordan (TX) and Andrew Young (GA) both won open seats. The Department of Justice made Young's path easier when it rejected the initial congressional plan from Georgia, because that plan removed Young's home from the district in which he hoped to compete. In 1974, Harold Ford Sr. upset a Republican incumbent to win the Memphis seat. No additional districts sent African Americans to Washington for more than a decade, and when Young resigned his Atlanta seat to become the U.S. representative to the United Nations in the Carter administration, a white replaced him and held the seat for a decade. In 1986, Mike Espy became the first African American to represent a largely rural district in the South in the twentieth century when he won Mississippi's Delta district.[14] In 1990, when Lindy Boggs retired, her New Orleans district elected a black.

The Justice Department demand that Section 5 states draw additional majority-black districts had its greatest impact in the region's congressional districts. The 103rd Congress welcomed an additional dozen blacks from the South, including the first 3 from Florida, 2 from North Carolina, and 1 each from Alabama, South Carolina, and Virginia. In addition, Georgia increased the size of its black delegation from 1 to 3, and Louisiana and Texas each sent a second African American.

The sixteen years that followed the dramatic increase in black congressional representation have witnessed little change in the South's number of African American members. The stability in the numbers of black representatives persisted despite a series of court challenges that forced the redrawing of many of the Max Black districts. In a series of decisions beginning with the North Carolina case *Shaw v. Reno,* the Supreme Court invalidated plans that legislatures had created by assigning top priority to considerations of race.[15] Since the DOJ had demanded that districts maximize minority populations, southern jurisdictions found it impossible to argue successfully that race had not dominated their decision process.

Some critics of these decisions saw in them the potential for a decline in black progress akin to the end of a Second Reconstruction, much as Woodward anticipated. Following these decisions, states, or in some cases the courts, when state legislatures failed to act, had to design new plans, and invariably the new plans reduced concentrations of black voters in the districts represented by African Americans. Jesse Jackson described the Supreme Court decisions invalidating the Max Black districts as a "kind of ethnic cleansing" that would reduce the size of the Congressional Black Caucus until it could "meet in the back seat of a taxi cab."[16] Longtime Atlanta voting rights attorney Laughlin McDonald fretted, "I really fear that this court is sending us back to the dark days of the 19th Century."[17] Jackson and McDonald, like Woodward three decades earlier, proved too pessimistic. As table 6.3 shows, the decade ended with only one fewer black in Congress from the South than in 1993. Cleo Fields, who had held the newly created majority-black district in Louisiana, opted not to seek reelection after a court invalidated his racially gerrymandered district; the new plan placed him in the same district with a Republican incumbent who retained more of his old district than Fields retained of his district.

New districts drawn following the 2000 census opened the way for Georgia to elect a fourth African American, and the "DeLay" middecade redrawing of Texas congressional districts saw a third black representing the Lone Star State.[18] The Ninth District of Tennessee, which had been held by two generations of the Ford family for more than three decades, elected a white in 2006 after the black vote splintered in the Democratic primary. Tennessee is one of the few southern states that does not require a majority vote for nomination, and a white won the decisive Democratic nomination with 31 percent of the vote. In 2008, a Vietnamese-born Republican upset William Jefferson to win the 60 percent black New Orleans district. Facilitating Joseph Cao's election was the indictment of the longtime black representative on charges of bribery, charges later proven in court. Cao also benefited from the low turnout caused by the need to postpone the election until December due to the threat of a hurricane. Cao lost his 2010 reelection bid to an African American.

Although language in Section 2 states explicitly that having minorities represented in a collegial body at the same rate as their share of the population is not necessary, civil rights activists and some of those who work in the Voting Section of the Justice Department have frequently sought proportionality.[19] Figure 6.1 shows the extent to which the incidence of African American legislators has come to equal the black share in the South's adult population. Following the redistricting carried out after the 1970 census, the shares of seats in upper and lower chambers of southern legislatures and the region's congressional delegation lagged far behind the black share in the voting-age population. By 1983, the shares of black representatives and senators had increased, but the black percentage in Congress declined slightly. After the racial gerrymandering following the 1990 census, blacks held almost identical shares of the congressional and state senate seats and slightly more of the state house seats. In the last two time periods, the share of congressional seats filled by African Americans dropped from the 1993 apex. The incidence of black state legislators continues to increase, with the house share a few percentage points above the senate figure. By 2009, the black share of house seats slightly exceeded the black share of the adult population. The current distribution and, indeed, the distribution for each year except 1993, show that the smaller the average constituency population, the greater the percentage of African Americans serving in the chamber. Most black legislators represent heavily black districts, and it becomes easier to fashion those kinds of districts as the population needed shrinks. For example, South Carolina had a 2000 population of 4,012,012, which resulted in an ideal or average population for a state house district of 32,355, an average senate population of 87,218, and an average congressional population of 668,669. A black majority would require 16,178 in a state house district, 43,609 in a senate district, and 334,335 in a congressional district.[20] South Carolina has far more places where 17,000 African Americans live in close proximity than where more than one-third of a million are concentrated. The relative ease of aggregating concentrations of African Americans to allow for blacks to elect their candidates of choice is evident in the share of seats held by African Americans across South Carolina's three legislative chambers—in 2009 blacks held 21.8 percent of the state house, 17.4 percent of the senate seats, and one-sixth of the congressional seats.

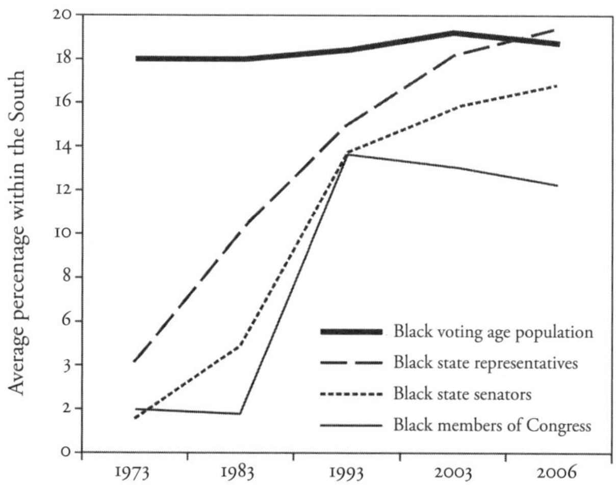

WHY DID WOODWARD GET IT WRONG?

Following the first Reconstruction, as Woodward himself described, the attention of the North shifted. As Woodward's student Morgan Kousser explains, multiple factors accounted for the loss of interest in maintaining black political participation. The legislators who had promoted congressional Reconstruction had left Congress by the time southern states adopted registration restrictions at the end of the nineteenth century. Other issues had come to the fore, and the depression of the 1890s relegated protection of black concerns to a low priority on the national agenda. Some members of Congress fretted that efforts to restrain southern actions that deprived blacks of their political rights might endanger programs having higher priorities, such as the tariff. Republican strength in Congress had declined, with Democrats having secured a majority in the House in the 1890 election and in the Senate two years later. The 1896 realignment restored Republican hegemony, but the new majority did not have to rely on Republicans winning seats in the South. Kousser sums up the situation as follows: "In such circumstances, Republicans might well feel it was not worth the trouble to prohibit racial and political discrimination in voting."[21]

In turning a blind eye to resurgent discrimination in the South, Republicans in Congress had little fear of a negative reaction from their voters. "The Democrats appealed to northern businessmen who had investments or customers in the South to assist them in preventing a return to Reconstruction."[22] With the nation's black population still overwhelmingly in the South, northern Republicans in Congress did not have to worry about alienating black voters in their constituencies.

The Supreme Court initiated what became something of a perfect storm by ceasing to provide a barrier against southern discrimination. In the best-known case from the turn of the century, the Court enunciated the separate-but-equal doctrine that soon led to segregation in public accommodations and other facilities. And in a pair of remarkable decisions handed down at the dawn of the century, the Supreme Court refused to intervene when Alabama arbitrarily refused to allow African Americans to register.[23] These decisions, in conjunction with judicial approval of the disenfranchising techniques incorporated into the Mississippi Constitution of 1890 and congressional refusal to approve the Lodge Force Act, all signaled to the South that the national government had little interest in regulating southern efforts to disenfranchise blacks.

The contrast between the disinterest of the North along with the congressional inattention at the turn of the twentieth century, on one hand, and the increased regulation in the last third of the century, on the other, is striking. Although the critical portion of the 1965 Voting Rights Act initially had a life of only five years, Congress has not allowed Section 5 to lapse. On four separate occasions between 1970 and 2006, the judiciary committees in the two chambers held extensive hearings and Congress debated the continuing need for requiring that changes relating to election laws be approved by federal authorities before implementation. Unlike its counterpart in the First Reconstruction, which ceased passing new legislation within a decade of the end of the Civil War, the contemporary Congress has continued to revisit the issue of voting rights.

Federal enforcement of statutory protections has been both more extensive and more persistent than during the initial Reconstruction. The Justice Department's Voting Rights Section has reviewed tens of thousands of proposed changes from Section 5 jurisdictions and has objected to hundreds of proposed changes. Only occasionally have submitting jurisdictions succeeded in getting court approval after having their submissions rejected by the DOJ. Even rarer have been charges of interference with a DOJ staff recommendation that a proposed change be denied.[24] Federal examiners still get dispatched to monitor elections in selected jurisdictions. The number of lawsuits brought by the DOJ has declined, but that may indicate not a failure of the federal will but the elimination of the problems that would give rise to litigation.

Another difference involves the response of the judiciary. The initial goals of the 1965 legislation, to remove barriers to registration and voting, had largely been achieved by the late 1960s. As a report from the U.S. Commission on Civil Rights demonstrated, black registration had risen dramatically across the South, with the greatest growth occurring in the states that had been most adamant in preventing black access to the ballot.[25] Despite the success in achieving the stated goals of the Voting Rights Act, the Supreme Court vastly expanded the reach of Section 5 in the *Allen* case when it interpreted Section 5 broadly to require federal approval of *all* laws that in any way impacted elections rather than simply those relating to registration and voting.[26] This enlarged the scope of federal authority by making redistricting plans, methods of selecting public officials, and the conduct of elections subject to federal approval in preclearance states. And while some civil rights groups criticized the Department of Justice for being insufficiently aggressive in enforcing Section 5, federal authority to review actions of governmental units that go far beyond regulations of registering and voting has become well established.[27]

The persistent involvement of federal courts, the bureaucracy, and Congress contributed to the development of a sufficiently large, active black electorate that no Democratic officeholder and very few Republicans would risk alienating it by attempting to turn back the clock, as occurred following the First Reconstruction. While votes on the initial version of the Voting Rights Act and early votes to extend it revealed a significant regional divide, the 2006 renewal drew few opposition votes. In the Senate, the latest extension passed unanimously, and in the House only thirty-three members opposed the continuation of Section 5 for another quarter century. Of those voting against final passage, nineteen came from the South.

Following the First Reconstruction, more than 90 percent of the black population resided in the South. Consequently, few officeholders outside of that region needed to be responsive to the concerns of black constituents. After the exodus of blacks from the South during the twentieth century, African Americans gained political influence in a wider array of states and congressional districts than in the latter years of the nineteenth century. Any efforts by southern racists to maintain white supremacy drew criticism from black political and religious leaders who lived outside the South.

Within the South, the black population had become far more urbanized than a century earlier. Even during the most repressive days of Jim Crow, urban southern blacks frequently fared better than their rural cousins. In some cities, such as Memphis and New Orleans, blacks had voted at a time when rural blacks living in the nearby Mississippi Delta were almost wholly barred from the polling place. During the two decades before passage of the Voting Rights Act, black participation in the urban South gradually increased. For example, black registration and voting had begun increasing in Atlanta immediately after the demise of the white primary.[28] African Americans had also become important in the politics of Durham, North Carolina, well before the protections of the Voting Rights Act.[29]

Urbanization and better communication allowed civil rights leaders in the latter part of the twentieth century to stay in touch. In the nineteenth century a black activist in a rural community would be isolated, but in the years after the Voting Rights Act, civil rights workers could exchange ideas about what worked, and they also had access to national and even international media when confronted by local racists.

Federal protections weakened in the late nineteenth century in part because of public disinterest. While civil rights have long since fallen from lists of the most important issues confronting the nation, they remain a concern for many citizens across the nation. The media have helped keep civil rights, if not in the forefront of people's minds, a topic that periodically resurfaces, such as on the anniversary of Martin Luther King's assassination, during Black History Month, and, on the local level, at the anniversary of significant civil rights events.

The differences outlined above help explain why history did not repeat itself as Woodward feared it would. Instead, African Americans have continued to make progress in the political sphere. Not only does the United States have a black president; in addition, during the 109th and 110th Congresses, the third-ranking Democrat in the U.S. House was an African American from South Carolina. In 2012 Massachusetts has a black governor and the Congress and state legislatures have record numbers of black members. As shown in figure 6.1, African Americans have achieved *more than* proportional representation in the lower chambers of southern legislatures. In 2011, eight southern legislative chambers had more black than white Democrats. In some states, black turnout in the 2008 election reached a record level.[30] For the first time since early in the First Reconstruction, when many who had served in the Confederate army remained disenfranchised, the share of the votes coming from African Americans in Alabama, Georgia, and South Carolina exceeded the black percentage of the adult population in those states.

The challenges facing African Americans today bear no resemblance to the concerns Woodward raised. Rather than confronting challenges to the gains ushered in by the Voting Rights Act and other civil rights legislation, the challenge now is to participate in an increasingly diverse political environment. Latinos have replaced African Americans as the nation's largest minority group. Despite efforts going back to the presidential campaign of Jesse Jackson to fashion a rainbow coalition that included blacks, Latinos, and others, elections often find African Americans more isolated than other groups. An extensive analysis of municipal elections finds that "to a certain extent, local elections are pitting African American voters against voters from the other three [white, Latino, and Asian American] racial and ethnic groups."[31] For African Americans to expand their influence and increase their number of officeholders, they will need to be more successful in finding coalition partners, since blacks have largely exhausted the potential for increased numbers of officials elected from overwhelmingly black districts.

NOTES

1. C. Vann Woodward, "What Happened to the Civil Rights Movement," in *The Burden of Southern History*, rev. ed. (New York: Mentor Book, 1968), 126.

2. J. Morgan Kousser, *Color Blind Justice: Minority Voting Rights and the Undoing of the Second Reconstruction* (Chapel Hill: University of North Carolina Press, 1999).

3. Everette Swinney, "Enforcing the 15th Amendment, 1870–1877," *Journal of Southern History* 28 (May 1962): 202–18.

4. Harrell R. Rodgers Jr. and Charles S. Bullock III, *Law and Social Change: Civil Rights Laws and Their Consequences* (New York: McGraw-Hill, 1972).

5. Ibid., 32.

6. Charles S. Bullock III and Ronald Keith Gaddie, *The Triumph of Voting Rights in the South* (Norman: University of Oklahoma Press, 2009).

7. Charles S. Bullock III, "Barack Obama and the South," *American Review of Politics* 31 (Summer 2010): 3–24.

8. In Texas the percentage of blacks among voters as estimated by the Census Bureau exceeded the percentage of blacks among eligible voters; however, these figures are often inflated (see Bullock and Gaddie, *The Triumph*).

9. *National Roster of Black Elected Officials* (Washington, DC: Metropolitan Applied Research Center, 1968).

10. *National Roster of Black Elected Officials* (Washington, DC: Joint Center for Political and Economic Studies, 2001).

11. *Baker v. Carr,* 369 U.S. 186 (1962).

12. *Georgia v. United States,* 411 U.S. 526 (1973).

13. While I refer to elections held in even-numbered years, Louisiana, Mississippi, and Virginia hold elections in odd-numbered years. For the sake of conformity, the numbers of black legislators in these states are shown in the subsequent even-numbered-year elections held in the other eight states.

14. Frank R. Parker, *Black Votes Count: Political Empowerment in Mississippi after 1965* (Chapel Hill: University of North Carolina Press, 1990).

15. *Shaw v. Reno,* 509 U.S. 630 (1993).

16. David G. Savage, "Despite Redistricting Dispute, Black Law Makers Win Reelection," *Los Angeles Times,* November 9, 1996, A10–A11.

17. Mike Christensen, "Blacks Fear Return to 'Dark Days of the 19th Century,'" *Atlanta Constitution,* June 30, 1995, A1.

18. See Steve Bickerstaff, *Lines in the Sand: Congressional Redistricting in Texas and the Downfall of Tom DeLay* (Austin: University of Texas Press, 2007). As described by Bickerstaff, U.S. House Majority Leader Tom DeLay, who represented a suburban Houston district, persuaded the Texas legislature to devise a new congressional plan designed to defeat most of the white Democrats then serving from the Lone Star State. This plan took effect with the 2004 election.

19. Abigail Thernstrom, *Voting Rights and Wrongs: The Elusive Quest for Racially Fair Elections* (Washington, DC: AEI Press, 2009).

20. These figures are for illustrative purposes. When districts are drawn, the emphasis is on the black percentage in the voting-age population.

21. J. Morgan Kousser, *The Shaping of Southern Politics: Suffrage Restriction and the Establishment of the One-Party South, 1880–1910* (New Haven, CT: Yale University Press, 1974), quotation on 33.

22. Ibid., 21.

23. *Giles v. Harris,* 189 U.S. 475 (1903); and *Giles v. Teasley,* 193 U.S. 146 (1904).

24. See Dan Eggen, "Politics Alleged in Voting Cases," *Washington Post,* January 23, 2006.

25. U.S. Commission on Civil Rights, *Political Participation* (Washington, DC: Government Printing Office, 1968).

26. *Allen v. State Board of Elections,* 393 U.S. 544 (1969).

27. See Howard Ball, Dale Krane, and Thomas P. Lauth, *Compromise Compliance: Implementation of the 1965 Voting Rights Act* (Westport, CT: Greenwood Press, 1982).

28. Clarence A Bacote, "The Negro Voter in Georgia Politics Today," *Journal of Negro Education* 26 (Summer 1957): 307–18; Jack Walker, "Negro Voting in Atlanta: 1953–1961," *Phylon* 24 (1963): 376–87.

29. William R. Keech, *The Impact of Negro Voting* (Chicago: Rand McNalley, 1968).

30. David A. Bositis, "Resegregation in Southern Politics?" 2011, Joint Center for Political and Economic Studies, Washington, DC.

31. Zoltan L. Hajnal, *America's Uneven Democracy* (New York: Cambridge University Press, 2010), 43.

7

Woodward's New Intellectual Stream

The Enfranchisement of the Freed Slave Population

HANES WALTON JR.
JOSEPHINE A. V. ALLEN
SHERMAN C. PUCKETT
DONALD R. DESKINS JR.

> Of all the revolutionary proposals that eventually received the sanction of law in the upheaval of Reconstruction, the proposal to give the freedmen the unrestricted right to vote was one of the most difficult for contemporaries to accept, in the North as well as in the South.
>
> —C. Vann Woodward, *The Burden of Southern History* (1968)

In the final chapter of this collection, Hanes Walton Jr., Josephine A. V. Allen, Sherman C. Puckett, and Donald R. Deskins Jr. reconsider Woodward's predictions regarding the impact that African American voters would have on the country and the region. They contend that underlining Woodward's discussion of southern identity is an innovative perspective on democracy and democratic theory. Specifically, they examine Woodward's pioneering concept of the enfranchised freedman as a political neophyte in the American electorate. Concentrating on voter registration and behavior in three periods characterized by a large influx of African American participation (Reconstruction, the period following the Smith v. Allwright *decision, and 2008), they ask, "Did this neophyte's voting behavior and political participation demonstrate characteristics expected of citizens in a democracy?" They conclude by citing Woodward's analysis of Reconstruction, in which he argues that "no red glow of anarchy lit up the southern horizon as a consequence of the [Reconstruction] revolution, and the enfranchised freedmen did not prove the unleashed beast of federalist imagination."[1] Their efforts highlight not only Woodward's optimism regarding African American enfranchisement, but also his vision regarding the strength and capacity of the American democratic system, which remains relevant in contemporary politics.*

C. Vann Woodward's book *The Burden of Southern History* is rich with themes and ideas regarding the budding intellectual streams of American democracy and exceptionalism. In epistemology one thinks in terms of a single model, theory, or paradigm; but in analyzing Woodward's book, what one finds is not a single idea but multiple ones. He offers scholars and academics literally a stream of ideas and concepts that challenge as well as undercut dominant and ruling orthodoxies, enriching and enhancing the definition of American democracy with his inclusionary principle. This chapter focuses on the intellectual political stream launched in chapter 5 of *The Burden of Southern History,* placed in the context of a reform movement in chapter 7, shown as being revitalized in the civil rights movement in chapter 8, and starting to structure the political landscape both regionally and nationally in chapter 11. Embedded in this intellectual stream are component parts not only of an innovative perspective on democracy and democratic theory, but of American exceptionalism as well.[2] In point of fact, Woodward's theoretical formulations are a profound epistemological breakthrough, given the historical facts and the intense and voluminous opposition against them, not only within his discipline, but also in the popular and public spheres of opinion. Like so many of his ideas, this intellectual stream was moving against the historical and public opinion mainstream. The tremendous reception his book received is a testament to its impact on the old orthodoxy and the disciples thereof. This orthodoxy still lingers, and that is surely true in political science, history's sister discipline. Thus, our research hypothesis for this chapter is drawn from Woodward's pioneering concept of the enfranchised freedman as a political neophyte in the American electorate. Did this neophyte's voting behavior and political participation demonstrate characteristics expected of citizens in a democracy? Or did the democratic experiment of enfranchising the newly freed slaves, as Woodward puts it, "discredit both the experiment itself and democratic faith in general?"[3] An empirical rendering of this research hypothesis will offer some testable assumptions about new voters in a democracy where race and ethnicity are powerful variables in and of themselves.

THE ENFRANCHISEMENT OF A FREED SLAVE POPULATION IN A DEMOCRACY: WOODWARD'S NEW INTELLECTUAL STREAM

Woodward's new set of ideas and insights challenged the prevailing orthodoxy, much as his well-known innovation the "Second Reconstruction" generated reflections on the First Reconstruction and on his less-well-known Third Reconstruction. Creating this new intellectual stream and setting it into motion went well beyond the preoccupation of political science with the destruction of slavery and the granting of freedom to the slaves. True, American democracy has liberty as one of its key features; however, coupled with this birthright tenet is the empowerment of the people. Liberty had been only partially realized by the time of the Civil War, because of the nation's attachment to and received legacy from the English concept of a "stake-in-society" requirement for suffrage rights. This became the guiding principle for the establishment of suffrage rights in both Colonial and Revolutionary America. Of suffrage rights, scholar Alexander Keyssar writes: "The lynchpin of both colonial and British suffrage regulations was the restriction of voting to adult men who owned property. On the eve of the American Revolution, in seven colonies men had to own land of specified acreage or monetary value in order to participate in elections; elsewhere, the ownership of personal property of a designated value (or in South Carolina, the payment of taxes) could substitute for real estate." Keyssar continues to make his point with the following remarks about how this received legacy from British society shaped colonial suffrage rights: "Both in England and in the colonies, property requirements had long been justified on two grounds. The first was that men who possessed property (especially 'real property,' i.e., land and buildings) had a unique 'stake in society'—meaning that they were committed members of (or stakeholders in) the community and that they had a personal interest in the policies of the state, especially taxation. The second was that property owners alone possessed sufficient independence to warrant their having a voice in governance."[4]

Basically speaking, this concept continued through Colonial America into Revolutionary America with little modification. This crucial inheritance from both British and Colonial America that "only men with property, preferably real property, were deemed to be sufficiently attached to the community and sufficiently affected by its laws to have earned the privilege of voting . . . became a major focus of controversy during the revolutionary era."[5] Therefore, both up to and throughout the constitutional debates at the Grand 1787 Constitutional Convention in Philadelphia, "arguments for and against a more democratic suffrage were voiced in newspapers, broadsides, provincial assemblies, town meetings, gatherings of militiamen, and constitutional conventions, as well as taverns, inns, city streets and privates homes."[6]

This should come as no surprise, because "under the Articles of Confederation, the states had retained complete control over the franchise. But the Constitution of the United States forged a link between state suffrage rules and the right to vote in national elections." In fact, at the 1787 convention, the Negro suffrage matter was assigned to the Committee on Detail, and "in the end, the committee's recommendation was to tie suffrage for the House of Representatives to state franchise requirements in elections to the lower house of each state legislature."[7] (This is stated in article 1, section 2, of the Constitution.)[8] Because suffrage rights had remained in the hands of first the Colonial governments and then the states during the Revolutionary era, the decision at the 1787 Constitutional Convention "left the federal government without any clear power or mechanism, other than through constitutional amendment, to institute a national conception of voting rights, to express a national vision of democracy" and universal suffrage. Thus, Revolutionary America's fledgling democracy left basically intact the stake-in-society principle regarding the country's suffrage rights. The principle applied not only to the thirteen new state governments; it was also true in the federal territories administered by the federal government. According to Keyssar, "in the largest piece of terrain directly controlled by the federal government, citizens and aliens alike had to own fifty acres of land in order to vote."[9]

Hence, one of the first tasks faced in antebellum America was the broadening and expansion of suffrage rights, and along with it came the need for a newer vision of democracy in America. Notable in this effort is the movement before and during the Jacksonian era, 1828–32, when the common man acquired suffrage rights. But this was also the very same period in which free men and women of color lost suffrage rights in Tennessee (1834), North Carolina (1835), and Pennsylvania (1838), in addition to Kentucky (1799), Connecticut (1818 and 1845), Delaware (1792 and 1831), and New Jersey (1807 and 1844); those rights were restricted in New York in 1821 via a property qualification not imposed on white males.[10] However, "by the end of the 1850s, only two property requirements remained in force anywhere in the United States, one applying to foreign-born residents of

Rhode Island and the other to African Americans in New York."[11] While the stake-in-society suffrage principle had been almost eliminated on the very eve of the Civil War, the barrier of race had not abated, rendering both the expansion of suffrage and a newer vision of American democracy highly circumscribed. Only six states (Maine, Massachusetts, New Hampshire, Rhode Island, Vermont, and New York) allowed free men of color to vote.

The coming of the Civil War led African Americans to expand their National Negro Convention Movement with the creation of another protest organization, the National Equal Rights League, which began lobbying for their suffrage rights.[12] Along with this national organization, there were numerous state organizations making the same demands. Yet, just as the Revolutionary War had not expanded suffrage rights as it did freedom for northern free men and women of color and slaves, the Civil War did not expand suffrage rights for the freedmen and freedwomen. On this particular matter, William Gillette found: "Voters in the North, in referendum after referendum, rejected Negro suffrage by a generally substantial vote. . . . During 1865 five jurisdictions voted down Negro suffrage in popular referendums. . . . in September, it was defeated in the . . . Territory of Colorado. . . . In October, in Connecticut. . . . During November, in Wisconsin . . . and . . . finally . . . in the southern-oriented District of Columbia."[13] Two years later, in 1867, the situation worsened when referenda were defeated in Kansas, Minnesota, Ohio, Michigan, and Missouri; the same thing happened in 1869 in New York. Of all of the states where African American suffrage referenda were held, only in Iowa and eventually Minnesota—and, by the state supreme court, in Wisconsin—did suffrage rights expand to include free men of color. According to Gillette, "By the end of 1868, then, no northern state with a relatively large Negro population had voluntarily accepted full Negro suffrage." None of the southern states readmitted under the Reconstruction plan of President Andrew Johnson provided for suffrage rights in their highly restrictive "Black Codes," nor had the Reconstruction proclamations of either President Lincoln or President Johnson provided for suffrage rights for the freed slaves. But all of that was about to change.[14]

The lesson from the numerous state referenda is that "unfortunately there was no ground swell of popular support or any decisive change in public opinion between 1865 and 1868 as registered in referendums on Negro suffrage. Instead, white Americans resented and resisted it."[15] States and their electorates, the two Republican presidents, the old Confederate South, and the Democratic Party opposed suffrage rights for African Americans, but Congress had not made a declaration up to this point. In the November 1866 midterm elections, the Republican Party gained enough seats to have dominant majorities in both the House and the Senate. One month later, on December 13, 1866, the Senate passed a bill granting freed slaves suffrage rights in the District of Columbia, and on the next day the House of Representative passed the measure. However, on January 7, 1867, Republican president Johnson vetoed the legislation. A day later, the Republican majorities in both houses of Congress overrode the presidential veto; the consequence was that African American freedmen could now vote in elections for president and Congress. After the passage of the District of Columbia suffrage bill, the Senate called up a House of Representatives bill from May 15, 1866, that proposed the granting of suffrage rights to freed slaves and free men of color in all of the federal territories. "On January 10, 1867, the Senate passed a similar measure. On the same day the House supported it. President Johnson, apparently in a state of resignation after the District of Columbia defeat, acquiesced, and Negroes after January 31, 1867, had the formal right to vote in federal territories." Next, the Republican Congress became a harbinger of things to come when it insisted that the conditions of statehood for the Nebraska Territory include the enfranchisement of African American free men of color. In 1867, Congress voted to override President Johnson's veto, granting statehood to Nebraska. Thus, as Woodward notes succinctly, "in one month all the territorial subdivisions under the direct control of Congress had received Negro suffrage."[16] Congress was now breaking away from the customary way of dealing with the suffrage question, which had been to let the states address the matter. But Congress's approach is built into American exceptionalism,[17] and the country had reached one of many critical junctures where it took a different set of choices and policies.

On March 2, 1867, Congress passed, over President Johnson's veto, the First Military Reconstruction Act, which divided the ten unreconstructed states into five military districts and described the process by which southern governments could regain their congressional representation. The initiative was left up to the southern governments. Nothing happened. Thus, on March 23, the Second Military Reconstruction Act was passed, giving power to the generals in command of the military districts "to register eligible voters and to set the machinery in motion for the election of delegates to (new state) constitutional conventions. . . . The army undertook the task of registering voters, including freed slaves."[18] The Third Military Reconstruction Act, passed on July 19, 1867, made southern provisional governments subordinate to the military commanders, while the Fourth Military Reconstruction Act, passed on March 11, 1868, made a simple majority of those voting sufficient for ratification of new state constitutions. Overall, it is the first and second military reconstruction acts that became the centerpiece of Woodward's intellectual stream on the enfranchisement of the freed slaves.

Of this enfranchisement of the freed slaves, Woodward writes: "Enfranchisement came in belatedly, surreptitiously, almost disingenuously advanced by its proponents, grudgingly accepted by a North that moved under duress and the argument of necessity and greeted with gloomy forebodings of failure, if not disaster. These attitudes were widespread, and they were not confined to copperheads, doughfaces, and mossback conservatives."[19] But those dominant sentiments were not only among the contemporary ones noted by Woodward. They had existed with the very birth of democracy in Greece, from Plato and Aristotle to the Federalists. Woodward states emphatically:

> Not Athens, nor Rome, or Paris at greatest turbulence had confronted their like. Here was the Federalist beast who would turn every garden into a pigsty. Here was old John Adams' shiftless and improvident Demos, pawn of demagogues and plutocrats and menace to all order. Here in the flesh was Hamilton's "turbulent and changing" mass who "seldom judge or determine right" and who made it necessary to give to "the rich and well born" that "distinct, permanent share in the government," which alone would insure stability. Here was the ultimate test of the democratic dogma in the most extreme form ever attempted.[20]

Thus, both contemporary and historically dominant sentiments and public attitudes were against what Congress had done in the first and second military reconstruction acts—specifically, it had enfranchised freed slaves. According to Woodward, the step was not only unprecedented; it was another prime example of American exceptionalism, since it redefined and reconceptualized the very nature, scope, and significance of democracy, especially American democracy.

Of the import and impact of this pioneering congressional legislative action, Woodward notes: "A political revolution was under way in the

Southern states, a revolution that is the first chapter in the history of the Negro voter in America. The initial step under military government, after the destruction of the old civil governments, was the creation of the new electorate in 1867 and 1868. In all, more than 703,000 Negroes and some 627,000 whites were registered as qualified voters in the reconstructed states. The processes of disfranchisement and enfranchisement were going on simultaneously." As a consequence of this simultaneous disenfranchisement of Confederate whites and enfranchisement of freed slaves, several electoral transformations occurred in the ten unreconstructed southern states. As Woodward explains: "While some states with white majorities in population were given colored majorities in their electorate, others had had their white majorities drastically reduced, and the two states with a preponderance of Negroes in population, South Carolina and Mississippi, had overwhelming majorities of colored voters."[21]

After providing the reader with the political geography of this electoral revolution in the enfranchisement of freed slaves set into motion by the first and second military reconstruction acts, Woodward enhances his intellectual stream by demonstrating what occurred to this new electorate at the very moment it was legally created. "This new-born electorate of freedmen was plunged immediately into action by the election of delegates to constitutional conventions. They followed by electing legislative bodies, state and local officials, and by full-scale and continuous participation in all phases and aspects of political life in a period that was abnormally active in a political way." Having described the demands and pressures of the southern political context awaiting the freed slaves, Woodward then gives us a vivid description of freed slave voters at the moment of their legal creation: "That the mass of these people had less education, less experience in public affairs, and less property of all sorts than white voters is obvious. As for the more intangible endowments of status and inner security . . . their relative impoverishment was appalling, unprecedented among American or any other known electorates. Their very appearance at the polls in mass, wearing the rags of slave days and bearing the ancient stigmata of oppression, conjured up every gloomy prognostication of the fate of democracies from Aristotle to the Federalists."[22]

After offering this remarkable demographic, political, and psychological portrait of the "new-born freedman electorate," Woodward, using the historical record, develops a behavioral evaluation of the electorate that is both balanced and carefully unbiased in relation to other writers' views: "The records left by that revolutionary experiment have been widely used to discredit both the experiment itself and democratic faith in general. Yet those records need not put democracy out of countenance, nor are they wholly devoid of comfort for those of that faith. . . . the enfranchised freedmen did not prove the unleashed beast of Federalist imagination. Moral pigsties undoubtedly developed, but they were oftener than not the creation of the other race, and more of them were to be found outside the South than within."[23]

He continues with the comment, "The new electorate of freedmen proved on the whole remarkably modest in their demands, unaggressive in their conduct, and deferential in their attitude. In no state did they hold place and power in anything approaching their actual numbers and voting strengths." But this isn't where Woodward leaves the matter. Before he closes his fifth chapter, "The Political Legacy of Reconstruction," he places his argument into the larger context of both the nation's history and its future, by noting that the inexperienced freedmen were not the only and last group of citizens who became instantly enfranchised in America and had to grow into political maturity.[24]

In fact, according to Woodward, the real political neophytes of the American electorate were the "twelve million white immigrants who poured into the stream of American citizenship in the fifty years after 1880 from southern and eastern European countries. [Their] record of . . . inexperience, naïveté, and ineptitude . . . in the big city slums is worse than the voting behavior of the freed slaves during the Reconstruction era."[25] Woodward's intellectual stream of studying the enfranchisement of freed slaves and then reducing this stream to the parsimonious behavioral concept of the political neophyte offers political scientists a new approach to assessing African American political behavior in the twentieth and twenty-first centuries. His book follows them from the Reconstruction era to the Populist era in chapter 7, on into the civil rights era in chapter 8, and finally to chapter 11 and the drive into the Third Reconstruction era. His intellectual stream is ever dynamic, ever flowing, ever changing, and ever reshaping both southern and national politics and the continually evolving vision of democracy in America.

DATA AND METHODOLOGY: THE POLITICAL NEOPHYTES' VOTING BEHAVIOR

Using Woodward's behavioral concept concerning the enfranchised freed slaves, this work analyzes their voter registration and voting behavior, first from the time of their political creation in 1868 up until 1920, then during the time of their political recreation and rebirth with the *Smith v. Allwright* decision in 1944, and finally from the beginning of the Third Reconstruction with the election of an African American president in 2008. Each one of these critical periods, during which vast numbers of former slaves and their descendants entered the southern electorate, provides a framework within which we can evaluate and assess some of the findings noted by Woodward in chapters 5, 7, 8, and 11 of *The Burden of Southern History*. This analysis does not include political neophytes who came of age after the 1965 Voting Rights Act, because doing so would necessitate similar explorations after the act's renewals in 1970, 1975, 1982, and 2006. Including all of these would require the abandonment of some other critical time points, given the space limitations of this study. The three time points that have been selected provide diversity in coverage.

This research encompasses all of the eleven former Confederate southern states. Woodward's study covered only these eleven states. Originally, Tennessee was excluded from his analysis because it had adopted a new state constitution that allowed freed slaves to vote, only one day before the First Military Reconstruction Act was passed by Congress, but it is included in this analysis because it, like all of the other southern states, disenfranchised the freed slave voters. Thus, presented here is a regional analysis of the entire South.

Since this analysis focuses upon voter registration and voting behavior in presidential elections and one statewide election, it relies mostly on election return data from African American majority counties and white majority counties in the South. This data allows us to search for patterns or trends of both democratic and antidemocratic behavior in the electorate or in the candidates and parties that this electorate supported as political neophytes. Woodward did not find such characteristics in his studies of these political neophytes at different stages in American political history. Hopefully, our empirical analysis will further illuminate any strengths or weaknesses in Woodward's historical and logical approach.

Woodward says that these political neophytes prove beneficial to American democracy simply because "here was the ultimate test of the democratic dogma in the most extreme form ever attempted." He claims that the enfranchisement of the freed slaves eventually wrought reform and improvement in the South, in both the electorate and the party system. By following Woodward's intellectual stream across time, this research concludes, as he did, that these political neophytes allowed the South in the modern era to elect southern Democratic presidents Johnson, Carter, and Clinton and southern Republican presidents Bush and Bush, as well as playing a major role in the election of the nation's first African American president in 2008.[26]

Finally, this data and methodology allow scholars to see not only how the political neophytes are defining the Third Reconstruction era with the election of the first African American president, but also the great relevance of Woodward's ideas for the present and the future. By including the 2008 Barack Obama election in the South, one sees not only a rising biracial electorate but also, in it, some of the great possibilities (more triumphs than tragedies) that Woodward saw in the irony and burden of southern history. Here is the continuing relevance of Woodward for the Third Reconstruction and beyond. Although the central focus of this research is on the registration and voting of the free men of color, one should be ever mindful of the political participation that took place before, during, and after the casting of ballots.[27]

WOODWARD'S POLITICAL NEOPHYTES IN RECONSTRUCTION AND POST-RECONSTRUCTION SOUTHERN PRESIDENTIAL ELECTIONS

In Chapter 5 of *The Burden of Southern History,* Woodward establishes quite early in quantitative terms how the First Military Reconstruction Act of 1867 restructured the one-dimensional uniracial white southern electorate into a biracial multidimensional electorate: "In all, more than 703,000 Negroes and some 627,000 whites were registered as qualified voters in the reconstructed states."[28] He captures for the reader the size and scope of this newly enfranchised freed slave population and draws from this static portrait his ideas about the role and function of these political neophytes. Using extant election return data from both the African American and white majority counties in these eleven southern states over time, we want to capture some of the dynamics of the newly enfranchised freed slaves. Such an approach allows us to determine in different time frames some of the relevance of Woodward's theories.

Figure 7.1 demonstrates that the vote for the Republican Party peaked in 1872, years after Mississippi, Texas, and Virginia were readmitted into the Union. Florida, which was readmitted in 1868, did not allow popular voting in the presidential election that year but fully participated through votes cast by its state legislature. All of the other southern states had been readmitted in 1868 as well. Figure 7.1 shows that the Republican vote declined precipitously and continually until 1920, when African American and southern white women became part the electorate. Once the freed slave vote began its decline shortly after the 1876 presidential election, a concomitant rise, up through 1888, for the white supremacist Democratic Party occurred in the vote of counties with African American population majorities.

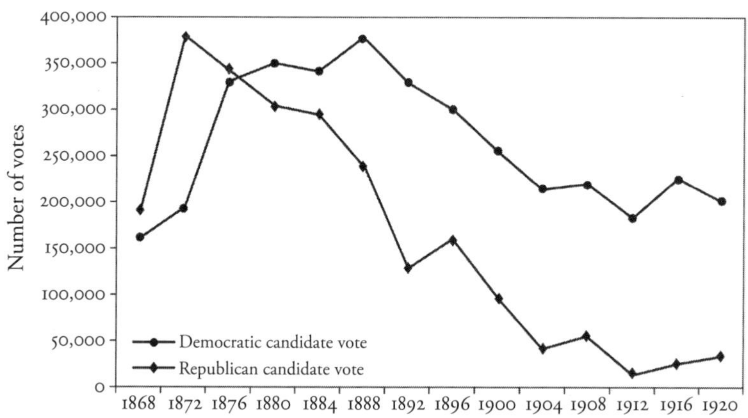

FIG. 7.1. The vote of African American majority counties for presidential candidates in the South, 1868–1920

As the era of disenfranchisement came into existence and was legally fastened upon each of the southern states, there was a decline in the vote for Democratic Party candidates that nearly parallels the decline in votes for Republican presidential candidates. Although both declines took place in the same counties, one occurred because there was a vigorous effort to curtail the enfranchisement of the freed slaves, while the other was in part a byproduct of the new state constitutional designs. Such a longitudinal trend reveals that in the areas of African American population dominance, there were votes for the white supremacist Democratic Party as well as for the Republican presidential candidate. Thus, by inference, there is a degree of diversity in the voting behavior of the enfranchised freed slaves. But most importantly, these voters were not restricting the southern white electorate, for with their declining vote, the freedmen also were seeing a decline in the numbers of African American elected local and state officials. Hence, the former slaves had no chance to legislate against the sundry disenfranchising techniques and procedures that the new state constitutions were putting in place.

In point of fact, African American southern politicos had the opportunity to participate in only two of the eleven new state constitutional conventions that established the era of disenfranchisement: Mississippi's convention had one African American delegate and South Carolina's had six. Historian Michael Perman describes this situation, beginning with South Carolina: "Besides these 154 white Democrats, [there were] 6 black Republican delegates, except for Mississippi's convention, in which Isaiah Montgomery, the founder and leader of the black settlement of Mound Bayou, had been the lone representative of his race."[29] Nevertheless, despite the larger African American delegation in South Carolina, the result was the same: the state constitutional conventions disenfranchised the freed slaves.

The techniques put in place in the South to reduce African Americans' electoral base of participation did not originate within the actual African American electorate or the meager state legislative representation that the restricted African American electorate could possibly generate. Simply put, a declining electorate in the African American majority counties could not have effectuated the simultaneous decline of the white electorate in the region. Placing the vote in the African American counties into the political context of the white majority counties and of all of the counties, one finds in figure 7.2 that after the 1876 presidential election, the total Democratic vote in all of the counties and that in the white counties began to parallel each other over time, while the Republican vote in white counties as well as the Republican vote in all counties nearly disappeared in 1912 then started to converge and become nearly one. Additionally, the Democratic vote in the black counties and the Republican vote in the black counties are both disappearing. Thus, this rising one-party dominance was due neither to the voting behavior of the freed slaves nor to the voting behavior of the white electorate. That the Democratic vote coming from the African American counties declined along with the Republican vote is an indication not of the white electorate's effectuating the growing one-party nature of the region but of the enabling of a one party system, as V. O. Key Jr. and others have shown, by the elected political elites from these counties.

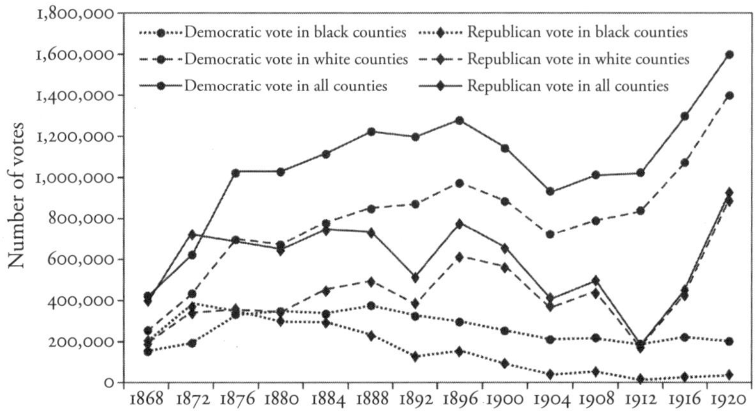

FIG. 7.2. The vote of southern counties for presidential candidates, all and by race, 1868–1920

Moreover, this dualistic decline in both the Democratic and Republican party vote in the African American counties in the South is another empirical example of the sophisticated veteran type voting behavior of the African American political neophytes. This decline highlights and suggests the fact that there was not just singular Republican partisanship voting in these African American majority counties but dual party voting. For whatever reasons and motivations, this initial African American electorate voted for both parties, to say nothing about their vote also for third-party candidates. Thus, there is no monolith at this first legal chance to cast ballots. Seemingly, depending upon the locale, the types of candidates, the aloofness of the Republican Party, and the nature and scope of the political candidates and their stance on issues, one finds diversity in the voting behavior of the African American political neophytes. Many scholars in their analyses of the Reconstruction and post-Reconstruction periods have overstated their findings in declaring that the voting African American was essentially a Republican partisan. Such findings need to be reexamined.

In addition, figure 7.2 reveals that the growing Republican vote was coming from the white majority counties. However, it was not large or strong enough to leverage competitive presidential elections in the region. A one-party system prevailed. This lack of party competitiveness resembled the decline in voting by the freed slaves and other groups. Therefore, the collapse of the white electorate, the two-party system, and party competitiveness—and the restrictive vision of democracy thus engendered—were not, and could not be, rooted in either the voter registration or the voting behavior of the political neophytes.

Figure 7.3 shifts from an analysis of total votes to the mean vote and demonstrates additional support for Woodward. Again this indicator shows a peak in 1872 for the Republican Party in the African American majority counties as well as a parallel decline for the Democratic Party vote. The pattern and trends hold, with only slight variations. The remaining electorate after the era of disenfranchisement was shrinking. It could not be influenced by the elected officials of the newly enfranchised freed slave voters, because these officials were being pushed out of the electoral process. As a consequence, they also could not have been responsible for the rise of a one-party structure in the region. The source of these occurrences has to be elsewhere in the South's political system, as Woodward opines in his commentary on the political legacy of Reconstruction.

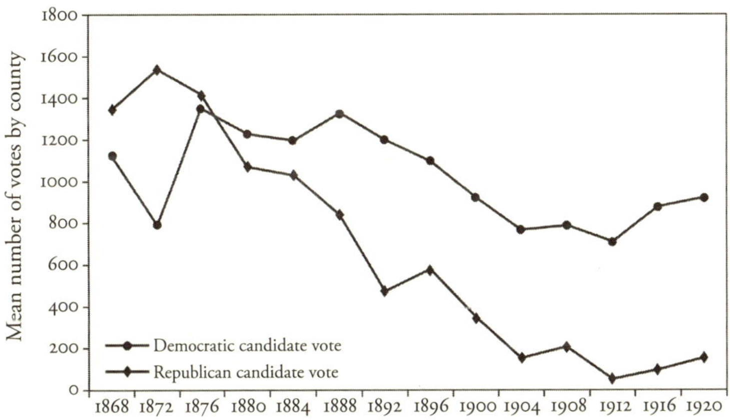

FIG. 7.3. Mean vote of African American majority counties for presidential candidates in the South, by county, 1868–1920

Figure 7.4 reveals to us that the mean Democratic vote coming from all of the counties in the South has dominated every election except that of 1872, the one point where the region had a competitive moment and an instance of a two-party system. It never approached competitiveness again during this period, and an essential factor was the continual absence of the freed slave voters from the system. The Republican vote from the white counties could not and did not make the party system competitive, and as a consequence, there was an enduring Democratic Party dominance. It took a while, as Woodward's discussions in other chapters show, for both the regional electorate and the political party system to recover from the exclusion of the enfranchised freed slaves.

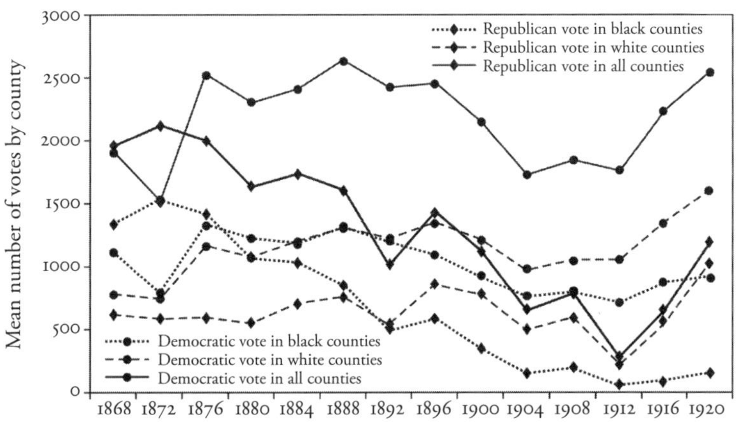

FIG. 7.4. Mean vote of southern counties for presidential candidates, all and by race, by county, 1868–1920

The dynamic changes revealed by figures 7.1–7.4 help one to fully grasp Woodward's thesis—namely, that there was both triumph and tragedy associated with the enfranchisement of the freed slave population in America's fledgling electoral process and democratic system. There is empirical support for his intellectual stream as a consequence of this unique political neophyte; that support emerged during the Reconstruction era and continued in varying degrees during other moments in America's political history, such as that set into motion by the Supreme Court decision on the all-white primaries.

There are several political socializing factors that helped these African American political neophyte voters behave more like sophisticated veteran voters. First, there were internal state factors, such as the fact that Tennessee and North Carolina allowed free men of color to legally vote until 1834 and 1835, respectively. Louisiana allowed free men of color to vote in Rapides Parish from 1839 to 1860, and free blacks in New Orleans petitioned President Lincoln and Congress for the right to vote in early 1865. As a consequence of their voter activism, President Lincoln sent a letter to Reconstruction governor Michael Hahn urging him to consider giving this right at least to those African Americans who had fought in the Civil War. Virginia was affected by the activities of John M. Langston, one of a very few African Americans to be elected to office before the Civil War (this occurred in Ohio). He became president of the National Equal Rights League in 1865 and spent his time traveling the country advocating for voting rights for African Americans. After moving to Virginia, Langston mobilized the African American electorate to vote and became in 1888 the first African American elected to the House of Representatives.

Externally, there were the Republican-led Union Leagues that came to each of the southern states and politically socialized the freed slaves into the Republican Party and political participation. Then the army, acting under the Second Military Reconstruction Act, gave the freed slaves actual electoral experiences by registering them to vote, monitoring their participation in the new state constitutional conventions, and supervising their voting for delegates to these state conventions as well as their voting for the state legislatures and statewide elections. The army was assisted by northern African American voter activists who came south and assisted the political neophytes' inclusion into the electoral and the political process. Finally, there was the endless opposition and violence from the white Democrats.

WOODWARD'S POLITICAL NEOPHYTES IN POST–WHITE PRIMARY SOUTHERN LOCAL AND PRESIDENTIAL ELECTIONS

The abolition of the white primaries by the Supreme Court's *Smith v. Allwright* decision on April 3, 1944, unleashed an entirely new group of African American political neophytes in the eleven states of the South. Although all women acquired the right to vote in 1920, African American women had never been allowed to vote in any of the southern states prior to this decision. The leading scholar of the white primary technique, Darlene Clark Hine, writes: "*Smith* was the watershed in the struggle for black rights. It signaled the beginning of the so-called Second Reconstruction and the modern civil rights movement. The political and social advances of blacks could not have occurred without the changes that came in the wake of the overthrow of the Democratic white primary." She discusses the entry of political neophytes into the southern political process first from a regional perspective, highlighting the fact that initially only 5 percent of the voting-age African American electorate was registered to vote, whereas after the 1944 Supreme Court decision, some 12 percent became registered. Focusing on Texas, she explains that in 1940 about 30,000 black Texans were registered, compared to 100,000 that were registered after the Court decision. Only the African American electorate in Georgia had a greater increase, growing from 20,000 in 1940 to 125,000 in 1947.[30]

A legal scholar looking at the same case declared that *Smith* had launched a quiet revolution: "In Southern Politics and life [the rise of black political power across the South], that revolution did happen. And the first step on this road to social and political revolution was the defeat of the Texas AWP (all-white primary)."[31] Earlier, political scientist Steven Lawson sized up the impact of the ruling by noting that "since the white primary had erected a solid fortress keeping blacks out of the polling booths, its demolition opened the iron clad doors to the most important election in southern politics." In his electoral portrait of these new political neophytes, Lawson notes: "In 1940 Ralph Bunche guessed that 250,000 Negroes were registered to vote in southern states; by 1947, the estimated number had jumped to 777,000."[32] Woodward comments on the disappearance of the white primary as well as on the reactions that many white southerners had to the disappearance of what they considered "unique" southern landmarks and monuments, such as the poll tax, the Jim Crow car, the lynching tree, one-party politics, racial demagogues, and segregation.[33] With this new vacancy on the southern landscape, there was a chance for the region to grow and expand in numerous other ways. But the disappearance of these landmarks opened the door for African American political neophytes, many of whom heped to generate new regional identity and political distinctiveness.

Table 7.1, using the most reliable and accessible extant voting data, provides African American southern state voter registration data before and after *Smith v. Allwright.* It also indicates the increases in numbers and percentages. The "Increase" column reveals that many new political neophytes came forth after the Supreme Court's ruling, when the number of new African American voters on the registration rolls more than tripled to 416,267. African Americans stepped up and placed their names on the voting rolls in these eleven states. In addition, the increases, which occurred in every one of the southern states, provide quite an impressive set of summary information, revealing huge increases in the numbers of political neophytes. The mean number of voters in 1940 stood at 15,353, and in 1947, after *Smith,* it was 53,196, an increase of 37,842. The median moved from 18,000 to 49,000 during the same period, an increase of 33,000. Every indicator points to how vigorously these new voters moved into the southern electoral process.

Table 7.1. Before and after *Smith v. Allwright:*
The estimated number of African American registered political neophytes

State	*1940*	*1947*	*Increase*	*% Increase*
Alabama	2,000	6,000	4,000	200.0
Arkansas	21,888	37,155	15,267	69.8
Florida	18,000	49,000	31,000	172.2
Georgia	20,000	125,000	105,000	525.0
Louisiana	2,000	10,000	8,000	400.0
Mississippi	2,000	5,000	3,000	150.0
North Carolina	35,000	75,000	40,000	114.3
South Carolina	3,000	50,000	47,000	1,566.7
Tennessee	20,000	80,000	60,000	300.0
Texas	30,000	100,000	70,000	233.3
Virginia	15,000	48,000	33,000	220.0
Total	168,888	585,155	416,267	246.5
Mean	15,353	53,196	37,842	359.2
Median	18,000	49,000	33,000	220.0
Maximum	35,000	125,000	105,000	1,566.7
Minimum	2,000	5,000	3,000	69.8

Source: Steven F. Lawson, *Black Ballots: Voting Rights in the South, 1944–1969* (New York: Columbia University Press, 1976), 134. Calculations by the authors

Turning to the percentage increases in voter registrations, figure 7.5 demonstrates that six of the eleven states more than tripled their African American registrations, while three other states at least doubled their previous marks. Arkansas was the only one with less than a 100 percent increase, but even Arkansas increased by 69.8 percent over its registrations before *Smith*. South Carolina led the region with its more than sixteenfold increase; there African Americans created their own political party, the South Carolina Progressive Democratic Party, in 1944 because they wanted to vote for incumbent president Franklin Delano Roosevelt and the state legislature had voted not to put him on the state ballot.[34] South Carolina was the only southern state in which an African American satellite political party emerged. It had a significant impact on voter mobilization as well as offering the people of the state a chance to vote for the incumbent president. In addition, an African American, Osceola McKaine, ran for the U.S. Senate in South Carolina in 1944, and many of the political neophyte registrants voted for him.

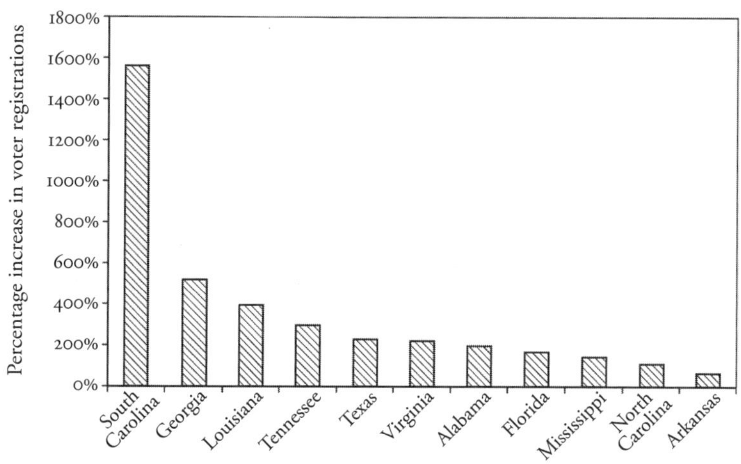

FIG. 7.5. Before and after *Smith v. Allwright:* Percent increase in African American political neophyte voter registrations. *Source:* Steven F. Lawson, *Black Ballots: Voting Rights in the South, 1944–1969* (New York: Columbia University Press, 1976), 134. Calculations by the authors.

Table 7.2 rank-orders the number of registered African American political neophytes in each of the southern states both before and after the *Smith v. Allwright* ruling. It also displays the increase in the number of registered voters made possible by the case, and it indicates the states that had the highest and lowest increases. Before the ruling, North Carolina and Texas led the South in the total number of African American voters, whereas after the ruling it was Georgia and Texas that led. Mississippi, and eventually Alabama, the states providing the most difficulty for African American registrants, rested at the bottom. The unique factor here is that although the vast majority of white primary court cases occurred in Texas, the greatest increase came in Georgia, where organizing and political mobilization leadership may have made the difference.

TABLE 7.2. Before and after *Smith v. Allwright:* Rank orderings of the southern states by the estimated number of African American registered political neophytes

State	*1940*	*State*	*1947*	*State*	*Increase*
North Carolina	35,000	Georgia	125,000	Georgia	105,000
Texas	30,000	Texas	100,000	Texas	70,000
Arkansas	21,888	Tennessee	80,000	Tennessee	60,000
Georgia	20,000	North Carolina	75,000	South Carolina	47,000
Tennessee	20,000	South Carolina	50,000	North Carolina	40,000
Florida	18,000	Florida	49,000	Virginia	33,000
Virginia	15,000	Virginia	48,000	Florida	31,000
South Carolina	3,000	Arkansas	37,155	Arkansas	15,267
Alabama	2,000	Louisiana	10,000	Louisiana	8,000
Louisiana	2,000	Alabama	6,000	Alabama	4,000
Mississippi	2,000	Mississippi	5,000	Mississippi	3,000

Source: Steven F. Lawson, *Black Ballots: Voting Rights in the South, 1944–1969* (New York: Columbia University Press, 1976), 134. Calculations by the authors.

Extant election data for Georgia allow more detailed analyses both statewide and at the local level for these political neophytes, in terms of both voter registration and voting behavior.[35] The data source for table 7.3 does not offer voting registration data prior to *Smith* (however, Paul Lewinson's book *Race, Class, and Party* does),[36] but there is reliable registration and actual voting data in the years after the Court's ruling for five statewide elections.

The median ratio of reported to estimated voters is 12 percent, and the mean number is 11 percent. Thus, the critical mass of African American leadership mobilizing in the state of Georgia maintained a steady level of new registrants during each of these five elections.

TABLE 7.3. Before and after *Smith v. Allwright*: The registered African American political neophytes in Georgia

Year	*Estimated number of black voters*	*Number of black voters reported*	*Reported number as % of estimated number*
1944	10,000	unknown	unknown
1946	85,000	10,871	13
1948	86,000	6,864	8
1950	45,000	4,424	10
1952	60,000	9,035	15
1954	60,000	7,021	12
Mean	67,200	7,643	11
Median	60,000	7,021 12	12

Sources: Adapted from Hanes Walton Jr., "Black Voting Behavior in the Segregation Era: 1944–1964," in *Black Politics and Black Political Behavior: A Linkage Analysis*, ed. Hanes Walton Jr. (Westport, CT: Praeger, 1994), 123. 1944 estimate from Paul Lewinson, *Race, Class, and Party: A History of Negro Suffrage and White Politics in the South* (London: Oxford University Press, 1932), 218.

Table 7.4 provides information on the diverse voting behavior of the African American political neophytes in terms of each individual white candidate running in the four statewide gubernatorial races and the one referendum held during the period. The majority of the African American vote always was cast for the candidate who expressed the most interest in the issues and political concerns of the African American community. In the referendum balloting, African Americans also voted for the issue of most concern to their community. Clearly, in these five statewide elections, African Americans did not vote to destroy or undermine the political system, but to assert their choice among possible outcomes. In the 1950 gubernatorial election and the 1952 referendum election, the interests of the white electorate and the African American electorate in Georgia converged, providing a glimpse of a biracial electorate not seen there since the Reconstruction era.

TABLE 7.4. After *Smith v. Allwright:* The voting behavior of registered African American political neophytes in Georgia

Year	*Referendum or Democratic Candidate*	*Number of Black Votes*	*% of Votes*	*Outcome*
1946	James Carmichael	10,477	96.4	
	Eugene Talmadge	246	2.3	Winner
	E. D. Rivers	132	1.2	
	Hoke O'Kelly	14	0.1	
	Total	10,869	100.0	
1948	M. E. Thompson	6,765	99.1	
	H. E. Talmadge	23	0.3	Winner
	Hoke Willis	19	0.3	
	J. Rayburn	10	0.1	
	Hoke O'Kelly	8	0.1	
	Total	6,825	99.9	
1950	M. E. Thompson	4,298	97.2	
	Herman Talmadge	90	2.0	Winner
	C. O. "Fats" Baker	27	0.6	
	Mrs. J. W. Jenkins	5	0.1	
	Pat Avery	4	0.1	
	Total	4,424	100.0	
1952	For the County-Unit Amendment	1,166	12.8	
	Against the County-Unit Amendment	7,919	87.2	Defeated
	Total	9,085	100.0	
1954	M. E. Thompson	5,426	77.4	
	Charles Gowen	792	11.3	
	Marvin Griffin	328	4.7	Winner
	Grace Thomas	263	3.8	
	Fred Hand	72	1.0	
	Tom Linden	64	0.9	
	Ben Garland	37	0.5	
	Ed Barfield	20	0.3	
	Arthur Neeson	11	0.2	
	Total	7,013	100.1	

Source: Adapted from Hanes Walton Jr., "Black Voting Behavior in the Segregation Era: 1944–1964," in *Black Politics and Black Political Behavior: A Linkage Analysis*, ed. Hanes Walton Jr. (Westport, CT: Praeger, 1994), 125–26.

Figure 7.6 visually displays the voting behavior of the African American political neophytes in the five statewide elections in Georgia. Although in every one of these Democratic primary elections, they cast votes for other candidates, after the Supreme Court ruling they cast the majority of their votes for a particular type of candidate that mandated their participation. This "particular type of candidate" refers to "the lesser of the two evils" in southern parlance, and to those outside of the South it means those southern candidates who were "moderate or progressive" on the race/segregation issue. As this type of voting behavior continued, the diversification inherent in it increased, as shown in the 1954 Georgia gubernatorial election. Again, this is clearly an empirical example of sophistication on the part of the African American political neophyte as conceptualized by Woodward.

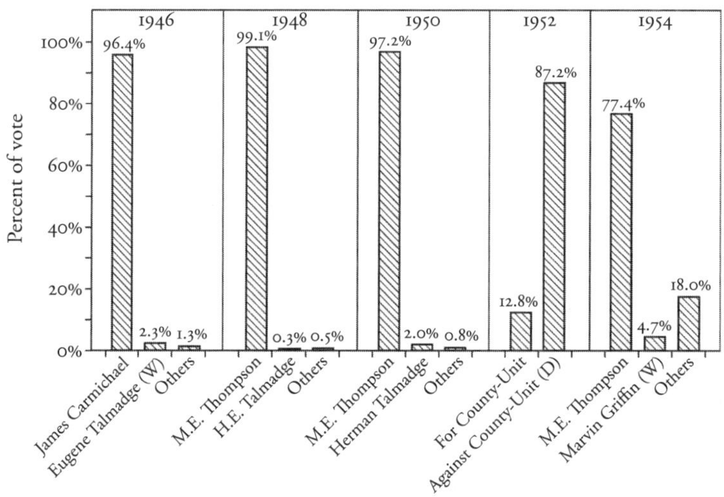

FIG. 7.6. After *Smith v. Allwright:* Voting behavior of African American political neophytes in Georgia, 1946–1954. *Source:* Adapted from Hanes Walton Jr., "Black Voting Behavior in the Segregation Era: 1944–1964," in *Black Politics and Black Political Behavior: A Linkage. Analysis,* ed. Hanes Walton Jr. (Westport, CT: Praeger, 1994), 125–26.

In addition to the statewide voting trends and patterns, there is city-level voting data for Macon, Georgia,[37] for nine elections after 1944, for both voter registration and voting results. Table 7.5 displays the actual number of African American political neophytes who registered to vote there and indicates how stable this number remained over these nine elections. The median percentage is 14, while the mean is 14.3 percent, and the range runs from 8 percent in 1962 to a high of 20 percent in 1948.

TABLE 7.5. After *Smith v. Allwright:* Voter registration of African American political neophytes in Macon, Georgia

Year	*Reported number of black voters*	*Black voters as % of total electorate*
1948	3,749	20
1950	2,154	13
1952	2,991	14
1954	2,813	16
1956	1,570	13
1958	3,372	15
1960	2,911	14
1962	594	8
1964	5,311	16
Mean	2,829	14.3
Median	2,911	14

Source: Adapted from Hanes Walton Jr., "Black Voting Behavior in the Segregation Era: 1944–1964," in *Black Politics and Black Political Behavior: A Linkage Analysis,* ed. Hanes Walton Jr. (Westport, CT: Praeger, 1994), 131.

Moving from voter registration to actual voting behavior, as shown in table 7.6, one finds that African Americans in Macon voted strongly against the Talmadge faction and the candidates of its political machine. Instead, they voted for candidates who were associated neither with the Talmadge faction nor with any identifiable opposition to it during these nine elections.[38] Again, one sees in the actual data the voter diversity and the voters' support for a wide range of candidates and issues.

Table 7.6 also reveals the voting behavior of these neophytes in presidential elections. Their support for the Democratic Party rose in the 1948 and 1952 elections but then declined abruptly in 1956 and switched to the Republican Party. This temporary switch to the Republican Party and candidate Dwight D. Eisenhower is another empirical example of the political sophistication among the African American political neophytes. In the 1956 presidential election, African Americans broke with a long tradition that went back to the 1936 presidential election, when they realigned with the Democratic Party. Thus, when they shifted their support to the Republicans in this election there were few positive factors that generated their temporary realignment. One of the main factors was that Governor Adlai Stevenson became even more vocal in his support of the South than he had been in the 1952 election, even though he had a white southerner, Senator John Sparkman of Alabama, as his vice-presidential candidate. In 1956, he let the Democratic National Convention choose his running mate, another southerner, Estes Kefauver of Tennessee. The difference this time was that Senator Kefauver was an outspoken liberal. Yet, it was Stevenson's conservatism on race that defined the ticket, and not Kefauver's liberalism. The second main factor was the endorsement of Eisenhower by African American Democratic congressman Adam Clayton Powell of Harlem. In addition, President Eisenhower had desegregated the Armed Services and promised more efforts for civil rights. Using these political cues, the Republican Party landslide brought the African American electorate into its winning coalition. Yet, support immediately switched back in 1960, when Democratic presidential candidate Senator John Kennedy had his brother Robert Kennedy call Mrs. Coretta Scott King and offer to help get her husband out of his heavy jail sentence. African Americans in Macon realigned their voting behavior, as did other African Americans in the state and elsewhere in the nation.[39] Once again African American neophytes showed that they could vote in a sophisticated manner.

TABLE 7.6. After *Smith v. Allwright:* African American voting behavior in Macon, Georgia

GUBERNATORIAL ELECTIONS						
	Talmadge faction		Anti-Talmadge faction		Other	
Year	*Number*	*%*	*Number*	*%*	*Number*	*%*
1948	15	0.4	3,670	97.9	64	1.7
1952	31	1.4	2,114	98.1	9	0.4
1954	58	2.1	2,220	78.7	543	19.2
1958	86	3.0	2,701	92.8	124	4.3
1962	51	1.0	5,146	96.9	114	2.1

TABLE 7.6. (*continued*)

PRESIDENTIAL ELECTIONS

	Democratic Party		Republican Party		Progressive Party		States' Rights Party	
Year	*Number*	%	*Number*	%	*Number*	%	*Number*	%
1948	1,828	61.9	958	32.4	160	5.4	8	0.3
1952	1,754	85.6	295	14.4	NR		NR	
1956	1,224	36.3	2,148	63.7	NR		NR	
1960	2,351	63.4	1,355	36.6	NR		NR	

REFERENDUM ELECTIONS

		"For" Vote		"Against" Vote	
Year	*Issue*	*Number*	%	*Number*	%
1952	County-Unit Amendment	113	3.8	2,878	96.2
1954	School Amendment	192	12.2	1,378	87.8
1960	Free or pledged electors	349	58.8	245	41.2

Source: Adapted from Hanes Walton Jr., "Black Voting Behavior in the Segregation Era: 1944–1964," in *Black Politics and Black Political Behavior: A Linkage Analysis,* ed. Hanes Walton Jr. (Westport, CT: Praeger, 1994), 132. Calculations by the authors.

Note: NR = not reported.

Finally, there are the three referendum votes. In this form of direct local-level voting, one can see that the Macon vote, at least on the County Unit Amendment, is similar to the statewide result that appears in table 7.4. On the other two referenda, these political neophytes voted specifically for issues that they perceived to be in their group interest, but they also offered their support for issues that some would not necessarily agree were in their best interest. Again, there was unmistakable diversity in voting.

Overall, data from the southern states. including Georgia, the state with the largest increase in political neophytes, supports the insights and contentions about the African American voter set forth by Woodward in his book. The events came long after Reconstruction and hold for his findings about that era. This leads us to analyze a third period with an increase in African American political neophytes, the 2008 presidential election, simply because this was a moment when all American voters, including African Americans, had their first opportunity to vote for an African American presidential candidate nominated by a major political party.[40]

Unlike the African American political neophytes of the Reconstruction and the post-Reconstruction period, this group that emerged after the white primary destruction had had numerous electoral successes throughout the northern, midwestern, and western states, as well as a few in the South. By this time there were African American congressmen, William Dawson from Chicago and Adam Clayton Powell from New York, as well as African American state legislators (both women and men) and city councilpersons. Behind these individuals, there had been a long historical struggle throughout the South to destroy the white primaries. Voter activism was and had been rising. And ever present was white opposition.

WOODWARD'S POLITICAL NEOPHYTES IN THE 2008 PRESIDENTIAL ELECTIONS: PRIMARY AND GENERAL

It all came together in the Iowa Democratic Caucus on January 3, 2008, where Senator Obama's stunning victory in Iowa sent a message to the African American electorate the likes of which had never been seen before. First, the victory demonstrated that Senator Obama was electable. Next, it solidified the support of the African American voter for him. Finally, and perhaps most importantly, it mobilized the African American community for him. Journalists Chuck Todd and Sheldon Gawiser captured the moment with their comment, "When African-Americans saw Obama win that very white state of Iowa, it sent the message that maybe their vote wouldn't be wasted on the young rising star of the Democratic Party."[41] The Iowa victory allowed Senator Obama to win South Carolina by a landslide, which further spurred the support of African American voters, especially in the southern primaries, all of which enabled him to win those states. He won some of them by such margins that they generated more delegates for him than for Senator Hillary Clinton. These margins were a result of the proportional rule developed by the Democratic National Committee in order to allocate delegates to both winners and losers of the primaries and caucuses.[42] In fact, because of the numbers and the self-mobilization of the African American voters, Clinton was able to win only the Arkansas, Tennessee, and Texas primaries (but not the Texas Caucus), while Obama swept the other southern states.

Figure 7.7 analyzes the voting percentages in all of the African American majority counties in the southern states. Only Texas had no such counties. In the other ten southern states, the number of such counties ranged from one in both Florida and Tennessee to twenty-five in Mississippi, for a total of ninety-one. The figure demonstrates that in these counties there was voter diversification. The political neophytes voted for several different candidates in the Democratic presidential primaries. Such voting factors were found in 1976 at the regional level and in Georgia at the state level, and they simply endured up to the 2008 primaries. In addition, the percentages in each of the ten states were greater for Senator Obama than for Senator Clinton or for the other candidates. Even in Arkansas, where Clinton had the advantage of being a native daughter, the political neophytes clearly voted for the African American.

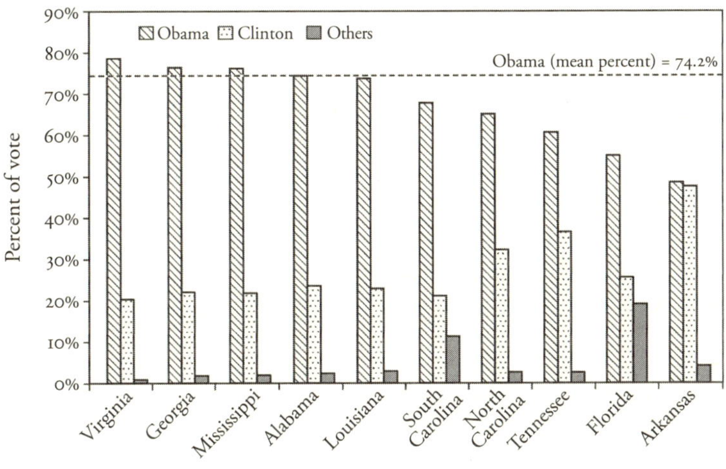

FIG. 7.7. Percent of the 2008 Democratic Party primary vote in black majority counties of the South

The overall and mean percentage of the vote in these counties for Obama is 74.2 percent. Counties in three states exceeded that level. Black majority counties in nine of the ten states gave more than 50 percent of their votes to Obama in the Democratic primaries, thus playing a major role in aiding his victory.

Moving from the party primary elections to the general election, figure 7.8 provides voting behavior in these same counties for Democrat Obama, Republican John McCain, and a host of third-party presidential nominees. Again there is diversity of voting, albeit a clear pattern of support for Obama, less than majorities in support of McCain, and small percentages for the third-party nominees, particularly in Louisiana and Arkansas. The mean county vote for Obama stands at 71.8 percent, and counties in all ten of the states show support above 60 percent. Nevertheless, McCain won eight of these states, while Obama won three: Florida, North Carolina, and Virginia. The fact that only one of these three states as shown by figure 7.8 was above the mean for Obama suggests that perhaps a biracial electorate helped him to win in Florida and North Carolina. Thus, in at least three states, the African American vote provided the balance of power in Obama's victory. The descendants of the freed slaves proved crucial in the elections of white southern Democratic presidents, first Carter and Clinton, and now a black Democratic president, Obama.

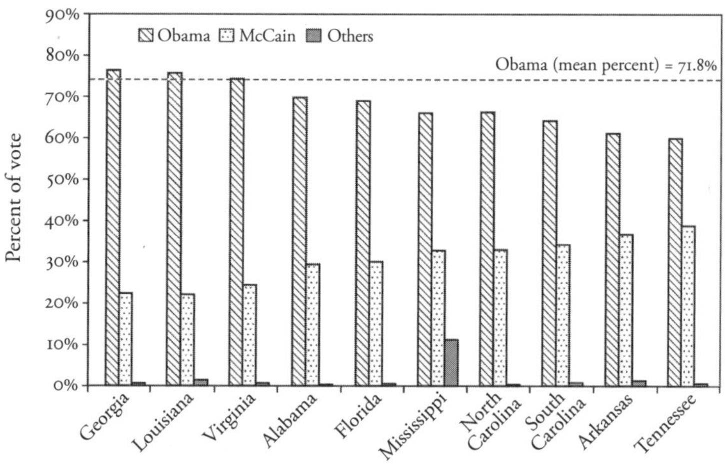

FIG. 7.8. Percent of the 2008 presidential election vote in black majority counties of the South

In 2008 the African American political neophytes experienced a historic event, the first chance to literally help *nominate* the first African American of a major political party for president. Secondly, they had the first chance to *elect* the first African American president. Having long been beneficiaries of a voting rights struggle that began in Colonial America and continued until the present time, the political neophytes in this time frame had numerous factors both internally and externally to help them become sophisticated veteran voters. Examples abound everywhere, in contrast to the first and second periods under analysis here.

THE RELEVANCE OF C. VANN WOODWARD FOR THE FUTURE: THE COMING OF THE THIRD RECONSTRUCTION

C. Vann Woodward, as we have seen, posited a viable, thoughtful, and penetrating intellectual stream on the enfranchisement of freed slaves and their descendants in the South and traced this ever-evolving journey (in terms of both progress and setbacks) through different periods of southern and greater American history. In this case, the journey was from the Reconstruction era, the Populist period, and the civil rights movement through the maturation of the Second Reconstruction and its beneficiaries, that is, the rise of southern black elected officials and southern presidents and vice presidents. Of the latter transformation, Woodward writes: "All three leading candidates for President in the election of 1992 laid claim to the prize by personal identification with the South in one degree or another." He adds that the winning ticket of Clinton-Gore, both men being from the South, became historic and rare simply because no such presidential ticket had existed since the 1828 ticket of Andrew Jackson and John C. Calhoun of Tennessee and South Carolina, respectively.[43]

Before describing the three southern candidates from the region in 1992 (Bill Clinton, Al Gore, and incumbent Republican president George H. W. Bush), Woodward noted the victory in 1976 of President Jimmy Carter of Georgia. Had Woodward been living, no doubt in 2000 he would have noted Republican president George W. Bush's victory over another southerner, former vice president Al Gore.

Woodward did discuss in chapter 11 another beneficiary of the transformation taking place in the South during the Second Reconstruction, the region's one-party system. According to Woodward, white southerners realigned from the Democratic Party to the Republican Party while the southern African American electorate shifted from the party of Lincoln to the white-supremacy party of George Wallace of Alabama and Senator

Richard Russell of Georgia. And in this dual realignment in the region, the South became the most Republican of all of the regions in the nation and a major prize in presidential elections.[44]

In his perceptive analysis of the transformation of the South's party system, Woodward notes that "with the exception of Jimmy Carter's victory in 1976, the Republicans carried all or almost all the South's electoral votes from 1972 through the election of 1988."[45] He could have added that the party carried the electoral votes of seven states in 1992 and 1996 due to the presence of two Democratic native-son southerners at the top of the presidential ticket but rebounded with a Republican native son at the top of the presidential ticket who won all of the region's electoral votes in 2000 and 2004.[46] It is in these remarkable findings and insights about the manner in which the Second Reconstruction transformed not only political representation in the region but also the party system itself, from a one-party Democratic hegemonic region to an essentially one-party Republican hegemonic region, at least at the presidential level, that Woodward's intellectual stream laid claim to the future, the coming of the Third Reconstruction. And in each succeeding Reconstruction period, there were a greater number of factors shaping the sophistication of the African American electorate.

In his "Postscript, April, 1968" to chapter 8, "What Happened to the Civil Rights Movement," Woodward forecasts the coming of the Third Reconstruction. He writes of "the tragic loss of Martin Luther King. . . . as young as he was at the time of his death, King was still more identified with the Second Reconstruction, which had largely run its course, than he had yet come to be with the Third Reconstruction, which was struggling to be born."[47] Although he does not precisely define his concept of the future "Third Reconstruction," he implies that by then the descendants of the enfranchised freed slaves would be players and undertake a significant role in the American democratic system. He further predicts that the transformation of the South's party system would be a major feature in the Third Reconstruction, given the differences in the partisanship of the two racial groups in the region. One sees some of this in the 2000 presidential election's outcome in Florida, particularly the role played by felony disenfranchisement.[48]

Political scientist Richard Valley tells us how important Woodward's conceptualization of the Second Reconstruction was and is for the discipline, noting that he first used the term in 1957. A rising number of political scientists have used it to explain voting rights and governmental intervention on behalf of these rights in the recent historical period and currently, because of the distinct similarities between these different periods of time.[49] An understanding of the importance and potential of Woodward's initial concept of the Second Reconstruction speaks volumes about the possibilities of his more recent concept, the Third Reconstruction.

Woodward's closing remarks about the Second Reconstruction forecast the future coming of the Third Reconstruction period. He concludes by saying that it was the rise and evolution of the African American political neophyte that eventually undercut the white southerners' long tradition of obsession with race and their "fortress mentality of white supremacy" and caused them to consider other possibilities in their own genial culture.[50]

Maybe all of this will happen in the Third Reconstruction. One thing scholars will learn from this empirical analysis of African American political neophytes is that, at least at the voting and political participation levels in three different periods in the American political experience, they did not "discredit both the experiment itself and the democratic faith in general." We can conclude with the words of C. Vann Woodward: "No red glow of anarchy lit up the southern horizon as a consequence of the [Reconstruction] revolution, and the enfranchised freedmen did not prove the unleashed beast of federalist imagination."[51] If the past is any guide to the future, the Third Reconstruction will not see the complete discrediting of the experiment or the democratic faith.

NOTES

1. C. Vann Woodward, *The Burden of Southern History,* updated 3rd ed. (Baton Rouge: Louisiana State University Press, 2008), 100.

2. John Kingdom, *America the Unusual* (New York: St. Martin's / Worth, 1999); Seymour Martin Lipset, *American Exceptionalism: A Double-Edged Sword* (New York: W. W. Norton, 1996); and Bryon Shafer, ed., *Is America Different? A New Look at American Exceptionalism* (New York: Oxford University Press, 1991).

3. Woodward, *The Burden of Southern History* (2008), 100.

4. Alexander Keyssar, *The Right to Vote: The Contested History of Democracy in the United States* (New York: Basic Books, 2000), 5.

5. Ibid., 9, 15.

6. Ibid., 15.

7. Ibid., 21, 22.

8. See Alexander Hamilton, James Madison, and John Jay, *The Federalist* (New York: Barnes and Noble Classics, 2006), 489.

9. Keyssar, *The Right to Vote,* 24, 23.

10. Christopher Malone, *Between Freedom and Bondage: Race, Party, and Voting Rights in the Antebellum North* (New York: Routledge, 2008), 4, and chaps. 2 and 3, which focus in detail on New York and Pennsylvania, respectively.

11. Keyssar, *The Right to Vote,* 29.

12. See the National Equal Rights League, *Proceedings of the First Annual Meeting of the National Equal Rights League* (Philadelphia: E. C. Markley, 1865). Heretofore this rare volume has not surfaced in the sundry studies of the Negro conventions.

13. William Gillette, *The Right to Vote: Politics and the Passage of the Fifteenth Amendment* (Baltimore: Johns Hopkins University Press, 1969), 25–26.

14. Ibid., 26–27. For a detailed discussion of the restrictive and suppressive nature of the "Black Codes," see James McPherson, *Ordeal by Fire: The Civil War and Reconstruction* (New York: Alfred Knopf, 1982), 511–12.

15. Gillette, *The Right to Vote,* 27.

16. Ibid., 29–31, quotations on 30 and 31.

17. Kingdom, *America the Unusual,* 84.

18. McPherson, *Ordeal by Fire,* 524.

19. C. Vann Woodward, *The Burden of Southern History* (Baton Rouge: Louisiana State University Press, 1968), 89.

20. Ibid., 100.

21. Ibid., 98, 99.

22. Ibid., 99–100.

23. Ibid., 100.

24. Ibid., 101 (quotation), 103.

25. Ibid., 103.

26. Ibid., 256–59.

27. For more historical background information on this political activity, see Steven Hahn, *A Nation under Our Feet: Black Political Struggles in the Rural South from Slavery to the Great Migration* (Cambridge, MA: Harvard University Press, 2003), 178–211, 408.

28. Woodward, *The Burden of Southern History* (1968), 98.

29. Michael Perman, *Struggle for Mastery: Disfranchisement in the South, 1888–1908* (Chapel Hill: University of North Carolina Press, 2001), 101.

30. Darlene Clark Hine, *Black Victory: The Rise and Fall of the White Primary in Texas,* new ed. (Columbia: University of Missouri Press, 2003), 249 (quotation), 254.

31. Charles L. Zelden, *The Battle for the Black Ballot: Smith v. Allwright and the Defeat of the Texas All-White Primary* (Lawrence: University Press of Kansas, 2004), 131.

32. Steven Lawson, *Black Ballots: Voting Rights in the South, 1944–1969* (New York: Columbia University Press, 1976), 53.

33. Woodward, *The Burden of Southern History* (1968), 5.

34. Hanes Walton Jr., *Black Political Parties* (New York: Free Press, 1972), 69–77.

35. Joseph Bernd describes how he visited numerous Georgia counties and personally collected voter registration and voting data for African Americans. The data in many instances was collected and kept separate from the white data and was sometimes reported separately

shortly after these elections occurred. See his *Grass Roots Politics in Georgia* (Atlanta: Emory University Research Committee, 1960). Later the African American data was extensive analyzed in Hanes Walton Jr., "Black Voting Behavior in the Segregation Era: 1944–1964," in *Black Politics and Black Political Behavior: A Linkage Analysis,* ed. Hanes Walton Jr. (Westport, CT: Praeger, 1994), 115–34.

36. Paul Lewinson, *Race, Class, and Party: A History of Negro Suffrage and White Politics in the South* (New York: Oxford University Press, 1932), 218, table 3.

37. While a professor of history at the University of Georgia, Numan V. Bartley collected similar African American voter registration and voting data from the city of Macon, Georgia, for nine elections from 1948 to 1964 for his book *From Thurmond to Wallace: Political Tendencies in Georgia* (Baltimore: John Hopkins University Press, 1970). He shared with Walton his complete data files. See Walton, *Black Politics,* 131–32.

38. V. O. Key Jr., *Southern Politics in State and Nation,* new ed. (Knoxville: University of Tennessee Press, 1984), 107–12, for a complete discussion of the Talmadge faction in Georgia politics.

39. Ibid. See also Donald Deskins Jr., Hanes Walton Jr., and Sherman C. Puckett, *Presidential Elections, 1789–2008: County, State, and National Mapping of Election Data* (Ann Arbor: University of Michigan Press, 2010), chap. 58.

40. Hanes Walton Jr., Josephine A. V. Allen, Sherman C. Puckett, and Donald R. Deskins Jr., "Black Politicians: Paving the Way," in *African Americans and the Presidency: The Road to the White House,* ed. Bruce Glasrud and Cary Wintz (New York: Routledge, 2010), 167–86.

41. Chuck Todd and Sheldon Gawiser, *How Barack Obama Won* (New York: Vintage Books, 2009), 14.

42. Hanes Walton Jr., Josephine A. V. Allen, Sherman C. Puckett, and Donald R. Deskins Jr., "Barack Obama: The Making of the President, 2008," *Black Collegian,* January 2009, 7–14; and their "The Red and Blue State Divide in Black and White: The Historic 2008 Election of President Barack Obama," *Black Scholar* 38 (Winter 2008): 19–31.

43. Woodward, *The Burden of Southern History* (1968), 257.

44. Ibid., 256–57.

45. Ibid., 256.

46. On the role and function of the southern native-son variable in presidential politics, see Hanes Walton Jr., *The Native-Son Presidential Candidate: The Carter Vote in Georgia* (New York: Praeger, 1992); Hanes Walton Jr., *Reelection: William Jefferson Clinton as a Native-Son Presidential Candidate* (New York: Columbia University Press, 2000); and Hanes Walton Jr., *Remaking the Democratic Party: Lyndon Baines Johnson as a Native-Son Presidential Candidate* (Ann Arbor: University of Michigan Press, 2012).

47. Woodward, *The Burden of Southern History* (1968), 186.

48. See U.S. Commission on Civil Rights, *Voting Irregularities in Florida during the 2000 Presidential Election* (Washington, DC: Government Printing Office, 2001); and the companion volume, *Voting Irregularities in Florida during the 2000 Presidential Election: Appendix* (Washington, DC: Government Printing Office, 2001). See also Hanes Walton Jr. and Simone Greene, "Voting Rights and the Million Man March: The Problem of the Restoration

of Voting Rights for Ex-Convicts," *African American Research Perspectives* 3 (Winter 1997): 68–74.

49. Richard Valley, *The Two Reconstructions: The Struggle for Black Enfranchisement* (Chicago: University of Chicago Press, 2004), 251n1, preface.

50. Woodward, *The Burden of Southern History* (1968), 264.

51. Ibid., 100. For more on Woodward's Third Reconstruction concept, see Hanes Walton Jr., Josephine A. V. Allen, Sherman C. Puckett, and Donald R. Deskins Jr., "Beyond the Second Reconstruction: C. Vann Woodward's Concept of the Third Reconstruction in the South," *American Review of Politics* 32 (Spring 2011): 105–30.

CONTRIBUTORS

JOSEPHINE A. V. ALLEN is professor emerita of policy analysis and management at Cornell University and professor of social welfare policy in the College of Community and Public Affairs at Binghamton University. She holds a Ph.D. in political science and social welfare administration and policy from the University of Michigan.

CHARLES S. BULLOCK III holds the Richard B. Russell Chair in Political Science and is Josiah Meigs Distinguished Teaching Professor at the University of Georgia. He has been at the University of Georgia since 1968 with the exception of one year when he served as legislative assistant to Congressman Bill Stuckey and two years when he was professor of political science at the University of Houston. In 2005 and 2009, he was a senior fellow at Oxford University's Rothermere American Institute. Bullock is author, coauthor, or coeditor of twenty-five books and more than 150 articles. He has published in major political science, public administration, and education journals. His most recent books are *The New Politics of the Old South* (Rowman and Littlefield, 2009), 4th edition, coedited with Mark Rozell; *The Triumph of Voting Rights in the South* (University of Oklahoma Press, 2009), coauthored with Keith Gaddie; and *Georgia Politics in a State of Change* (Longman, 2009), also written with Keith Gaddie. *Runoff Elections in the United States* (University of North Carolina Press, 1992), a comprehensive analysis of runoff elections that Bullock coauthored with Loch Johnson, won the V. O. Key Award for the best book on southern politics.

JAMES C. COBB is the B. Phinizy Spalding Distinguished Professor of History at the University of Georgia. A former president of the Southern Historical Association, Cobb has written widely on the interaction between economy, society, and culture in the American South. His books include *The Selling of the South: The Southern Crusade for Industrial Development, 1936–1990*

(University of Illinois Press, 1993), *The Most Southern Place on Earth: The Mississippi Delta and the Roots of Regional Identity* (Oxford University Press, 1992), and *Away Down South: A History of Southern Identity* (Oxford University Press, 2006). His most recent book, *The South and America since World War II,* was published by Oxford University Press in 2010.

DONALD R. DESKINS JR. is professor emeritus of sociology at the University of Michigan. He is a coauthor of *Presidential Elections 1789–2008: County, State, and National Mapping of Election Data* and the forthcoming *African American Electorate: A Statistical History.*

LEIGH ANNE DUCK is associate professor of English at the University of Mississippi, where her research focuses on the literature and culture of the modern and contemporary United States and South Africa. She is interested in modernism, constructions of race and nation, and theories concerning space, narrative, and memory. She has published essays on the work of Zora Neale Hurston and William Faulkner, as well as on the study of "postplantation" literatures and representations of the South in film, in such journals as the *Journal of American Folklore, American Literary History,* and *American Literature.* Her book *The Nation's Region: Southern Modernism, Segregation, and U.S. Nationalism* was published by the University of Georgia Press in 2006. She has also served as a visiting associate professor at the University of Copenhagen.

ANGIE MAXWELL is the Diane D. Blair Professor of Southern Studies and an assistant professor of political science at the University of Arkansas, Fayetteville. She received her Ph.D. in American Studies from the University of Texas. She is the coeditor of *Unlocking V. O. Key, Jr.: Southern Politics for the Twenty-First Century* (University of Arkansas Press, 2011). Her recent publications have appeared in *Presidential Studies Quarterly, Southern Quarterly,* and the *Journal of Black Studies.* She is also under contract with the University of Tennessee Press to edit a volume of journalist James Agee's notebooks, and she is writing a new critical introduction to a reprint of Ralph McGill's Pulitzer Prize–winning civil rights movement editorials, *A Church, a School,* to be published by the University of South Carolina Press in 2012. She is currently revising her book manuscript entitled

"Why Do They Live There? How the White Southern Inferiority Complex Shaped Modern America." She is a cofounder of the Blair-Rockefeller Poll, an election-year survey that reveals national and regional voting behavior and preferences.

ROBERT C. MCMATH is dean of the Honors College and professor of history at the University of Arkansas. Between 1972 and 2005, McMath taught history at Georgia Tech and served in administrative posts ranging from chair of the History Department to vice provost. McMath has also served as the interim provost of the University of Arkansas. He is the author or coauthor of numerous articles and seven books on American history. He is best known among historians for his work on protest movements and politics in the United States and Canada, most notably his landmark work *American Populism* (Hill and Wang, 1990). Additionally, McMath was the lead author of *Engineering the New South: Georgia Tech, 1885–1985* (University of Georgia Press, 1985), which is still regarded as a model study of technological universities.

WAYNE PARENT is the Russell B. Long Professor of Political Science at Louisiana State University and has recently served as both department chair and associate dean of the College of Arts and Sciences. His research focus is on southern politics, elections, and Louisiana politics. He is a frequent commentator on national and Louisiana politics for the local, state, and national media. Parent's recent and notable publications include *Inside the Carnival: Unmasking Louisiana Politics* (Louisiana State University Press, 2006); "Louisiana's Stormy Politics," in the *Political Encyclopedia of U.S. States and Regions* (CQ Press, 2008); and *Blacks in the American Political System* (University of Florida Press, 1995). A graduate of Louisiana State University, he received his Ph.D. from Indiana University, Bloomington.

SHERMAN C. PUCKETT is a Ph.D. graduate of the University of Michigan in urban and regional planning. He was an appointee in the administration of Mayor Coleman Young in Detroit and is the retired director of geographic information systems in Wayne County, Michigan. He is also a coauthor of *Presidential Elections 1789–2008* and the pending *African American Electorate: A Statistical History.*

TODD SHIELDS is dean of the Graduate School and of international education at the University of Arkansas, where he is also a professor in the Department of Political Science and the director of the Diane D. Blair Center of Southern Politics and Society. His research interests lie broadly in American campaigns and elections, although he also conducts research in southern politics and research methods. He is the author or coauthor of dozens of articles and book chapters. His first book, *Money Matters: The Effects of Campaign Finance Reform on Congressional Elections* (Rowman and Littlefield, 1999), examined the likely effects of campaign finance reform on congressional elections. He is also coeditor of *The Clinton Riddle: Perspectives of the 42nd President* (University of Arkansas Press, 2004) and of *New Voices in the Old South: How Women and Minorities Influence Southern Politics* (Florida Institute of Government, 2008). His most recent book, *The Persuadable Voter: Wedge Issues in Presidential Campaigns* (Princeton University Press, 2008), coauthored with Sunshine Hillygus, won the 2009 Robert E. Lane Award for best book in political psychology. He is the coeditor of *Unlocking V. O. Key, Jr.: Southern Politics for the Twenty-First Century* (University of Arkansas Press, 2011). Shields has also served as chair of the Department of Political Science and as interim academic dean at the Clinton School of Public Service. He is a cofounder of the Blair-Rockefeller Poll, an election-year survey that reveals national and regional voting behavior and preferences.

HANES WALTON JR. is professor of political science and research scientist in the Institute for Social Research at the University of Michigan. He is a native of Athens, Georgia, and received his education at Morehouse College in Atlanta. His graduate work was undertaken at Atlanta University and Howard University, where he obtained a Ph.D. in government. Since earning his doctorate, Walton has held an American Political Science Congressional Fellowship, a Ford Foundation Fellowship, a Rockefeller Fellowship, and a Guggenheim Fellowship. He belongs to the Phi Beta Kappa, the Pi Sigma Alpha, and the Alpha Kappa Mu honorary societies. Walton's principal areas of interest are African American politics, presidential elections, and public policy. His research has appeared in the *American Journal of Political Science,* the *Journal of Politics,* the *Journal of Negro History,* and the *DuBois Review.* His latest published works include *Letters to President Obama* (Skyhorse, 2009) and *Presidential Elections, 1789–2008: County,*

State, and National Mapping of Election Data (University of Michigan Press, 2010). His current book explores and analyzes the manner in which the political context variable influences the political behavior of the African American community.

JEANNIE WHAYNE is professor of history at the University of Arkansas and adjunct curator of American history at Crystal Bridges Museum of American Art in Bentonville, Arkansas. She received her Ph.D. from the University of California, San Diego, in 1989. Whayne has published over a dozen articles and essays on Arkansas, African American, and southern history. She has coedited, authored, or coauthored nine books, including *A Whole Country in Commotion: The Louisiana Purchase and the American Southwest* (University of Arkansas Press, 2005) and *The Clinton Riddle: Perspectives on the 42nd President* (University of Arkansas Press, 2004). She is a two-time recipient of the Arkansas Library Association's Arkansiana Award for her book *Arkansas: A Narrative History* (University of Arkansas Press, 2002), coauthored with Thomas DeBlack, George Sabo, and Morris Arnold, and for *A New Plantation South: Land, Labor, and Federal Favor in Twentieth Century Arkansas* (University of Virginia Press, 1996). Her latest book, *Delta Empire: Lee Wilson and the Transformation of Agriculture in the New South,* was published in 2011 by Louisiana State University Press. She has been named a master teacher at the University of Arkansas and was elected to the university's Teaching Academy. In 2008 the Organization of American Historians selected her as a distinguished lecturer, and the Agricultural History Society recently selected her as a "Fellow of the Society" in honor of her scholarly achievements and her service to agricultural history. She has been a fellow at the Smithsonian Institution and at the Carter Woodson Institute at the University of Virginia. She is past president of the Conference of Historical Journals and a former editor of the *Arkansas Historical Quarterly.*

PATRICK G. WILLIAMS is associate professor of history at the University of Arkansas, Fayetteville. He received his B.A. from the University of Texas and his Ph.D. from Columbia University. He edits the *Arkansas Historical Quarterly* and is the author of *Beyond Redemption: Texas Democrats after Reconstruction* (Texas A&M University Press, 2007). He has published articles in the *Journal of Southern History* and the *Southwestern Historical Quarterly* and coedited *A Whole Country in Commotion: The Louisiana Purchase and the American Southwest* (University of Arkansas Press, 2005) with S. Charles Bolton and Jeannie Whayne. Williams has won the Fulbright College's Master Teacher Award, and in 2009 he was inducted into the University of Arkansas Teaching Academy.

INDEX

Abolitionism, 18
Adams, Henry, 40
Adams, John, 159
Adorno, Theodor, 92
Afghanistan, 88
African American literature, 31, 35, 42, 44–47
African Americans: current challenges of, 150; landmarks of history of, 45; in "Lost Cause" mythology, 41; as members of U.S. Congress, 141, 143–46, 150, 169, 178, 180; in middle class, 133; political participation of, 131–50, 153–85; population of, residing in South, 149; poverty of, in rural areas, 47; and school integration, ix, 6, 10, 15, 16, 20, 25–26; and state constitutional conventions during Reconstruction, 165; as state legislators, 132, 140–43, 145–46, 150; Woodward's "The Search for Southern Identity" on, 43–44. *See also* Civil rights movement; Obama, Barack; Segregation and racial discrimination; Voting; Voting Rights Act (VRA)
Afro-American studies programs, 22, 23
Afrocentrism, 22–23, 24
Age of Reform, The (Hofstadter), 81–82, 93–98, 111*n*36, 111*n*39, 111*n*48, 112*n*54
Agrarians, 31, 41, 42, 53, 56, 69, 76
Agricultural legislation, 124
Alabama: African American legislators in, 143; African American members of U.S. Congress from, 144; African American population in, 75; agrarian rural lifestyle of, 76; civil rights movement in, 10, 15, 19, 20; disenfranchisement of African Americans in, 147; Folsom in, 66, 73; impact of racial identity on political identity in, 75; industrialization in, 119; memory of Jefferson Davis in, 54; vote for 1964 presidential election in, 66; vote for 2008 presidential election in, 71–76, 78, 181–82; voter registration and turnout of African Americans in, 134–37, 150, 171–73; Wallace as governor of, 137
Alexander, Will, viii
Allen, Josephine A. V., xi, 153–89
Allen v. State Board of Education, 134
American Historical Association, ix, 36–37
American identity. *See* National identity
American Scholar, 94, 111*n*48
Antebellum America, 156–57. *See also* Slavery
Anti-Semitism, 92, 93, 96–97, 110*n*34, 112*n*54, 114*n*71
Aristotle, 159, 160
Arizona, 133
Arkansas: Diane Divers Blair in, xv–xvii; civil rights movement in, 16; Clinton's primary win in, 180; Covenant, the Sword, and the Arm of the Lord (CSA) in, 114*n*71; Democratic Party in, 121; Winthrop Rockefeller in, viii, xvii–xviii; Southern Tenant Farmers' Union in, 85; vote for 2008 presidential election in, 72, 127, 181–82; voter registration and turnout of African Americans in, 135–37, 171–73; Woodward from, vii, viii, 7, 95
Articles of Confederation, 156
Aryan Nation, 114*n*71

Asian Americans, 145, 150
Ayers, Edward L., 56
Baker v. Carr, 140
Baldwin, James, 24
Bartels, Larry, 67–68, 70, 71
Bartley, Numan V., 187*n*37
Battle for Leyte Gulf, The (Woodward), 6
Beale, Howard, 10, 13
Beard, Charles A., 5, 94
Beck, Glen, 105, 114*n*73
Bell, Daniel, 80, 91–92
Bernd, Joseph, 186–87*n*35
Bickerstaff, Steve, 151*n*18
Billings, Dwight, 119
Black, Earl and Merle, 68
Black Codes, 157
Black power and racial separatism, 2, 21–26
Blacks. *See* African Americans
Blair, Diane Divers, xv–xvii
Blum, John Morton, 3
Boggs, Lindy, 143
Bonner, Robert E., 59*n*40
Boorstin, Daniel, 27
Brinkley, Alan, 93
Brooks, Cleanth, 86
Brooks, David, 89, 110*n*23
Brown, David S., 110*n*31, 111*n*39
Brown v. Board of Education, ix, 6, 10, 12, 15, 20
Brundage, W. Fitzhugh, 45, 56, 61*n*62
Brunner, Emil, 109*n*14
Bullock, Charles S., III, xi, xiii, 131–52, 189
Bunche, Ralph, 170
Burden of Southern History, The (Woodward): critique of and critical acclaim for, vii–xiii, 2, 3, 31, 154; dedication of, to Warren, 41; first edition of, 18–19, 20, 38, 117; jacket copy for, 27; on lessons of history, 31, 34; literary influences on, 35–36, 40–44; misperceptions of, by others, 31; preface of, 38, 41; publication of, 7; relationship of *The Strange Career of Jim Crow* with, 1, 2; revised editions of, x, xi, xii, 2, 21–24, 27, 32, 47, 88, 101, 132, 141, 184; sales of, 3; Woodward's concerns for misuse of content of, xii–xiii
Burden of Southern History, The (Woodward). *See also* "Irony of Southern History, The" (Woodward); "Populist Heritage and the Intellectual, The" (Woodward); "Search for Southern Identity, The" (Woodward); "Second Look at the Theme of Irony, A" (Woodward); Segregation and racial discrimination; Southern identity and distinctiveness
Bush, George H. W., 163, 183
Bush, George W., 88, 104, 163, 184
Butler, Octavia, 46

Calhoun, John C., 5, 53, 183
California, 133
Cao, Joseph, 145
Carmines, Edward, 66
Carter, Dan T., 68, 70, 71, 126
Carter, Jimmy, 54, 61*n*56, 105–6, 127, 143, 163, 182–84
Cash, W. J., 64
Cell, John, 26
Celtic population, 76, 77
Chesnut, Mary, ix, 8
China, 100
Christian Identity movement, 103
Civil Rights Act (1964), 132, 133
Civil rights movement: black-power leaders of, 21, 24; and *Brown v. Board of Education,* ix, 6, 10, 12, 15, 20; goals of, 20, 21, 24, 48; and King's assassination, 2, 21, 48, 133, 149, 184; King's leadership of, 21, 24, 26, 48; and King's praise for *The Strange Career of Jim Crow,* 19–20, 76; museum on, 61*n*62; obstacles to, 13–14; organizations involved in generally, 100; protests during, 10, 15, 16, 19, 20; and race riots, 20–21, 23, 24, 25, 132; and Second Reconstruction, 20–21, 27, 32, 47, 131–50; and social movement theory, 110*n*28; and

Third Reconstruction, 21, 48, 51; violence in, 2, 20–21, 23, 24; white backlash against, 21, 25, 48, 51; Woodward's disappointment with, xi, 2, 23–27, 48, 131–32, 134; Woodward's optimism on, 10, 15–16, 19, 20, 21. *See also* Voting; Voting Rights Act (VRA)
Civil War: causes of, 49, 54, 60*n*44, 61*n*56; Confederate veteran of, 52; defeat and humiliation of, for South, 1, 2, 18, 33, 38, 43, 63; sesquicentennial of, 49, 59–60*n*43; Woodward on significance of, 119. *See also* Confederacy
Clayton Antitrust Act, 115*n*78
Clinton, Bill, vii, 67, 163, 180, 182, 183
Clinton, Hillary, 180–81
Cobb, James C., ix–x, xiii, 1–30, 48, 117, 132, 189–90
Cohn, Deborah, 49
Cold war, 1–2, 18, 80, 81, 84, 92. *See also* McCarthyism
Collective memory, 34–35, 39, 41, 45, 52–53, 57*n*11
Collins, Bruce, 39, 50
Colonial America, 155
Color Blind Justice (Kousser), 132
Columbia University, 3, 92, 93, 110*n*31, 111*n*43, 112*n*54
Commemorative monuments and events, 45, 61*n*62
Commission on Civil Rights, U.S., 148
Communism, viii, 9, 84, 85, 111*n*43. *See also* McCarthyism; Soviet Union
Compromise of 1877, 6
Confederacy: disenfranchisement of Confederate veterans, 150, 160; and "Lost Cause" mythology, 38, 39, 41, 50, 55; monuments and memorials to, 45, 61*n*62; pensions for Confederate veterans, 124; restoration of citizenship for leaders of, 54, 60*n*53, 61*n*56; and secession, 49–50, 60*n*44, 87; Tea Party movement compared with, 50–51. *See also* Civil War
Congress of Interracial Cooperation, viii
Congress, U.S.: African American members of, 141, 143–46, 150, 169, 178, 180; Black Caucus in, 144; divisions among Republicans in 112th Congress, 104; in late nineteenth century, 146–47; Pujo Committee in, 107, 115*n*78; reading of U.S. Constitution in, 60*n*44; and Reconstruction legislation, 147, 158–60, 163, 169; restoration of Jefferson Davis's citizenship, 54. *See also* Voting Rights Act (VRA)
Conservatism, 92–93, 98, 101–4, 114*n*71, 126–27. *See also* Tea Party movement
Constitution, U.S., 49, 53, 55, 60*n*44, 115*n*78, 127, 156
Contentious politics, 98, 99, 101, 104. *See also* Social movement theory
Couch, William T., 5
Coulter, E. Merton, 7, 9
Covenant, the Sword, and the Arm of the Lord (CSA), 114*n*71
Crespino, Joseph, 34, 48
Crouter, Richard, 109*n*10
CSA. *See* Confederacy; Covenant, the Sword, and the Arm of the Lord (CSA)
Czechoslovakia, 100

Dailey, Jane, 120, 122, 123
Davis, Jefferson, 49–55, 60*n*53, 61*n*56
Dawson, William, 180
Debs, Eugene V., 5
DeLay, Tom, 144, 151*n*18
Democracy and democratic theory, 154–57, 159, 163
Democratic Party: Dixiecrats in, 54, 66, 67, 68; in 1868–1920 elections, 162–69; election fraud by, 90, 116, 121, 122; in Georgia elections from 1946–1954, 174–80; internal politics of, 119–20, 128–29*n*10; in late nineteenth century, 146–47; "New South" Democrats, 118–19; in 1960s, 102;

Democratic Party (*continued*)
Populists versus, 90, 125–26; in presidential election (2008), 180–83; in presidential elections from 1948–1960, 177–79; and racial identity in the South, 65–66, 116, 121–22; Redeemer Democrats, x–xi, xiii, 11–12, 42, 116–29; solid Democratic South, 65–66, 116; and suffrage rights after Civil War, 158; tax policy of, 116, 123–25, 130*n*19; and Voting Rights Act, 66; and white primary, 45, 65, 117, 169–74; Woodward on, 117, 120. *See also* Presidential election *headings*
Desegregation. *See* Integration
Deskins, Donald R., Jr., xi, 153–88, 190
Discrimination. *See* Segregation and racial discrimination
Disenfranchisement of African Americans. *See* Voting
Dixiecrats, 54, 66, 67, 68. *See also* Democratic Party
DOJ. *See* Justice Department, U.S.
Dole, Bob, 139
Donaldson, Susan, 42
Donnelly, Ignatius, 98
Du Bois, W. E. B., xii, 9, 41
Dubey, Madhu, 46
Duck, Leigh Anne, x, xii, 31–61, 190
Dunbar, Leslie, 132
Durr, Virginia, 15

East Germany, 100
Economic crises, 102, 104, 107, 115*n*78, 126, 146
Education: African Americans' interest in separate schools, 47; Afro-American studies programs, 22, 23; funding of, 124; integration of schools, ix, 6, 10, 15, 16, 20, 25–26; minority students in higher education, 133; and southern studies, 36, 48–49, 59*n*37; textbook controversy in Texas, 32–35, 54, 56*n*1; textbook on Populism, 114*n*73
Edwards, Laura F., 38–39
Eisenhower, Dwight D., 14, 92, 177–78
Elazar, Daniel, 65
Elkins, Stanley, 7
Ellison, Ralph, 35, 44
Emory University, viii, 3, 4
Equal Rights Amendment, 126
"Equality: The Deferred Commitment" (Woodward), 51
Espy, Mike, 143
European Southern Studies Forum, 25

"Fall of the American Adam, The" (Woodward), 57*n*5
Farmers Alliance, 90. *See also* Populism
Farrakhan, Louis, 24, 25, 26
Faulkner, William, 36, 40, 42, 43, 47
Federal Reserve Act, 115*n*78
Ferkiss, Victor C., 93
Fields, Barbara, 9
Fields, Cleo, 144
Financial crises. *See* Economic crises
Florida: African American legislators in, 142; African American members of U.S. Congress from, 144; presidential election (2000) in, 184; presidential election (2008) in, 181–82; readmission of, to Union, 164; voter registration and turnout of African Americans in, 136, 137, 171–73; and Voting Rights Act, 133, 138
Folkways uber alles doctrine, 1, 13–14, 16, 19, 42
Folsom, Big Jim, 66, 73
Foner, Eric, 120
Ford, Harold, Sr., 143
Ford, Pearl K., 127
Fox News, 105
France, 97, 110*n*34
Frank, Thomas, 67
Frankfort School, 110*n*31
Franklin, John Hope, 10, 42, 83–84, 108*n*4
Frazier, E. Franklin, 16

Free people of color. *See* African Americans; Voting
Fugitive poets, 31. *See also* Agrarians
Future of the Past, The (Woodward), 57*n*5

Garton Ash, Timothy, 113*nn*62–63
Gawiser, Sheldon, 180
Gay, Peter, 112*n*54
Georgia: African American legislators in, 140, 142, 143; African American members of U.S. Congress from, 143, 144; agrarian rural lifestyle of, 76; Jimmy Carter from, 54; civil rights museum in, 61*n*62; Confederate commemorative markers in, 60*n*44; Redeemer Democrats in, 125; redistricting in, 140; vote for 1964 presidential election in, 66; vote for 2008 presidential election in, 72, 127, 181–82; voter registration and turnout of African Americans in, 134–37, 140, 149, 150, 170, 171–80, 186–87*n*35, 187*n*37; Tom Watson in, viii, 3
Georgia Institute of Technology, viii
German Historical Institute, 24–25
Germany, 87, 96–97, 110*n*34
Gilder, George, 89
Gillette, William, 157
Glazer, Nathan, 91
Goldwater, Barry, 66
Gore, Al, 67, 183
Graf, LeRoy, 108*n*4
Great Britain, 99, 102
Greenbackers, 120
Grovey v. Townsend, 65

Hackney, Sheldon, 55
Hahn, Michael, 169
Hahn, Stephen, 26, 120
Halbwachs, Maurice, 52, 57*n*11
Hamilton, Alexander, 159
Hampton, Wade, 126–27
Harpers, 8, 132
Harris, Carl, 125
Harvey, "Coin," 98
Hatfield, Mark, 54
Health insurance, 51
Helms, Jesse, 69
Henderson, George Wylie, 44
Herndon, Angelo, viii, 9
Hicks, John D., 94, 95
Hine, Darlene Clark, 170
Hispanics. *See* Latinos
Historians: African American historians, 22, 23; and "consensus history," 118; goal of, as shaping public opinion, 2–3, 10–13, 15, 27, 51; guilt of white historians, 22–23; and literary criticism generally, 36; mission for, 48; presentism of, 81–83, 101; regional historians, 38–39, 42. *See also specific historians*
Historical consciousness, 42–43
"Historical Dimension, The" (Woodward), 40, 58*n*27
"History of the present," 81–83, 101
History of the South Series, viii–ix, 5–6, 9
Hitler, Adolf, 92
Hobsbawm, Eric, 101, 112*n*52
Hodgson, Godfrey, 109*n*12
Hofstadter, Richard: friendship between Woodward and, 94–95, 111*n*36, 111*n*43; on Populism, 80, 81–82, 91–99, 110*n*34, 111*n*48, 112*n*54, 114*n*73; on pseudo-conservatism, 92–93; Pullitzer Prize for, 111*n*36. *See also Age of Reform, The* (Hofstadter)
Holmes, Oliver Wendell, 89
Huckabee, Mike, 127
Humphrey, Hubert, 66, 137
Hurston, Zora Neale, 44
Hyman, Michael, 129–30*n*19

Ibsen, Henrik, 89
I'll Take My Stand (Agrarians), 41, 42, 56, 69, 76
Immigrants, 161
Industrialization, 17, 43, 45, 62, 63, 69, 119

Integration: of Armed Services, 178; black separatism versus, 2, 21–24; in North versus South, 21–24; of public accommodations and housing, 133; of schools, ix, 6, 10, 15, 16, 20, 25–26; of Southern Historical Association, 83–84, 108*n*4; and states' rights, 50. *See also* Civil rights movement
Iraq, 88
Irony: on backlash against civil rights movement, 47, 48; on integration in North versus South, 21–24; meaning of, 27, 86; Niebuhr on, 81, 82, 84–89, 102, 106, 109*n*8, 109*n*14; on restoration of Jefferson Davis's citizenship, 54; on slavery narratives not referenced by Woodward, 44; on southern distinctiveness, 17–18, 39, 40; on southern writers, 42, 45–46; of title of *The Burden of Southern History,* 27; usefulness of, 80, 86–87; on Vietnam War, 47, 88; Woodward's essays on, x, 1–2, 17–18, 21–22, 23, 80–81, 83–89; Woodward's ironic rhetorical style, 86
Irony of American History, The (Niebuhr), 85–86, 102, 106, 109*n*8, 109*n*14
"Irony of Southern History, The" (Woodward), x, 1–2, 17–18, 21–23, 38–39, 47, 48, 80–89, 108*n*4. *See also* "Second Look at the Theme of Irony, A" (Woodward)

Jackson, Andrew, 156, 183
Jackson, Jesse, 60*n*44, 144, 150
James, Henry, 40
Japan, 6, 87, 110*n*20
Jefferson Davis (Tate), 49–50, 53, 54
Jefferson Davis Gets His Citizenship Back (Warren), 51–54, 60*n*53
Jefferson, William, 145
Jim Crow. *See* Segregation and racial discrimination; *Strange Career of Jim Crow, The* (Woodward)
John Birch Society, 100, 105
Johns Hopkins University, ix, 3, 6, 9–10, 15
Johnson, Andrew, 157–58
Johnson, Leroy, 140
Johnson, Lyndon, 47, 65, 66, 88, 134–35, 137, 163
Johnson, Richard, 68
Johnston, Richard, 68, 70–71
Joint Center for Political and Economic Studies, 140
Jones, Gayl, 46
Jordan, Barbara, 143
Journal of Southern History, 17, 23, 120
Joyner, Charles, 48, 55
Justice Department, U.S., 139–40, 143–45, 148

Kafka, Franz, 65
Kantrowitz, Stephen, 122
Kefauver, Estes, 178
Keizer, Arlene, 46
Kennedy, John, 178
Kennedy, Paul, 59*n*38
Kennedy, Robert, 178
Kerry, John, 69, 71–72, 127
Key, V. O., Jr., vii, 11, 65, 166
Keynes, John Maynard, 123
Keyssar, Alexander, 155, 156
Kierkegaard, Soren, 65
King, Coretta Scott, 178
King, Martin Luther, Jr.: assassination of, 2, 21, 48, 133, 149, 184; imprisonment of, 178; as leader of civil rights movement, 21, 24, 26, 48; praise by, for *The Strange Career of Jim Crow,* 19–20, 76
Klarman, Michael J., 26
Klein, Kerwin, 34
Kousser, J. Morgan, 132, 146–47
Kreyling, Michael, 40–41, 45, 53

Labor movement, 110*n*27, 111*n*43, 126
Lamm, Donald, 24–25
Langston, John M., 169
Lassiter, Matthew, 34, 48, 50
Latinos, 133, 150
Lawson, Steven, 170

Lee, Robert E., 61*n*56
Legislatures. *See* Congress, U.S.; State legislatures
Leuchtenburg, William, 92
Lewinson, Paul, 173
Liberalism, 21, 50, 64–65, 82, 85, 102, 109*n*12, 109*n*14, 127. *See also* New Deal; Populism
Libertarianism, 55, 103, 105
Limbaugh, Rush, 105
Lincoln, Abraham, 53, 54, 157–58, 169
Lipset, Seymour Martin, 91, 96
Literacy test for voting, 134, 135
Lodge Force Act, 147
Logan, Rayford W., 16
Long, Huey, 66, 73
"Look Away, Look Away" (Woodward), 47, 49
"Lost Cause" mythology, 38, 39, 41, 50, 55
Louisiana: African American legislators in, 141, 142, 143, 151*n*13; African American members of U.S. Congress from, 143, 144, 145; African American population in, 75, 121; agrarian rural lifestyle of, 76; antebellum period in, 169; Cao as Congressman from, 145; Huey Long in, 66, 73; Pujo as Congressman from, 107, 115*n*78; Reconstruction in, 121, 169; vote for 2008 presidential election in, 71–76, 78, 181–82; voter registration and turnout of African Americans in, 134–37, 149, 171–73
Louisiana State University, 6
Louisiana State University Press, ix, 5, 7
Lynching, 45, 117, 170

MacDonald, Andrew. *See* Pierce, William
MacLean, Nancy, 55
Mannheim, Karl, 92
Marshall, Thurgood, ix
Marxian class analysis, 3, 92
Mary Chesnut's Civil War (Woodward), ix, 8
Max Black approach, 139–40, 142, 144
Maxwell, Angie, vii–xiii, 127, 190–91
McAdam, Doug, 101
McCain, John, 182
McCarthyism, 1, 18, 90, 91, 92, 93, 95–96, 116, 118. *See also* Cold war
McDonald, Forrest, 14–15
McDonald, Laughlin, 144
McKaine, Osceola, 172
McMath, Robert C., x, xii–xiii, 80–115, 120, 128*n*4, 191
McVey, Timothy, 114*n*71
McWhiney, Grady, 76
Mda, Zakes, 46
Meier, August, 108*n*4
Melville, Herman, 40
Memory. *See* Collective memory
Military Reconstruction Acts, 158–59, 162, 163, 169
Mississippi: African American legislators in, 141, 142, 143, 151*n*13; African American members of U.S. Congress from, 143; African American population in, 75, 121, 160; agrarian rural lifestyle of, 76; Delta Cooperative Farm in, 85; disenfranchisement of African Americans in, 147, 148; readmission of, to Union, 164; Reconstruction in, 121, 165; vote for 1964 presidential election in, 66; vote for 2008 presidential election in, 71–78, 181–82; voter registration and turnout of African Americans in, 134–37, 171–73; Richard Wright in, 44
Montgomery, Isaiah, 165
Moore, James Tice, 125
Morgan, Edmund, 3
Morgan, J. P., 107
Morgan, J. P., Jr., 107
Morrison, Toni, 46
Moynihan, Daniel, 59*n*36
Murray, Albert, 59*n*36
Myths, 36–39, 48

NAACP Legal Defense Fund, 10, 12
Nashville Agrarians. *See* Agrarians

Nation, 16
National Equal Rights League, 157, 169
National identity and nationalism: and economic crisis of 1970s, 102; and material-ambition ideal, 69, 70; and myth of innocence and power, 18, 31, 33, 34, 47, 51, 53, 55, 63, 86; myth-based ideas of generally, 37; Niebuhr on, 85–86, 88, 102; and September 11 terrorist attack, 88; southern identity versus, 32–34, 51, 55, 62, 63; Tanenhaus on, 32–34; tenets of, 85; Woodrow's criticisms of, and South's experiences as corrective for, 1–2, 18, 25, 33, 38–39, 43, 47, 80, 82–84, 87, 102
National Negro Convention Movement, 157
Naylor, Gloria, 46
Nevins, Allan, 5
New American Right, The (Bell), 80, 91–94, 101, 103, 111*n*48
New Deal, x, 80, 84, 90, 92, 94, 95, 98, 106, 125. *See also* Liberalism
New York Review of Books, 8
New York Times, 5, 8, 32–33, 59*n*43
New York Times Book Review, 8
New Yorker, 54
Niebuhr, Reinhold: distrust of liberalism by, 85, 109*n*14; and foreign policy guidance, 110*n*23; influences on, 109*n*10; on irony, 81, 82, 84–89, 102, 106, 109*n*8, 109*n*14; and liberals, 65, 109*n*10; on national identity, 85–86, 88, 102
Nixon, Richard, 67
Nora, Pierre, 39, 57*n*11
Norquist, Grover, 91
North Carolina: African American legislators in, 140, 143; African American members of U.S. Congress from, 144; antebellum period in, 156, 169; Democratic Party in, during late 19th century, 121; industrialization in, 119; vote for 2008 presidential election in, 69, 71–75, 78, 181–82; voter registration and turnout of African Americans in, 134–37, 149, 171–73
Novak, Michael, 89
Nugent, Walter T. K., 112*n*54

Obama, Barack, 43, 69, 71–73, 89, 104, 105, 127, 133, 163, 179–83. *See also* Presidential election (2008)
O'Brien, Michael, 7
Odum, Howard, 3, 5
Organization of American Historians, ix, 22
Origins of the New South, 1877–1913 (Woodward): compared with *The Strange Career of Jim Crow,* 13; epigraph of, 84; labor movement not focuse of, 110*n*27; presentism as approach of, 82; publication of, viii–ix, 6, 83; on Redeemer Democrats, 11–12, 42, 117, 118, 120; research for, 9, 15
Orwell, George, 65
Oxford University, 6
Oxford University Press, 6–7, 13

Parent, Wayne T., x, xiii, 62–79, 191
Parry, Janine, 130*n*26
Parsons, Talcott, 91
People's (Populist) Party, 90, 100, 107. *See also* Populism
Perman, Michael, 128–29*n*10, 165
Phillips, U. B., 17, 19, 69–70
Pierce, William, 114*n*71
Pierson, George W., 3
Plato, 159
Poland, 100
Political culture of the South: and Dixiecrats, 54, 66, 67, 68; and racial identity, 64–68, 71, 72–73, 75–76, 121–22; and Redeemer Democrats, x–xi, xiii, 11–12, 42, 116–29; and solid Democratic South, 65–66, 116–28; and upward mobility, 72, 73–74; variation in, among states, 75, 78; variation in, within states, 75–77; and white primary, 45, 65, 117, 149, 169–74; and youth, 74. *See also* Democratic

Party; Presidential election (2008); Republican Party; Voting; Voting Rights Act (VRA)
Poll tax, 9, 45, 117, 122, 170. *See also* Voting
Pollack, Norman, 110*n*29, 112*n*54
Populism: and African American voters, 11; American history textbook on, 114*n*73; Bell's *The New American Right* on, 91–94; and contentious politics, 98; demise of, 11, 121; Democrats versus, 90, 125–26; Hofstadter on, 80, 81–82, 91–99, 110*n*34, 111*n*48, 112*n*54, 114*n*73; as interest politics, 96; irrational Populists, 80, 91–93, 96; and labor movement, 110*n*27; McCarthyism associated with, 90, 91, 92, 93, 95–96; and People's (Populist) Party, 90, 100, 107; in South versus West, 91, 110*n*29, 112*n*54; Tea Party movement compared with, x, xiii, 80–81, 104–8; tenets of and programs supported by, 90–91, 106–8, 112*n*54, 125; Woodward on, x, 80, 82, 83, 89–91, 93–99, 116–18, 128*n*4. *See also* Watson, Tom
"Populist Heritage and the Intellectual, The" (Woodward), x, 80, 90–91, 93–98, 116–18, 127
Posse Comitatus, 114*n*71
Postel, Charles, 106–7, 120
Potter, David, 3, 14, 15, 19
Poverty: Johnson's War on Poverty, 47; of rural African Americans, 47; in South historically, 1, 2, 18, 33, 38, 43, 96; Third Reconstruction as benefiting the poor, 21, 48, 51; and underclass, 59*n*36
Powell, Adam Clayton, 178
Presentism, 81–83, 101
Presidential election (1952), 177–78, 179
Presidential election (1956), 177–78, 179
Presidential election (1960), 178, 179
Presidential election (1964), 66, 134, 136–37
Presidential election (1968), 136–37
Presidential election (1976), 183, 184
Presidential election (1980), 103, 104
Presidential election (1992), 183
Presidential election (2000), 67, 183, 184
Presidential election (2004), 67, 69, 71–72, 127, 151*n*18, 184
Presidential election (2008): in Arkansas, 72, 127; and distinctive southern identity, 62–63, 68–75, 77, 78; Obama's appeal in different southern states, 69, 71–72; and Obama's primary victories, 180; significance of generally, x, xi, 78, 133, 150, 163, 182–83; state-by-state presidential election vote in the South, 71–75, 127, 182; state-by-state primary vote in the South, 181; statistics on African American vote for Obama, 72–73; white support for Obama in, 72–74
Presidential elections (1868–1920), 165–68
Presidential elections (1936–1948), 172, 178, 179
Progressivism, 94, 106, 114*n*76, 120, 176, 179
"Proto Dorian convention," 64
"Pseudo-Conservative Revolt, The" (Hofstadter), 92–93
Puckett, Sherman C., xi, 153–88, 191
Pujo, Arsène, 107, 115*n*78

Race and racial identity: black power and racial separatism, 2, 21, 22, 23, 24, 25–26; and black power and racial separatism, 2, 21–26; and opposition to Obama, 127; and southern political identity, 64–68, 71, 72–73, 75–76, 121–22; and white supremacy, 17, 19, 45, 64–65, 69–70, 117, 121–22, 125, 149, 185; and white-only Democratic Party, 65–66. *See also* African Americans; Civil rights movement; Integration; Segregation and racial discrimination; Southern identity and distinctiveness
Race riots, 20–21, 23, 24, 25, 132
Radical Republicans, 18, 116. *See also* Republican Party
Rainey, Glenn, 4

Rand, Ayn, 103, 108
Randall, Alice, 46
Randolph, John, 5
Readjusters, 120, 124
Reagan, Ronald, 67, 103, 104, 106, 126
"Recent Paradoxes of American Race" (Woodward), 24
Reconstruction: Carpetbaggers during, 42; disenfranchisement of Confederates during, 150; end of, 6, 121; federal legislation during, 147, 158–60, 163, 169; fiscal policy of Radical Reconstruction, 124–25; Johnson's plan of, 157–58; Lincoln's plan for, 157–58; state constitutional conventions during, 165; voting rights for former slaves during, 134, 153; white southerners' response to, 38, 51; Woodward on, 131–32, 134, 153, 158–61; Woodward's proposed book on, 7, 8. *See also* Radical Republicans; Redeemer Democrats; Second Reconstruction; Third Reconstruction
Redeemer Democrats, x–xi, xiii, 11–12, 42, 116–29
Redistricting, 140, 142, 144–45
Regional identity. *See* Southern identity and distinctiveness
Republican Party: and conservatism, 103, 104; divisions among Republicans in 112th Congress, 104; in 1868–1920 elections, 162–69; in late nineteenth century, 146–47; in 1960s, 102; in presidential election (1980), 103, 104; in presidential elections from 1948–1960, 177–79; Radical Republicans, 18, 116; and reading of U.S. Constitution in Congress, 60*n*44; and social issues, 67; in the South, x, xii, 47, 50, 62–63, 66–68, 183–84; and suffrage rights for African Americans after Civil War, 158; and Tea Party movement, 103, 105; and textbook controversy in Texas, 32; and Union Leagues for freed slaves, 169. *See also* Presidential election *headings*
Resource mobilization theory, 113*n*64
Reunion and Reaction (Woodward), 6, 9, 12
Revolutionary America, 155–56
Rhett, Robert Barnwell, 87
Rhode Island, 156–57
Riesman, David, 91
Roberts, Adam, 113*n*63
Rockefeller, John D., 107
Rockefeller, Winthrop, viii, xvii–xviii
Rockwell, Georgia, 114*n*71
Romine, Scott, 38
Roosevelt, Franklin Delano, viii, 110*n*20, 172. *See also* New Deal
Roosevelt, Theodore, 96, 106, 114*n*76
Rosenfeld, Gavriel, 35
Russell, Richard, 184

Said, Edward, 41
Saturday Review, 8
Schlesinger, Arthur, Jr., 85, 109*n*10
Schools. *See* Education
"Search for Southern Identity, The" (Woodward), 1–2, 16, 19, 32–33, 36–45
"Second Look at the Theme of Irony, A" (Woodward), 21–22, 47, 48, 88. *See also* "Irony of Southern History, The" (Woodward)
Second Reconstruction, 20–21, 27, 32, 47, 131–50, 155, 170, 183–85
Segregation and racial discrimination: and *folkways uber alles* doctrine, 1, 13–14, 16, 19, 42; of Johns Hopkins Faculty Club, 9; in northern cities, 21–22, 23, 47; in post-civil-rights-era South, 32; in public accommodations, 10, 108*n*4; separate-but-equal doctrine of, 22, 147; southern identity linked with, 13–14, 17, 37, 42, 62, 69–70, 117, 170; Warren on, 41; Woodward's optimistic view of demise of, 16, 19, 37–38; Woodward's *The Strange*

Career of Jim Crow on, ix, 1, 2, 12–17, 42; Woodward's uncoupling of southern identity from, 16–19, 69. *See also* Civil rights movement; Integration; Race and racial identity; White supremacy
SHA. *See* Southern Historical Association (SHA)
Shafer, Byron E., 68, 70–71
Shaw v. Reno, 144
Shields, Todd, vii–xiii, 127, 192
Shugg, Roger, 7
Simpson, O. J., 24–25
Sixteenth Amendment, 115*n*78
Slavery: African American writers on, 46; Agrarians on, 41, 44; as cause of Civil War, 49, 54, 60*n*44, 61*n*56; defense of, 18, 38, 49–50; irony of proslavery orthodoxy, 87; as linked with southern identity and distinctiveness, 17, 19, 33, 38, 75; proslavery constitutionalism, 50, 59*n*40; in Styron's *The Confessions of Nat Turner,* 22; Tate on, 42; U.S. Constitution on, 60*n*44; Warren on, 53; Woodward on, as social evil, 55; Woodward's neglect of slavery narratives, 44
Smith, Henry Nash, 2, 94, 111*n*39
Smith, Jon, 49
Smith v. Allwright, 65, 162, 169–74
Social movement theory, 80–81, 98–108, 110*n*28, 113*n*59, 113*n*61, 113*n*64. *See also* Civil rights movement; Populism; Tea Party movement
South Africa, 113*n*63
South Carolina: African American legislators in, 142, 143, 146; African American members of U.S. Congress from, 144, 146, 150; African American population of, 121, 145–46, 160; agrarian rural lifestyle of, 76; Progressive Democratic Party in, 172; Reconstruction in, 121, 165; secession by, 87; vote for 1964 presidential election in, 66; vote for 2008 presidential election in, 72, 181–82; voter registration and turnout of African Americans in, 134–37, 150, 171–73
"Southern Critique for the Gilded Age, A" (Woodward), 40
Southern Historical Association (SHA), ix, 6, 9–10, 17, 83–84, 108*n*4
Southern identity and distinctiveness: and agrarian economy, 62, 69, 76, 117; based on shared history, 62, 69–71; and Celtic population, 76, 77; and cold war, 1–2, 18; and defeat- and poverty-ridden historical experiences, 1, 2, 18, 33, 38, 43, 63, 96; desire and anxiety in Woodward's quest for, 36–41; disadvantages of focus on, 48; Du Bois on, xii; emergence of, from historical experience, 34–35; Fugitives/Agrarians on, 31, 41, 42; globalization as threat to, 49; and industrialization and urbanization, 17, 43, 45, 62, 63, 69, 119, 149; and "Lost Cause" mythology, 38, 39, 41, 50, 55; as memory-based, 36, 39–40, 54, 70, 78; misinterpretation of Woodward's vision of, 31; and monuments to the Confederacy, 45; national identity versus, 32–34, 51, 55, 62, 63; original nature of, 62; and political identity, xii, 62–78; potential of misuse of Woodward's writings on, xii–xiii, 15–16; and "proto Dorian convention," 64; relevance of, and as corrective for postwar Americans, 1–2, 18, 25, 33, 38–39, 43, 47, 80, 82, 83, 84, 87, 102; and religious and family values, 69, 76; search for authentic but usable southern past, ix–xii, 14, 17–19, 26–27, 31, 33, 36–37; and slavery, 17, 18, 19, 33, 38, 53, 75; and southern literature, 35–36, 40–47; uncoupling of racial discrimination from, 16–19, 69; value of, 32, 48–49; and values of modesty, caution, and justice in national politics, 2, 32, 55; Warren on, 51–54; Woodward on generally, vii,

Southern identity and distinctiveness (*continued*)
ix–x, xii–xiii. *See also Burden of Southern History, The* (Woodward); Race and racial identity; Segregation and racial discrimination; White supremacy
Southern literature, 35–36, 40–47
Southern political culture. *See* Democratic Party; Political culture of the South; Presidential election (2008); Republican Party; Voting
Southern studies, 36, 48–49, 59*n*37
Soviet Union, 1–2, 18, 80, 81, 84, 88, 92, 100, 109*n*8, 113*n*62
Sparkman, John, 178
Spaulding, A. Timothy, 46
State legislatures, African Americans in, 132, 140–43, 145–46, 150
States' rights, 49–50, 54
Stevenson, Adlai, 14, 178
Stimson, James, 66
Stowe, Harriet Beecher, 104
Strange Career of Jim Crow, The (Woodward), ix, 1, 2, 6–7, 12–17, 19–20, 25, 33, 38, 42, 76, 82
Styron, William, 22
Suffrage rights. *See* Voting
Supreme Court, U.S.: on government discrimination, 139; on redistricting, 140, 142, 144; on school desegregation, ix, 6, 10, 12, 15, 20, 25–26; on separate-but-equal doctrine, 147; and Voting Rights Act, 133, 134, 148; on white primaries, 169–70

Taft, Howard, 92
Talmadge faction in Georgia, 175–76, 178
Tanenhaus, Sam, 32–34, 49
Tarrow, Sidney, 99, 100, 101, 112*n*57
Tate, Allen, 31, 42, 44, 49–50, 53, 54
Taxation, 91, 103, 116, 119, 122–25, 130*n*19. *See also* Poll tax
Tea Party movement, x, xiii, 50–51, 60*n*44, 80–81, 93, 104–8, 114*n*76, 127
Tennessee: African American legislators in, 142; African American members of U.S. Congress from, 143; antebellum period in, 156, 169; Clinton's primary win in, 180; congressional elections in, 144–45; constitution of, after Civil War, 162; Supreme Court case on legislative districts in, 140; vote for 2008 presidential election in, 72, 181–82; voter registration and turnout of African Americans in, 136–37, 149, 171–73; Richard Wright in, 44
Tenth Amendment, 127
Terrorist attacks, 88, 110*n*23, 114*n*71
Texas: African American legislators in, 141, 142, 143; African American members of U.S. Congress from, 143, 144; African American population in, 125, 151*n*8; Clinton's primary win in, 180; Democratic Party in, 119, 121, 124–25; readmission of, to Union, 164; redistricting in, 144, 151*n*18; Winthrop Rockefeller in, xvii; textbooks in, 32–35, 54, 56*n*1; Tower as Congressman from, 65; voter registration and turnout of African Americans in, 136–38, 170–73; and Voting Rights Act, 133, 138; white primary in, 170
Textbook controversy in Texas, 32–35, 56*n*1
Think Back (Woodward), 57*n*13
Third Reconstruction, 21, 48, 51, 155, 162, 163, 184–85
Thomas, Clarence, 25
Thornton, J. Mills, III, 23, 124–25
Thurmond, Strom, 54
Till, Emmett, 33
Tillman, Ben, 126–27
Tilly, Charles, 101, 103, 106, 113*n*59, 113*n*61
Tindall, George, 15
Todd, Chuck, 180
Tom Watson, Agrarian Rebel (Woodward), viii, 3–5, 10–11, 64, 66, 82, 90, 93, 110*n*27

Tower, John, 65
Toynbee, Arnold, 84, 102
Turner Diaries, The, 103, 114*n*71
Turner, Frederick Jackson, 94

Union Leagues, 169
University of Chicago Press, 7
University of Florida, viii–ix, 5
University of Georgia, 7
University of London, 6
University of North Carolina, Chapel Hill, viii, 3–5
University of Texas, 5
University of Tokyo, 6, 110*n*20
University of Virginia, 6, 9
Valley, Richard, 184
Vance, Rupert, 5
Vanderbilt University, 31, 53. *See also* Agrarians
Viereck, Peter, 93
Vietnam War, 47, 88, 131, 132
Virginia: African American legislators in, 141, 142, 151*n*13; African American members of U.S. Congress from, 144, 169; Readjusters in, 120, 124; readmission of, to Union, 164; Redeemer Democrats in, 116, 123; vote for 2008 presidential election in, 69, 71–76, 78, 181–82; voter registration and turnout of African Americans in, 134, 136–37
Virginia and Kentucky Resolutions, 127
Voting: by African American voters, xi, 66–67, 131–40, 153–85; by African Americans from 1868–1920, 162–69; by African Americans from 1944–1964, 169–80; in antebellum America, 156–57; before and after abolition of white primaries, 169–80; in Colonial America, 155; defeat of suffrage referenda for free people of color in northern states from 1865–1869, 157; and disenfranchisement of African Americans, xiii, 9, 45, 116, 117, 120, 134, 135, 146–47, 148, 157, 164–74; disenfranchisement of Confederates during Reconstruction, 150, 160; election fraud by Democratic Party, 90, 116, 121, 122; literacy test for, 134, 135; and political socializing factors for African Americans after Civil War, 169; and poll tax, 9, 45, 117, 122, 170; property requirements for, in antebellum period, 156–57; Reconstruction legislation on, for African Americans, 158–61; and redistricting, 140, 142, 144–45; in Revolutionary America, 155–56; voter registration and turnout of African Americans, 134–38, 148–50, 170–82; and white primary in South, 45, 65, 117, 149, 169–74; by women, 169–70; Woodward on enfranchised freedmen as political neophytes, 159–64, 183, 185. *See also* Voting Rights Act (VRA); Presidential election *headings*
Voting Rights Act (VRA), xi, xiii, 10, 21, 66, 78, 131–40, 148–50, 162

Walker, Alice, 46
Wall, Ben, 108*n*4
Wallace, George, 68, 137, 183
Wallenstein, Peter, 125
Walton, Hanes, Jr., xi, xiii, 153–88, 187*n*35, 192–93
War on Poverty, 47
Warren, Robert Penn, 31, 35, 41, 51–54, 60*n*53, 86
Watson, Tom, viii, 3–5, 10–11, 64, 66, 82, 84, 90, 93, 98, 109*n*7
Weber, Max, 92
West, Don, 111*n*43
Wharton, Vernon, 15
"What Happened to the Civil Rights Movement?" (Woodward), 21, 48
Whayne, Jeannie, vii–xiii, 193
Whisnant, David E., 49
White primary, 45, 65, 117, 149, 169–74

White supremacy, 17, 19, 45, 64–65, 69–70, 117, 121–22, 125, 149, 185. *See also* Segregation and racial discrimination
Wiener, Jonathan, 119
Williams, John Bell, 108*n*4
Williams, Patrick G., x–xi, xiii, 116–30, 193–94
Williamson, Joel, 36
Wilson, Joe, 127
Wilson, Woodrow, 114*n*76
Woodward, C. Vann: academic career of, viii–ix, 2–10, 25, 83; achievement of, vii–xiii, 6, 26–27; autobiographical essay by, 81, 89; biographical information on, viii–ix; death of, ix, 26; essays and essay reviews by, 8, 36; Festschrift honoring, 124–25; friendship between Hofstadter and, 94–95, 111*n*36, 111*n*43; papers of, at Yale University, 8; presentism of, 81–83, 101; and proposed book on race relations in 1990s, 24–25; research practices of, 2–6, 8–9, 13–15, 95; revisionist critique of writings by, 26, 34, 36; self-description of, 81; as social activist, viii, 9–10, 81; as "therapist of public mind," 2–3, 10–13, 15, 27; as World War II veteran, ix, 83. *See also Burden of Southern History, The* (Woodward); Southern identity and distinctiveness; *and other writings by Woodward*
Woodward, Glenn, 7
World War II, ix, xvii, 65, 82, 83, 87
Wright, Richard, 35, 44

Yale University, ix, 3, 7–8, 15
Young, Andrew, 143

Zinn, Howard, 81, 108*n*2, 108*n*4